Semiotics of Deceit

Semiotics of Deceit

THE PATHELIN ERA

Donald Maddox

With a new English Prose translation of Maistre Pierre Pathelin
by ALAN E. KNIGHT

Lewisburg
Bucknell University Press
London and Toronto: Associated University Presses

© 1984 by Associated University Presses, Inc.

Associated University Presses
440 Forsgate Drive
Cranbury, N.J. 08512

Associated University Presses
25 Sicilian Avenue
London WC1A 2QH, England

Associated University Presses
2133 Royal Windsor Drive
Unit 1
Mississauga, Ontario, Canada L5J 1K5

Library of Congress Cataloging in Publication Data

Maddox, Donald.
  Semiotics of deceit.

  Includes index.
  1. Farce de maître Pierre Pathelin. 2. Deception in literature. 3. Truthfulness and falsehood in literature. 4. Semiotics and literature. I. Farce de maître Pierre Pathelin. II. Title.
  PQ1573.M3   1983   842'.2   82-74491
  ISBN 0-8387-5040-0

Printed in the United States of America

for Jeff, Margot, and Greg

Contents

Illustrations and Acknowledgments 9
Preface 11
  1. Semiopathelin 17

      Part I. The Narrative Dimension of Deceit

  2. Infrapathelin, the Deceived Deceiver 29

      Part II. The Verbal and Semantic Structures of Deceit

  3. Paremiopathelin the Sententious 43
     Excursus: The Three Faces of Logopathelin 59
  4. Pathegyrics, or the Subversive Encomium 62
  5. Thanatopathelin and the Art of Dying 72
  6. Antipathiquelin and the Rhetoric of Torts 95
  7. Manipathulin, the Delusive Persuader 109
  8. Illocupathelin, Speech Actor 118

Part III. *Pathelin* and the Discourse of Deceit in Medieval French Drama

  9. Protopathelin: The Medieval Dramatic Heritage of Deceit 135

      Part IV. The Cultural Dimension of Deceit

10. Ideopathelin: The Signs of the Times 157
Conclusion 171
Master Pierre Pathelin, translated by Alan E. Knight 173
Appendix: Narrative and Discoursive Semiotics 200
Notes 206

Illustrations and Acknowledgments

The six photographic reproductions in Chapter Five are taken from *The Ars moriendi (Editio Princeps, circa 1450). A Reproduction of the Copy in the British Museum.* Edited by W. Harry Rylands, F.S.A. With an Introduction by George Bullen, F.S.A., Keeper of the Printed Books in the British Museum (London: Wyman, 1881). The photographs are courtesy of Brown University Library.

Plate I.	Temptation against Faith
Plate II.	Temptation to Despair
Plate III.	Temptation to Impatience
Plate IV.	Temptation to Vainglory
Plate V.	Temptation to Avarice
Plate VI.	The Death of Moriens

Portions of Chapter Two originally appeared in *L'Esprit Créateur*, pp. 55–68. The Author and publishers gratefully acknowledge permission from the Editor to use material from that article in this book.

For permission to cite passages from *Maistre Pierre Pathelin (Farce du XVe siècle)*, deuxième édition revue par Richard T. Holbrook, Classiques Français du Moyen Age, 35 (Paris: Champion, 1963), grateful acknowledgment goes to Librairie Honoré Champion, Paris.

Preface

You know the type. Shifty eyes, a smooth line, a yen for the finer things in life, always on the prowl for a bargain, never gives a sucker an even break. You may know him from the play written about him five centuries ago, the one in which he never really died. But you have probably seen him yourself dozens of times. For Pierre Pathelin is among us yet. You can still find him on a Saturday morning stalking the flea markets, or drifting through the bargain basements, junk yards, antique stores, and used car lots of this world. When he sees him coming, the wary merchant will close for lunch or call it an early day. He once told the clothier that the world would be a better place, with less deceit and double-dealing than there is nowadays, if there were more people like that merchant's late father. No one will ever say that about him when his eulogy is read. Yet without him, or rather, without the imperious acquisitive drive that keeps him going, century after century, the world would be a *different* place, for there likely would be far less free enterprise and certainly no wheeling and dealing. Or, if you will, only the *laissez* and no *faire,* for there is a little of the Pathelin in all of us consumers. Moreover, there is a lot of Pathelin in this book, and I should like to take this opportunity to thank him for his collusion, without which it could not have been written.

Maistre Pierre Pathelin is the masterpiece of late medieval French comic drama. The play is justly celebrated both for its technical perfection and its human insight. Many critics have legitimately ranked it as an important precursor to some of the greatest comedies of Molière, and persuasive evidence has been adduced that it merits the distinction of being called the first genuine comedy in the French language.[1]

During the past seventy-five years, *Pathelin* has received a considerable degree of attention from literary historians eager to identify its author and his milieu. The play has also been a veritable gold mine for philologists because the anonymous playwright, like his contemporary François Villon, had a keen sense of the ludic potential of Middle French. He exploited this vein with exuberance and verve, creating elaborate verbal fantasies from proverbs, shreds of archaic dialects, professional and popular idioms, and curious neologisms;[2] in this, he foreshadows Rabelais, Joyce, and Beckett no less than Molière. This linguistic and literary vitality has elicited many short articles and notes devoted to obscure and difficult aspects of the play, but only a few longer studies emerged, early in this century.[3] Of the latter, questions of authorship were a major preoccupation, and the critical battlefield is still strewn with the remains of heated skirmishes over this issue that animated a transatlantic quarrel during the years between the two world wars.[4] And now that philology and literary history have established many basic facts about specific details in this work, now that it has been repeatedly edited, and now that medieval French drama has recently evoked a resurgence of critical attention, a comprehensive study of *Maistre Pierre Pathelin* is timely, indeed, long overdue.

The present analysis of the play is multifocal. It begins with an examination of intrinsic features and works outward toward a sense of the relationship between the play and its dramatic and cultural heritage. Although a literary study at its inception, the project was inspired by the kind of cross-disciplinary awareness established as a basic tenet of the emerging field of semiotics of culture. Formal study of literary texts cannot indefinitely be carried out without reference to their intertextual resonance and to the manner in which they integrate features of extraliterary cultural models. Not long ago, Daniel Poirion contrasted a "'scientifistic', 'mutilative' semiology" with a "semiotics that would respect the originality of societies and earlier mentalities," advocating the latter as an appropriate perspective from which to examine medieval texts.[5] Inasmuch as a semiotics of culture affords a means of situating literary discourse within a broader typology of discourses in a given culture, it adopts such a perspective, so as to enable the literary scholar and critic to achieve a greater sense of how a particular cultural event, such as a literary text or a dramatic work, participates in the cultural coherence of its age.

By no means least among the cultural functions evident in *Pathelin* is its objective to entertain and to delight. Numerous recent translations and amateur productions of the play, in both Europe and America, prove that modern readers and spectators, no less than medieval Schoolmen, are subject to the power of sign-functions in the production of laughter. Without sacrificing serious analytical objectives, therefore, care has been taken in this study to avoid losing that crisp vitality which has assured the play an enthusiastic reception down through the ages. Although Pierre Pathelin would never have *purchased* this book, one delights in imagining that its appeal would have prompted him to slip a copy under his cloak while browsing through the bookstalls.

The word *pathelin* itself means "language," especially the particularized usage of language to achieve particular ends, most of which, in the case of Pierre Pathelin, are dubious in the extreme.[6] For Pathelin is a pathological liar, hence a pathological user of signs, or a *semiopath*, as it were. As a semiopath, Pathelin is a manipulator of signs to the detriment of others; he is a character who has mastered the techniques of verbal forgery; he is a disrupter of discourse and a (double-) dealer in deceptive appearances. In the chapter headings, I have attempted to capture the spirit of Pathelin as pathological user of signs, as in his role as declaimer of pathologically barbed panegyric, or "pathegyric"; as manipulator ("Manipathulin"); as a pseudomoribund ("Thanatopathelin"); as a litigious adversary ("Antipathiquelin"), etcetera. These headings will help to evoke the protean nature of Pathelin, whose languages constantly subject his identity to all sorts of colorful distortions and extensions. These neologistic permutations of his name will serve to remind us that no aspect under study is impervious to the discursive verve of this semiopath.

To ensure that the citations from the play are understood by readers untrained in Middle French and its related dialects, each citation that appears in the study is accompanied by a translation. These are all excerpted from a new English prose translation of *Master Pierre Pathelin* by Alan E. Knight, who followed the Holbrook edition of the play. I am most pleased that this sprightly, accurate, and much needed translation appears in its entirety in this book, and I am indeed grateful to Professor Knight for his kind permission to publish it here for the first time. It was originally made for a fresh production of the play, and this proximity to the scene, as well as the fact that the translator is himself a distinguished specialist in medieval drama, make it a welcome companion to this study.

In an effort to clarify the conceptual foundation of my analyses, I have added a brief appendix containing a bibliographical and terminological discussion of major aspects of narrative and discursive semiotics. Inasmuch as my multifaceted semiotic approach sometimes goes beyond current theoretical perspectives in semiotics, or deals with fundamental concepts in specialized ways, I have been attentive throughout to the needs of the reader and have, whenever possible, supplied brief definitions of terms and concepts while attempting to avoid unduly long detours from the subject at hand. The appendix represents a further effort to clarify and to evoke a theoretical background that may prove to be of interest in its own right.

The original draft of this study was written while I was a fellow-in-residence at the Fondation Camargo in Cassis, France. I wish to thank the administration and staff of the Fondation for their invaluable assistance during that initial writing stage in France; I wish also to evoke here the memory of the late, much regretted Reinhard Kuhn, a Fondation colleague whose friendship and encouragement were deeply appreciated. For my early interest in medieval French drama, I owe much to the inspired teaching of Barbara M. Craig and Patrick R. Vincent. To my reviewers—Peu d'Aquest, Martin Garant, Guillaume and all the others, past and future—I raise a tankard. And to my wife, Sara, who read and critiqued parts of this book more than once and still managed to laugh with me in my levity, I promise six yards of that light blue fabric Pathelin so much admired, the very next time I go to the mercantile fair.

Semiotics of Deceit

1
Semiopathelin

"In the beginning was the Word." And the Word was good. It was not good enough, however, to prevent deceit and transgression from becoming a way of life for those too easily swayed from its precepts. A case in point involves the medieval French drama. On the evidence of its earliest known play, *Le Mystère d'Adam,* it began in the late twelfth century with the temptation of Adam and his spouse, who break faith with their Creator as a result of Satan's manipulative, delusive persuasion of Eve. Nearly three centuries later, in the mature twilight of its flourishing, the medieval scene is animated by a lowly shepherd who successfully deludes his lawyer, Maître Pierre Pathelin, using the very same tactics with which the latter has just deceived the court. In the case of Adam and Eve vs. the divine Figura, the deceptive behavior initiated by Satan is eventually recognized for what it is because the Judge is omniscient, while in *Pathelin* the judge is human, fallible, and therefore susceptible to manipulation that leads to erroneous judgment. Similarity outweighs contrast, however. As a result of the first, divine Judgment, mankind was obliged to move beyond the confines of Terrestrial Paradise, away from harmony with the Celestial City and into that proto-urban alienation from God decried by Saint Augustine in *De civitate Dei.*[1] Thereafter, according to medieval avatars of the myth, deceit became commonplace among mankind. A late medieval biblical exegete might construe the deceptive conduct and the erroneous verdict in *Pathelin* as merely particular instances of this general propensity of fallen man. In the play it is twice implied, aphoristically, that only Judgment Day itself will ring down the curtain on such deceptive behavior.[2] If there is a message for the medieval theatrical public in these two plays as juxtaposed, it is perhaps that man in his postlapsarian state is destined to repeat variants of the transgression which brought him into that fallen condition in the first place.

It would seem rather pointless to dwell on these two scenes in medieval French drama were it not for the fact that *deceit,* in a wide variety of guises, is a common occurrence in this repertory. A number of pertinent images come readily to mind. Having lured his brother into the fields, Cain brandishes his cudgel behind a prayerful Abel; in the Mysteries, the mouth of

Hell gapes in anticipation of those undone by the arch-deceiver, beginning with Adam and Eve; consider the kiss of Judas in the Passion plays—another instance of abortive deceit foreknown by the Omniscient. Then there is Théophile's Faustian collusion with the Devil in the early miracle of the Virgin. Our Lady will come to the aid of more than one victim of deceit in the *Miracles de Nostre Dame*. We also recall the delusion of the pagans by false idols and the dark projects of three thieves in the *Jeu de Saint Nicolas* of Jean Bodel. Remember the two tavern wenches who fleece the Prodigal Son in the *Courtois d'Arras?* Nor can we forget the roguish knight and (not so) naïve shepherdess in the *Jeu de Robin et Marion;* the medical and religious frauds in the *Jeu de la feuillée;* poor Griseldis deliberately misled by her insensitive spouse; the cruel boy and the avaricious blind man in the earliest known French farce; and a host of similar deceptive types and tactics in subsequent congeners. The list of Pathelin's precursors and distant cousins could go on at length, but the point has already been made: French plays from the late twelfth through the fifteenth century are rich in figures of deceit.

Of all medieval French plays involving strategies of deceit, however, *Maistre Pierre Pathelin* must take pride of place. There can be no doubt that deceit, in a wide variety of forms, is the very mainstay of this play. We meet the crooked lawyer, Pathelin, whose practice is a curious blend of *avocacïon* and *trompacion,* and whose wife, Guillemette, by her very name evokes the guile of her delusive collusion with Pathelin. In need of attire, Pathelin goes to the mercantile fair and cons the clothier, Guillaume, out of a bolt of cloth by flattering his family and promising him not only gold but a meal of roast goose when he arrives to collect. This clothier, Guillaume—whose name means "gullible" in Middle French usage—is likewise devious. Yet he is never paid for his overpriced merchandise, because when he arrives at the residence of Pathelin later in the day, he finds neither gold nor goose but only a sick and dying replica of his client. After a long scene in which Pathelin feigns terminal illness as his wife insists that her husband has been at death's door for eleven weeks, the deluded clothier finally concludes that he is in error and relents in his effort to collect. Frustrated, he brings suit against his shepherd, another deceiver, who has slaughtered some of his master's sheep. The shepherd engages Pathelin as his attorney, promising him gold in payment. By having his client bleat throughout the trial, Pathelin manages to get him absolved on grounds of mental incompetence. Yet he fails in turn to collect his fee, for the shepherd, ceaselessly bleating, beats a hasty retreat. So the master deceiver is finally deceived, and by his own device at that.

No matter how elaborate, any summary of the play would fail to provide an adequate account of the myriad changes rung on the act of lying and deceit, whether by false statement or misrepresentation. "How do I lie to thee?" wonders Pathelin. Let me count the ways. There is lying by limning, lying by dying, lying by litigation. There is fleecing by overpricing; deceiving by greeting; delusion by collusion; stealing and mealing; caviling and babbling; rambling and raving; cheating and bleating. The list is virtually endless. It would seem that everything in the play surges from the fundamental energy generated by delusion and lying. Analysis of *Pathelin*, whether as drama, literary artifact, or cultural object, is drawn magnetically to disclosure of the means, whether verbal; gestural; proxemic (relying on the semantic qualities of space); paralinguistic (involving qualities of intonation in performance); kinesic (concerning body movements); psychological, and so forth, by which to lie. Purposefully. Manipulatively. Effectively. Creatively. To gain an end, which is, precisely, to "work" the systems of culture by beating them at their own game, in order to obtain goods, services, verdicts, even a new identity now and then in return for nothing but lies, wicked, lovely lies.

What, then, is lying?

To a Robertsonian, of course, lying is a function of *cupiditas*, thus a perversion of the chief Pauline virtue.[3] "If I speak in the (forked) tongues of men—aye, and of devils, too—but have not *cupiditas*," cries the Deceiver, "I have become mere sounding brass or a noisy cymbal. . . . *Cupiditas* is impatient and unkind. *Cupiditas* is envious, sometimes boastful, always conceited, often behaves underhandedly. She is self-seeking, easily provoked, and she reckons up the wrongs she has suffered. She has great empathy with *deceit*, but has no sympathy with truth. . . . Consequently, her victims see things dimly, as does the clothier, Guillaume Josseaulme, through a glass darkly, even when face to face!" In this context, lying, driven by *cupiditas*, is the work of the Devil.

To a semiotician, however, lying is the work of the sign. For it was Umberto Eco who said, as if *Pathelin* had been uppermost in his mind at the very moment of utterance, that:

> . . . if a liar pretends to be sick by behaving in a certain way, the semiotic functioning of this behavior can be analyzed irrespective of the fact that he is actually lying. *Every time there is possibility of lying, there is a sign-function:* which is to signify (and then to communicate) something to which no real state of things corresponds. . . . The possibility of lying is the *proprium* of semiosis just as (for the Schoolmen) the possibility of laughing was the *proprium* of Man as *animal rationale*.[4]

For the fifteenth-century Schoolmen who enjoyed this farce, *Pathelin* would certainly have assured the "possibility of laughing" and thus have demonstrated their concept of Man. For the modern critic, on the other hand, *Pathelin* would seem to provide a well-equipped laboratory of the lie in which to explore the nature of sign-functions in dramatic discourse. Like the alchemist before his alembic in the dark and drafty recesses of some long forgotten Gothic tower, the semiotician poring over his material rejoices to discover therein the processes of semiosis that produce new and unforeseen meaning and significance out of baser elements: verbal and semantic properties. Moreover, a "theory of the lie" may be the touchstone of his enterprise, if we subscribe to Eco's view of sign-production.

> Semiotics is concerned with everything that can be *taken* as a sign. A sign is everything which can be taken as significantly substituting for something else. This something does not necessarily have to exist or to actually be somewhere at the moment in which a sign stands for it. *Thus semiotics is in principle the discipline studying everything which can be used in order to lie.*[5]

As even a casual reading of the play reveals, *Pathelin* is in essence a carnivalesque festival of deceit. Thus, a discipline which studies "everything which can be used in order to lie" is, or would seem to be, ideally suited to our needs as we examine its figures of deceit.[6]

In order to foreclose on this hastily drawn analogy between alchemists and semioticians, however, it is necessary to set forth method, not madness. Alchemists pour; semioticians pore. Yet it is a systematic kind of poring that is most likely to yield significant results. It was John Locke whose seventeenth-century "doctrine of signs" identified semiotics as a branch of scientific study "the business whereof is to consider the nature of signs the mind makes use of for the understanding of things, or conveying its knowledge to others" (1960). Despite a wide variety of theoretical refinements currently being made by semioticians, Locke's statement remains a generally valid description of the fundamental "business" of semiotics. The semiotician systematically seeks to disclose the signs, both verbal and nonverbal, used in relational patterns so as to signify and to communicate. At issue, then, are not only meanings, but also, and primarily, the modes of their production and of their reception, or semiosis. In our quest for the productive ingredients of a dramatic semiosis of the lie, it will therefore be necessary to do more than simply describe, compare, contrast, or otherwise locate instances of deceit in *Pathelin*.

Obviously, deceit has many different types of incarnations in *Pathelin*, including delusive utterances, misleading appearances, deceptive behavior, and not all of these varieties of deceit are restricted to verbal structures. Although the play exists by virtue of the verbal medium, this medium in turn signifies other verbal and nonverbal media essential to dramatic coherence. Rather than accord undue privileges to any one of these media by defining deceit uniquely with respect to it alone, one must begin by recognizing deceit as a minimal unit of signification independent of any particular discursive context yet susceptible of identification according to specific criteria which will be set forth presently. In order to distinguish this specialized term from casual usage of the word *deceit*, the former shall hereafter be identified as /deceit/, using the graphic convention of single slashes. We now have a minimal signifying category—a *classeme*—called /deceit/, which we may use as a means of identifying the verbal and nonverbal signs and systems of signs in the play that use the same elementary signifying configuration to organize specific varieties of deceit. The objective is thus to identify as many of the figures of deceit in the play as possible by showing that their uniquely intricate structures are founded by the same invariant configuration of /deceit/.

Having determined how /deceit/ is variously manifested in the signifying systems of the play, we may then proceed to a broader consideration of how the play is situated with respect both to identifiable norms of medieval French dramatic discourse and to the late medieval cultural context in which it is embedded. Thus, after having defined, at the end of this chapter, the elementary nucleus of signification which constitutes the classematic category /deceit/, we shall trace configurative manifestations of /deceit/ throughout the play at various levels of discourse, using the results of this inquiry to characterize the status of the work as at once a constituent of literature, drama, and culture. Study of the figures of deceit in the play according to a methodological apparatus inspired by theoretical developments in literary semiotics will ultimately afford an opportunity to offer certain limited observations pertinent to a semiotics of late medieval European culture.

It goes without saying, of course, that /deceit/ is richly manifested in literature and drama of all times and places. Yet it is so fundamental to nearly every important aspect of *Pathelin* that any extensive analysis of the play cannot fail to accord it special attention. As will become apparent later in this essay, /deceit/ also serves as a valuable analytical category for the situation of the play within a broader medieval dramatic and cultural context. This is obviously not meant to imply that /deceit/ is necessarily a dominant classeme in medieval drama or culture, but rather to suggest that by studying the manner in which a culture represents deceit in its dramatic projections, we may be in a position better to understand significant cultural aspects that do not directly pertain to the deceptive mechanisms themselves. Rather than becoming an end in itself, then, extensive study of figures of deceit may lead to the disclosure of other perspectives, such as those which concern the coherence of medieval French drama as a signifying medium (Chapter 9) or the tension between signification and representation in late medieval culture (Chapter 10).

A survey of the critical reception of *Pathelin* through the centuries would reveal that the play has never been singled out for extensive study of its delusive strategies and figures alone, while on the other hand it has been consistently admired for other qualities deemed atypical of late medieval comic drama. Scarcely a decade ago, Jean Frappier admired the way in which *Pathelin* combines perfection of intrigue with psychological depth.[7] Similar views have been expressed by many generations of critics who find that the work stands apart from other comic plays of its time because technical virtuosity of plot is equaled by penetrating human insight. Four centuries ago, in fact, Henri Estienne referred to the play in a manner already prefigurative of Frappier. Philausone, a character in a dialogue by Estienne, discusses the merits of the play in specifically generic terms: "Il me souvient encore de plusieurs bons mots, voire de maints bons et beaux traicts, et de la bonne disposition conjointe avec l'intention gentile, tellement qu'il me semble que je luy fay grant tort en l'appelant une farce, et qu'elle mérite bien le nom de comédie."[8] (I still recall several witticisms, indeed many fine and beautiful touches, and the orderly disposition of parts conjoined with a noble intent, so that I would do it a grave injustice to call it a farce, for it truly merits being called a comedy.) By "intention gentile," Philausone designates a certain depth and substance that would distinguish it from the more mechanical, psychologically meager techniques of much farce.[9]

Although figures of deceit are not explicitly evoked in the critical attitude first expressed by Estienne, this early appraisal affords a valuable directive in the formulation of guidelines for intrinsic analysis of mechanisms of deception in *Pathelin*. Noteworthy in this regard is the phrase "la bonne disposition conjointe avec l'intention gentile," with its twofold categorization expressed in terms of poetic theory. By 1578, the year in which Estienne made this observation, *disposition* was already a well-established term in the lexicon of poetics, designating the second part of rhetoric *(dispositio)*, concerning determination of the best order possible for that which has been found by *invention,* as in the disposition or distribution of the parts of a discourse.[10] Though not constituents of the five basic parts of rhetoric, *intention* and *conjointe* also evoke earlier terms used in poetics, especially those found in exordial statements by Chrétien de Troyes and other vernacular narrative authors of the late twelfth century. Like Chrétien's *antancïon, intention* most likely connotes "the investing of a thought and a will of the author," whence its importance as a reference to the verbal and semantic aspects of discourse.[11] Within the etymological lineage of Chrétien's "conjointure", and, before that, of the term "iunctura" used by Horace, *conjointe* is most likely an allusion to the articulation or linking of units of narrative.[12] Thus, in a vein similar to that of Frappier, Estienne seems to suggest that it is the fundamental harmony between linear structure—the play's technical virtuosity—and meaning, or verbal and semantic richness, which accounts for the remarkable qualities of *Pathelin*. General orientation of the analysis of /deceit/ and its configurations might therefore be made in terms of these two broadly conceived dimensions, the one designating narrative structure, the other, verbal and semantic texture.

Although resonant with basic concepts in traditional poetics, this early formulation is also anticipatory of the conceptual framework of narrative and discursive semiotics.[13]

Narrative semiotics concerns itself with what Vladimir Propp had called the "morphology," or fundamental architecture, of story. Culture "texts" of all types, be they fiction, drama, ballet, pantomine, even episodes in real life, all unfold according to certain logical patterns of actions that may be identified and plotted independently of the specific features of the performers and of their milieu. By subjecting the text to a kind of "fluoroscopic" analysis which penetrates the various external layers of sociohistoric detail, the narrative semiotician, or narratologist, seeks to locate and describe the abstract network made up primarily of "functions" (e.g., departure, arrival, combat, marriage, etc.) and "actants" (performers of specific roles with regard to the functions) that constitute the narrative infrastructure—what French analysts call the *récit*—of the text and enable it to "tell the story." In this semiotic context, *disposition* would correspond to the organization of narrative "syntax," whereby narrative components are distributed along the chronological axis of the plot. In our semiotic investigation of *Pathelin*, we shall first examine the narrative *disposition* of the play within a narratological framework in order to determine how this dimension signifies and/or communicates /deceit/ as it unfolds.

While narrative semiotics deals with a textual dimension which is essentially nonverbal and largely covert, discoursive semiotics is attentive to the manifest verbal and semantic features that adorn and particularize textual expression. (This is what A. J. Greimas, taking exception to Propp's much earlier usage, has recently termed *morphology*.)[14] It is now no longer a matter of the abstract structure of narrative expression that dynamically relays the components of story, but rather of the *content* of such expression as constituted by specific characters who behave according to the norms of their culture, represented by detailed settings and verisimilar events. This concern with the manner in which the text is invested with culturally specific verbal and semantic detail appears to be closely akin to the notion of *intention* as expressed by Estienne, and in later chapters, we shall scrutinize aspects of textual *intention* for evidence of how /deceit/ may inform the play's verbal and semantic configurations.

The distinction between a separate narrative and a separate discoursive dimension of the text is more for the sake of analytical convenience than it is an account of textual reality, for the narrative dimension is itself a constituent of the discourse, or coordinated language of the text. In fact, the dynamic structure of narrative is sometimes referred to as "narrative discourse" and is treated as perhaps *the* most important nonverbal language in the text—the language of plot. The notion of text as a stratified *coordination* of narrative and discoursive language recalls Estienne's comment that, in *Pathelin, disposition* and *intention* are *conjointe*. As do semioticians, Estienne already acknowledges the existence of a textual dimension characterized by a coordinated "conjoining" of narrative expression with verbal and semantic content. In our analysis of *Pathelin*, we must therefore consider the importance of /deceit/ to the play's conjoining configurations.

When approached from the perspective of narrative and discoursive semiotics, analysis of the latent implications in Estienne's observation would ultimately entail extended study of sign production in *Pathelin,* beginning with the most elementary articulation of meaning and proceeding through numerous levels of the syntactic, verbal, and semantic hierarchies. Such a comprehensive program far exceeds the limits of either the possible or, more significantly, the desirable, for either the analyst or the reader. Within the context of an intrinsic study of the ramifications of /deceit/ in the play, however, the perspective of narrative and discoursive semiotics, as sketched above, will serve admirably as a means of achieving a multifocal evaluation of the figures of deceit which inform and unify the whole, making *Pathelin* an early milestone of French comic drama.

Having identified two fundamental, complementary dimensions in which to carry out analysis, that of narrative discourse and that of verbal and semantic content, as well as the dimension of their interrelations, there remains the need to establish a working hypothesis with which to "anchor" and to focus the study. To further this objective, we may profitably revert to a logical model of cognitive states in order to define the elementary signifying nucleus of /deceit/ pertinent to both narrative and discoursive organization.

Recently, A. J. Greimas and Joseph Courtés have drawn a basic distinction between *action* and *cognition* in narrative.[15] They note that we recognize not only a series of events in a story, but also *knowledge* about these events. Any given story organizes its own intrinsic coherence so as to distinguish, always within its discoursive universe, that which is "true" from that which is "false." Often, the resolution of a story may entail recognition of knowledge previously held in abeyance by a secret or a lie. Knowledge of a truth or a falsehood is frequently withheld from certain of the characters while being jealously guarded by others who are in some way privileged. Sometimes knowledge is manipulated by the narrator so as to prevent even the reader or listener from achieving the correct perception of what is true and what false until the moment of recognition. The authors say that when deceit or delusion is excluded from relations between characters in a story, their exchanges occur according to a *fiduciary contract* involving mutual trust. In such instances, "there is no distance between events and knowledge about the events." When delusion or lying occurs, as in the story-type "deceiver deceived," the fiduciary contract is *abrogated* because knowledge about events no longer corresponds to the events themselves.[16]

Although Greimas and Courtés restrict their focus to the problem of knowledge in narrative, their logical model obviously has broader applications, including the disclosure of a useful hypothetical concept of the elementary signifying structure of /deceit/. This model is articulated in terms of the contrary opposition between reality and mere appearances. Briefly, when the categories "Being" and "Appearing" are both operative, we are in the realm of what is "True." When their subcontraries, "Not Appearing" and "Not Being" obtain, we are in the realm of the "False." When it is a matter of "Being" and "Not Appearing," a "Secret" is involved, while the "Delusion or Lie" is a product of "Appearing" and "Not Being." Whence the following logical organization of cognitive states:[17]

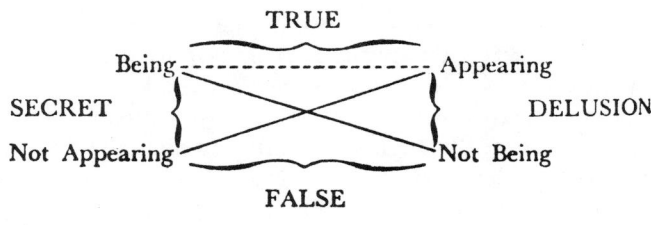

—TRUE (= being + appearing)
—FALSE (= not being + not appearing)
—SECRET (= being + not appearing)
—DELUSION (= not being + appearing) or LIE

Figure 1

In terms of this cognitive model, we may characterize the classeme /deceit/ as being minimally signified by a condition of "Appearing" and "Not Being" as constituted by the vertical relation, or *deixis*, of "Delusion" in the model. We see that /deceit/ results from a nondisjunction of the "True" from the "False," that is, the latter is confused with the former because the distinction, or disjunction, between the two categories is blurred.

Having identified /deceit/ with reference to this elementary signifying nucleus, we may go on to suggest that the model may be manifested variously in different discursive contexts. For example, a particular narrative may actualize the categories in the model by featuring a moment of recognition after which knowledge that was under the rubric of "Secret," or "False," or "Delusive," may then be known as "True." Knowledge as distributed in the discourse can thus be characterized by successive displacements of one of the axes in the model by another. It should be noted, of course, that "True" and "False" are not understood in any absolute ideological or philosophical sense, for they acquire meaning only within the specific discoursive context which constructs its own particular coherence with regard to these terms.

Having casually observed the importance of deceptive phenomena of all sorts in *Pathelin*, we may hypothesize that the dominant semantic category, or classeme, in the play is /deceit/. On the assumption of this broad field of investigation, we shall attempt to determine the extent to which the axis "Delusion or Lie" in the model, characterized by a state of "Appearing + Not Being," finds expression at numerous levels of narrative and discoursive organization. It is a matter, then, not only of identifying occurrences of this state, but also of describing the relations among these occurrences, as well as the properties that combine to make up any given state and constitute its identity as a figure of deceit. Whence the necessity to consider the figures of deceit in *Pathelin* in both the syntagmatic and the paradigmatic dimensions or, in other words, in terms of the linear distribution of the narrative as well as in terms of specific hierarchies of relations within this distribution. By way of a perhaps oversimplified analogy, if texts were railway trains, one would examine not only the boxcars and their linkage, but also the linear disposition of the track that conveys them.

In Part I (Chapter 2), the narrative infrastructure of the entire play will be examined in order to see how the basic structure of the axis of Delusion in the model is ramified in the syntagmatic organization of functions. Here we are dealing with the track, again on the analogy of trains, and, to some extent, with the disposition of the boxcars. Then Part II (Chapter 3) will discuss configurations of /deceit/ in the "conjoining" of narrative expression and content, while Chapters 4–8 will consider how /deceit/ informs prominent verbal and semantic levels of discourse tributary to the functions previously identified. It will be a matter of admiring the way in which the train moves along in conformity with the curvatures in the track as well as of looking into the boxcars with /deceit/ labeled on their sides.

In Parts III (Chapter 9) and IV (Chapter 10), the results of this intrinsic analysis of the discourse of deceit in *Pathelin* will be weighed in terms of a variety of medieval dramatic and cultural considerations. In this broader context, /deceit/ will serve as the criterion with which to determine the status of the play with regard to medieval theatrical discourse of an earlier period (Chapter 9) as well as with respect to the anticipation of post-medieval views of representation (Chapter 10). In this "classematic" approach, /deceit/ will serve as our point of departure and remain conceptually in focus throughout in order to keep the train of thought, as it were, on the right track.

PART I

The Narrative Dimension of Deceit

2
Infrapathelin, The Deceived Deceiver

According to the working hypothesis set forth in Chapter 1, /deceit/ is the dominant classeme of organization in *Maistre Pierre Pathelin*. To initiate the study of how /deceit/ is organized into recognizable figures at various levels of the dramatic discourse, the present chapter seeks to disclose the strategies of deceit conveyed by the narrative infrastructure.[1] This narratological approach was conceived in response to an observation by Henri Estienne who, as we have seen, singled out the "bonne disposition" as a particularly admirable quality of *Pathelin*. We observed that in the context of rhetorical tradition, "disposition" harks back to *dispositio,* second of the five parts of rhetoric, involving the arrangement of the elements of a discourse. In the present instance, it is a matter of the arrangement, or distribution, of elements of narrative discourse.

The distinction between narrative *disposition* and other elements of "discourse" has been made to conceptualize two distinct yet complementary areas of analysis, though, as we mentioned in the preceding chapter, the concept of "discourse" is theoretically inclusive of the narrative domain as well. As understood in a very broad context, discourse is constituted by the organized structures—grammatical, lexical, semantic, and so forth—that give coherence to a set of properties so that their relations constitute an organized system. Literary discourse comprehends not only verbal and semantic structures but, when story is involved, narrative structures as well.[2] It is thus not uncommon to find allusions to "narrative discourse," which, far from being a contradiction in terms, is simply an appropriate acknowledgment that a given discoursive universe may owe part of its organization and coherence to a narrative dimension. It is this dimension which has been designated as the *récit* by Claude Bremond and other French structuralists.[3] In its own right, this narrative level of discoursive organization is semiotic, that is, it "conveys a meaning in and of itself, separately from the story it tells us," as Seymour Chatman puts it.[4] In his illuminating synthesis, Chatman identifies narrative according to the criteria of "expression" and "content," each of which has its own "substance" and "form".[5] Expressed in terms of this familiar semiotic conceptualization, the present chapter is primarily concerned with the *form of narrative content,* as it appears in the linear, syntagmatic structuration of "events" and the "functions" of characters. Chapters 3 through 8, on the other hand, will deal with the ways in which this narrative form conveys the *substance of content* as manifested in numerous verbal and semantic discursive configurations made up of objects and actions that emanate from the author's cultural background.

The rapid development of narratology during the past two decades, greatly inspired by the earlier seminal work of Propp, has contributed to a tendency to isolate the narrative dimension from other levels of discourse so as better to identify the "morphology" of narrative armatures shared by a given corpus of stories.[6] Useful though they may be for this purpose, such narratological procedures invariably de-emphasize that which is unique in a single narrative work.[7] To compensate for this abstract, artificially isolated apprehension of the narrative dimension, I have elsewhere suggested that more attention be devoted to what could be called "narrative style," that is, to the complex relations between a specific narrative infrastructure and the hierarchy of verbal and semantic features which it relays.[8] In this study of *Pathelin,* I have chosen initially to analyze the narrative dimension, though the choice does not reflect a belief that this dimension is of greater importance than other levels of discourse. It is nonetheless a readily accessible dimension: "The narrative level is the most evident stratum of the theatrical system," observes Patrice Pavis.[9] Moreover, it is this dimension which provides the armature, or skeletal contours, of the whole. As in the study of "narrative style," where narrative is seen in *relation* to other levels of the discourse, we shall initially avail ourselves of the useful analytical tools of narratology and thus lay the foundation for other, complementary types of analysis pertinent to later examination of related verbal and semantic features.

Readers of *Maistre Pierre Pathelin* often savor the way in which Pathelin, the masterful deceiver, is himself deceived in the closing moments of the spectacle, whence an instance of the timeless narrative formula of "deceiver deceived." It will be recalled from Chapter 1 that Greimas and Courtés characterize this story type as one in which there is an invalidation of the "fiduciary contract" between characters because of a discrepancy between events and knowledge about them.[10] If deceivers are "have-nots" motivated by their victims who are "haves," the success of the former is often assured by making the victims into "know-nots." By controlling and limiting the knowledge available to the victim, the deceiver may conceal the truth regarding crucial events and thus attain his objective at the expense of the ignorant victim.

This sort of manipulation of knowledge so as to deceive a potential victim recurs at prominent moments throughout the play. In all, six such instances stand out as the most important narrative actions, or *functions,* in the entire play. Each of these is in fact a variant of the same function,

Deceit, and for the sake of convenience, we shall identify them as functions D^1 through D^6. Each is characterized by the presence, either explicit or implied, of a fiduciary contract, or bond of faith between characters, whereby promissory assertions and other statements are or will be authenticated by circumstances or events. Yet each is also *marred* by the invalidation, or abrogation, of the implicit or explicit fiduciary contract. Whence the function Deceit; whence also the regular recurrence, at the level of narrative discourse, of the elementary signifying structure of /deceit/ identified in the first chapter in terms of the cognitive model of Greimas and Courtés.

We may usefully list narrative functions D^1 through D^6, bracketing information on the nature of the fiduciary contract involved in each instance and briefly summarizing the manner in which each contract is abrogated:

D^1 [*Buyer / Seller Contract* = promissory purchase on credit]
Pathelin seals his promise to pay for cloth by giving the clothier a "denier à Dieu," or earnest, then departs, goods in hand, without intending to pay.

D^2 [*Seller / Buyer Contract* = honest valuation of merchandise]
The clothier delusively persuades Pathelin to agree to pay more for the desired cloth than it is worth on the current market.

D^3 [*Debtor / Creditor Contract* = acknowledged obligation to pay for purchase]
By the use of elaborate pretense, Pathelin and Guillemette convince the clothier that he errs in his identification of Pathelin as his debtor.

D^4 [*Employee / Employer Contract* = Protection and care of employer's property]
The shepherd kills the clothier's sheep for his own use and attempts (unsuccessfully) to misrepresent their fate. (This may presuppose underpayment of employee, if we accept the shepherd's opinion, vv. 1087–88.)

D^5 [*Mercantile Court / Plaintiff Contract* = opportunity for redress of legitimate grievance]
By delusive collusion, Pathelin and his "client" convince the judge to dismiss the clothier's case prematurely, alleging that the shepherd is mentally incompetent to stand trial.

D^6 [*Client / Attorney Contract* = promissory retainer of services]
Having promised to pay his fee in gold, the shepherd dupes Pathelin by continuing to play his role of bleating simpleton prior to fleeing.

Our summary of these six instances provides a nearly complete digest of the main events in the play, and this suggests the likelihood that Deceit is *the* dominant narrative function in *Pathelin*. Further, it is evident that the classeme /deceit/, marked by (not being + appearing) on the axis of Delusion in the cognitive model, categorizes each of these functions, so that each constitutes a variant investment of the same elementary signifying structure. Apparent in each of these six major functions is the same iterative, or recurrent, pattern, according to which *the abrogation of a fiduciary contract results from a delusive persuasive doing.* The identification of patterns of delusive persuasion is of capital importance to the study of figures of deceit. Its ramifications exceed the level of narrative discourse, however, and necessitate a separate discussion of the phenomenon of *manipulation,* which will be taken up in Chapter 7.

The six instances of deceit in this inventory may be subjected to additional analysis before we map out the network of relations among them. Of particular interest is that a further distinction may be drawn between *pragmatic* (or material) *deceptions,* in which capital or consumers' goods and assets are the primary object of deceit, and *cognitive deceptions,* in which delusive manipulation of knowledge alone is the object of deceptive conduct. The following inventory classifies the six instances of deceit in *Pathelin* according to the oppostion *pragmatic / cognitive:*

D^1 Pragmatic [P → C]
D^2 Cognitive (abortive); Pragmatic (abortive) [C → P]
D^3 Cognitive [P, G → C]
D^4 Pragmatic; Cognitive (abortive) [S → C]
D^5 Cognitive [P, S → C]
D^6 Pragmatic [S → P]

(P = Pathelin; G = Guillemette; C = clothier; S = shepherd; → designates victim)

The interdependence of cognitive and pragmatic factors is evident throughout this inventory. D^1, where Pathelin departs with the cloth under his arm, is essentially a pragmatic deception, yet its success depends upon Pathelin's delusive manipulation of knowledge, so that the clothier is actually convinced that he is to be paid later, after enjoying a fine meal of roast goose. Moreover, the ultimate success of D^1 is assured by a further cognitive deception, D^3, in which Pathelin and Guillemette play the death scene, finally convincing the clothier that the bedridden, moribund wretch could not have been the merchant's client earlier in the day. D^2 is cognitive to the extent that the clothier gives reasons for the high price of the cloth (see vv. 240–53), pragmatic to the extent that these reasons are offered in order to obtain more money for the merchandise. Of course, D^2 is abortive on both counts: Pathelin is hardly deluded by the clothier's arguments (see vv. 336–38) and eventually keeps the cloth for the mere price of a "denier à Dieu." The shepherd's pragmatic dupery of the clothier, D^4, was evidently successful until the accessory cognitive deceit—whereby the shepherd maintained falsely that the sheep had died of disease—was discovered by the clothier. Like D^3, D^5 (the courtroom scene) is essentially cognitive, involving a delusive dramatization, yet it is also accessory to the pragmatic swindling in D^1

and D^4: the clothier's two grievances, one against Pathelin, the other against the shepherd, both remain unredressed. The final deceit, D^6, is clearly pragmatic, yet Pathelin's failure to obtain his fee stems in part from an earlier cognitive self-deception when he underestimated the shepherd's potential for deceit. Basically cognitive deceptions like D^3 and D^5 are motivated largely by pragmatic objectives, while all of the pragmatic deceptions are to some extent dependent upon cognitive manipulation. We shall return to this matter in Chapter 7.

The identification of iterative functional manifestations of deception reinforces the postulation of a narrative structure organized by the axis of Delusion and strengthens the hypothesis that /deceit/ is in fact the organizing classeme of the entire play. To further our primary objective of testing this hypothesis with regard to narrative syntax, we must now analyze the superficial structure of pragmatic and cognitive deceptions according to their *distribution* in the text.

Study of the distribution of the function Deceit, retaining the information heretofore gathered concerning the identity of deceivers and victims and the distinction between cognitive and pragmatic deceit, will facilitate the subsequent identification of logical relations among the major functions. Analysis of distribution is best achieved by the division of the text into its constituent segments. Determination of the latter is not as arbitrary as one might imagine because the play seems naturally to fall into three relatively discrete segments. Michel Rousse has in fact identified three segments of roughly equivalent length: I (vv. 1–497); II (vv. 507–1006); III (vv. 1017–599). The two monologues of the clothier (vv. 498–506; 1077–16) effect the "transitions" from segments I to II and II to III.[11] My segmentation in Figure 2 differs from that of Rousse only inasmuch as, for reasons of narrative rather than dramatic structure in the play, I identify the closing reversal as a fourth segment, though as we shall presently see, since it is totally dependent upon Segment III, I shall refer to it as Segment III[a]:

SEGMENT I	SEGMENT II	SEGMENT III	SEGMENT III[a]
D^1—Pragmatic [P → C] D^2—Cognitive (abortive)/ Pragmatic (abortive) [C → P]	D^3—Cognitive [P, G → C]	D^5—Cognitive [P, S → C] D^4—Pragmatic/ Cognitive (abortive) [S → C]	D^6—Pragmatic [S → P]

(P = Pathelin; G = Guillemette; C = clothier; S = shepherd; J = judge; → victim)

Figure 2

In passing, we may note that in Figure 2 there is a significant contrastive relationship between Segment I and Segment III^a. In Segment I, Pathelin first appears as a deceiver and retains this role throughout Segments II and III. (He is a virtual victim of the clothier in Segment I, but the clothier's deceptive strategy is abortive.) Not until Segment III^a does Pathelin exchange his role of deceiver for that of deceived victim. Moreover, the only *successful*, nonabortive pragmatic deceits, D^1 and D^6, occur in Segment I and Segment III^a, respectively. The implications of these particular relationships between Segments I and III^a will be taken up later in this chapter.

Having determined how the six instances of deception, considered as discrete entities, are distributed among the four textual segments, we can then analyze the *concatenation* of these deceptions so as to determine their *relational* distribution, thus realizing our primary objective of showing how /deceit/ is organized at the level of narrative syntax. Analysis of relational distribution may be accomplished in two phases.

Initially, each instance of deception may be considered as a *comportment*, or discrete pattern of conduct, susceptible of analysis according to its constituent phases: the modalities of its origin; its development; its realization or nonrealization. This ternary view of the comportment has been characterized by Claude Bremond as an "elementary sequence";[12] yet it has been pointed out that further subdivisions of the sequence are logically feasible. Recently, Thomas Pavel has proposed a model of the Proppian function "deceit" *(tromperie)*, showing that the sequence organized around this function is in fact divisible into more than three components:[13]

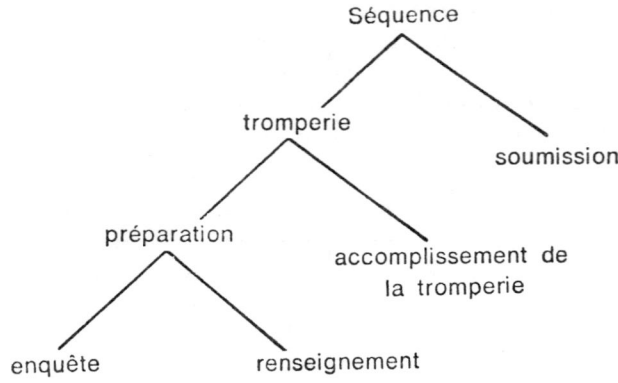

Here we can see that the comportment involving deception and submission is part of a more complex pattern which Pavel has analyzed regressively. Thus, prior to the victim's submission, the *tromperie* or deceit is itself marked by distinct phases of "préparation" and carrying out or "accomplissement." In turn, "préparation" may involve a prior search for necessary information, or an "enquête," followed by the acquisition of that information, or "renseignement," and so on, theoretically *ad infinitum*.

The six instances of deceit in *Pathelin* lend themselves to similar analysis, witness for example the sequence embedded in D^3, which we shall call "Deception Sequence 3," or DS^3:

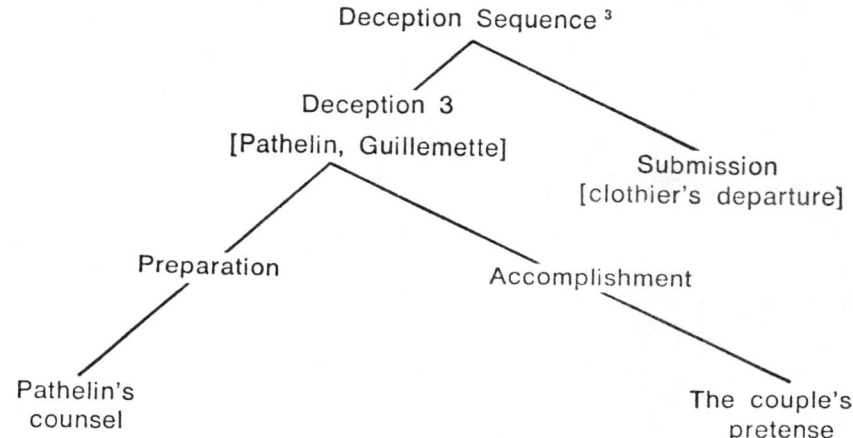

DS^3 is shown here in its conformity with Pavel's abstract representation of a deceptive comportment. This is by no means an exhaustive representation of the possible modalities presupposed by DS^3. Yet further subdivisions, such as the constituents of Pathelin's counsel or of the couple's pretense, would eventually culminate in tributary components not represented in the text and would therefore be of little practical value.

After identifying the components of the six major sequences based on the function "Deceit," designated as DS^1–DS^6, we may proceed to illustrate how these six functions are syntagmatically linked in the text, as in Figure 3.

This representation owes much to those made of Corneille's tragedies by Thomas Pavel in his *Syntaxe narrative*. The *Text* of *Pathelin* is depicted globally as being opened by an *Initial Situation* in which Pathelin is "deceiver" (T^r) and closed by a situation in which he is ultimately "deceived" (T^e). Each of the four segments tributary to this textual development are analyzed according to the major functions of deceit, D^1–D^6. These functions are in turn depicted in terms of the comportments involved in their realization. The diagram may thus be understood by *regressive* reading. Beginning with Segment I, *Preparation* of D^1 takes the form of Pathelin's *Displacement* (to the clothier's stall), followed by his bogus *Purchase* of cloth (with the *denier à Dieu*, or earnest). This *Purchase* it itself the occasion for the clothier's attempted deceit, D^2, *Preparation* for which is his *Lie* about the value of the cloth and the ensuing *Contract*. Having exhausted all aspects of the Prepa-

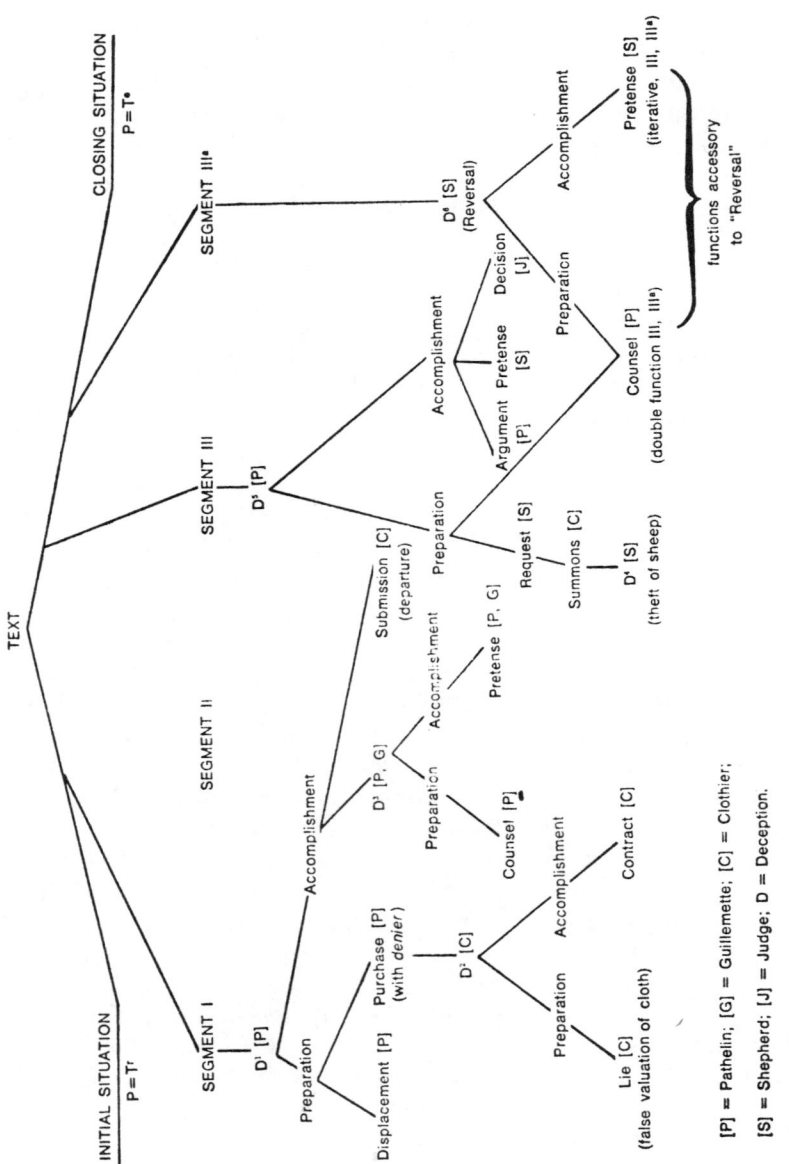

Figure 3

ANALYSIS OF NARRATIVE SYNTAX
Action: Deceiver Deceived ($T^r \rightarrow T^e$)

ration of D^1, we retrace our steps back to D^1 and proceed to its *Accomplishment* phase, which takes us to Segment II, D^3. The latter, involving Pathelin's feigned death, is prepared by his *Counsel* to Guillemette, accomplished by the couple's *Pretense,* and closed by the submissive second *Departure* of the clothier. Thus we can see how completion of D^3, a cognitive deception, is a necessary tributary to the *Accomplishment* of pragmatic deception D^1. Inasmuch as the clothier's deceptive program (D^2) is ultimately abortive, it comes to serve primarily as an index of his semiological status as "miser."[14]

Having "read" all of the ramifications of Segments I and II, we return to the upper "main artery" of the *Text* and proceed to Segment III, read it regressively as before, then go to III^a and do likewise. Segment III features the courtroom scene in which Pathelin defends the shepherd (D^5), but this scene has been prepared by an *extra-diegetic episode,* that is, by an episode which took place before the beginning of the events in the play. This was D^4, the shepherd's *Theft* of sheep, which culminates in the clothier's *Summons* to court and the shepherd's *Request* that Pathelin serve as his defender. Pathelin's *Counsel* that the shepherd bleat during the trial completes the *Preparation* stage of D^5, while its *Accomplishment* is brought about by Pathelin's *Argument,* the shepherd's *Pretense,* and the *Decision* of the Judge.

Like Segments I and II, III and III^a are interdependently conjoined. The *Reversal* (D^6) in III^a is contingent upon the double function of Pathelin's *Counsel* that the Shepherd bleat, as well as upon the redundance of this *Pretense* when Pathelin tries to collect from his "sheepish" client. The *Reversal* acquires much of its irony from the fact that, by virtue of his counsel to the shepherd in DS^5, Pathelin becomes the involuntary adjuvant, or facilitator, of his own deception in DS^6.

The foregoing analysis enables us graphically to see just how the widespread, popular, relatively simple story-type of "swindler" or "trickster" tale involving the theme of "deceiver deceived" is elaborated in the intricate network of deceits in the play. No one would ever prefer it to the actual performance of the play, yet it does provide an abstract illustration of the justice in Estienne's observation that the play is laid out according to a "bonne disposition." The diagram reflects the fact that, early in the play, Pathelin's thematic role as lawyer is devalued (vv. 1–13) while his background and competence as swindler or deceiver is valorized (esp. vv. 34–57). The initial situation in which Pathelin is a virtual deceiver gives rise to a series of his deceptive antics culminating in a reversal by which he in turn is deceived. The closure of the text is postulated on the transformation of the titular subject from the role of deceiver (T^r) to that of deceived (T^e).

It has long been recognized, as Stith Thompson pointed out in 1946, that the "trickster" figure is typically embroiled in adventures that make him either the duper or the victim, and Pathelin's exchange of roles identifies his kinship with this narrative type.[15] Yet this type of narrative normally involves two actors in the exchange, establishing "the well-known structure of the rogue and dupe (swindler tales) in which the two positions are interchangeable (defining man's fate as the eternally deceived deceiver), and the narrative endless."[16] Unlike the mythic story or folktale where an initial problematic situation is transformed into a closing situation from which the problem has been eliminated, and in which goodness and order are restored through the efforts of a subject-hero, the swindler tale confronts two antagonists neither of whom may be unambiguously "good." Moreover, he who dupes last may have duped best, yet his triumph leaves his adversary in a state of lack. Because closure occurs in this state of disequilibrium, it may seem arbitrary and susceptible of generating new adventures.

Despite the disequilibrium among antagonists engendered in the play by the type of narrative it incorporates, it is apparent in Figures 2 and 3 that *Pathelin* retains a textual equilibrium which is paradoxically evocative of the mythic story and folktale.

Consider in Figure 3 the harmonious complementarity between Segments I and II on the one hand and III and III^a on the other. Segments I and II form a self-contained unit, one that could constitute a play independently of what follows. At the end of Segment II, the clothier is clearly a "deceiver deceived," whence a satisfactory closing equilibrium. Pathelin retains free of charge the bolt of cloth which was, after all, the object of his initial "quest." Yet already at the end of Segment II the playwright has exploited the nondefinitive closure of his story type. The clothier is deceived, frustrated, and thus prepared for further segments in which he is the aggressor. Moreover, Pathelin is still a "deceiver" and remains to be deceived at the end of the two ensuing segments, III and III^a. Inasmuch as the clothier will remain frustrated and deceived at the end of the play, primary emphasis is placed on the titular character's ultimate reversal. This focus on the transformational perspective of the protagonist, so that his "story" encases those of the other characters, recalls the behavior of the "subject-hero" in the Greimassian analysis of the mythic story, the ironic difference being that the mythic story moves toward amelioration of the subject-hero, from disequilibrium to equilibrium, whereas Pathelin's story could be said to open with the precarious equilibrium of the "deceiver" and close with the disequilibrium (and degradation) of the "deceived."[17]

Whence the question: Is *Pathelin* a fusion of two separate farces, as some have maintained in view of the potential independence of Segments I and II, so that we have an example of primitive cycle-formation initiated by the disequilibrium at the end of Segment II? Or is this play really the work of a single playwright who cast his material according to the global format we know today?

The answer lies in the foregoing analysis of "la bonne disposition." We recall that the mythic story, folktale, and romance characteristically contain homologation of initial and final segments, so that the latter is quite similar to—sometimes even a virtual replica of—the former, except that it reflects the intermediary transformations that have occurred.[18] Likewise, a similar type of homologation of initial and final segments occurs in *Pathelin*. Earlier, we noted in Figure 2 the relationships between Segments I and III^a, which contain the only successful pragmatic deceptions in the play. These segments are especially reminiscent of the initial and final *contenus corrélés*, or homologous structurations of content, in Greimas's representation of the mythic story paradigm.[19] Homologation exists between D^1 and D^6, for Pathelin's pragmatic swindle of the clothier in Segment I is qualitatively counterbalanced by the shepherd's pragmatic swindle of Pathelin in III^a. The intermediary segments do not feature Pathelin as "deceived," and closure occurs *only* after he is finally deceived and, moreover, deceived in the same manner as he originally deceived, that is, *by the abrogation of a fiduciary contract stipulating the payment of gold* (cf. vv. 298–99 and 1125–26). Distributional analysis would thus seem to indicate that *Pathelin* was conceived, or at least unified from antecedent material, by a single author who, perhaps unconsciously, recuperated the paradigm of the *récit mythique* to the extent that closure is contingent upon the situational transformation of the titular actor from the status of "deceiver" to that of "deceived," as well as upon the achievement of a qualitative equilibrium between initial and final deceptions by the motif of nonpayment of promised gold. There is no question of a recuperation of the mythic *récit* in terms of content, but rather in terms of an empty content-form whose symmetry serves to shape the narrative closure of what is traditionally an open, ceaselessly alternating story-type in which protagonist and antagonist exchange their roles.

In this chapter, we have seen that the elementary signification of /deceit/ informs the six major functions of deceit around which the narrative infrastructure of the play is organized. The "bonne disposition" of the play's narrative dimension is a direct result of the artful way in which the complex narrative figures of deceit are developed from a story-type whose history stems back through remote centuries. Study of the submerged networks of "infra"-*Pathelin* must now give way in the following chapters to consideration of the play's "intention gentile," as we examine various aspects of verbal and semantic organization relayed by the narrative system. In this effort, we shall at last come face-to-face with the faces of Pathelin and begin to hear the languages and voices of his ideolects.

PART II

The Verbal and Semantic Structures of Deceit

Attention now shifts from Infrapathelin to Logopathelin or, in terms of the distinction drawn by Estienne, from the level of narrative *disposition* to multiple levels of verbal ornamentation and semanticization that reflect an *intention gentile*. Anatomically speaking, we shall see how the narrative "bones and cartilage" are filled out with the "flesh and blood" of verbal and semantic coherence.

The next six chapters examine different types of discursive "tissue" in *Pathelin*. First there is the level of *paremiological discourse* organized on the basis of proverbs in the play. Then devices of portraiture call into being an *epideictic* coherence, as in the oratory praise or blame of gods or men, known in ancient rhetoric as "epideictic" or "panegyrical" eloquence. The thematic importance of death and the law prompt analysis, respectively, of *thanatological* and *juridical* discursive elements. A chapter on *manipulative discourse* gives rise to another on the importance of speech acts, or *illocutionary discourse,* in the strategies of manipulation. In effect, these chapters deal with the six most important levels of discursive organization within the discourse of deceit, which is hypothetically the fundamental level of discoursive organization in the play. To this primary discursive order the six types of discourse are all tributary.

Of particular interest at the outset of this phase of study is the matter of how narrative and discursive features are interactively *conjoined* so as to elicit special praise from one of the earliest critics of the play. Inasmuch as it is in the elementary signifying universe of a *proverb* that such artful conjoining is most readily apparent, analysis of a paremiological configuration must take pride of place.

3
Paremiopathelin the Sententious

The narrative trajectory of *Maistre Pathelin* culminates in a proverb which metaphorically sums up the basic action of the story type itself. An exasperated Pathelin concedes defeat to the shepherd who has become his master's duper:

> Par Saint Jehan, tu as raison:
> *les oisons mainnent les oes paistre!*
> (vv. 1585–86)

(By Saint John, you're right: the goslings lead the geese to pasture.)

Just as apparently naïve goslings lead ostensibly experienced geese astray, so has this evidently simple rustic deceived the cunning lawyer. Although Pathelin adds that he will have the shepherd pursued by a "sergent," or officer, and imprisoned (vv. 1593–99), the spectator is acutely aware of just how empty this threat really is, for the judge has already acquitted Thibault Aignelet and even excused him, on grounds of mental incompetence, from all further legal liability:

> Va t'en, mon amy; ne retourne
> jamais, pour sergent qui t'ajourne.
> La Court t'assoult, entens tu bien?
> (vv. 1490–92)

(Go, my son, and don't ever come back, even if an officer serves you with a warrant. The court grants you full pardon.)

Thus Thibault may, in the final line of the play, offer to pardon any summoner Pathelin might send to fetch him, for, thanks to the lawyer himself, the shepherd is no longer subject to legal pursuit. These circumstances heighten the sense of finality conveyed by the proverb. The world of Pathelin is suddenly upside down,[1] and we savor the particular irony of this proverbial gaggle as we recall that Pathelin had earlier promised to cook the clothier's goose. If Guillaume was unable to find a fowl, the play nonetheless provides *us* metaphorically with one in this lawyer who laid the

43

golden egg for his client. A Rabelaisian Bridlegoose could not have done better.

In effect, then, the dramatic macrotext announces the fulfillment of its "deceiver deceived" story type by means of a proverbial microtext.[2] In the last chapter we discussed how this story type characteristically closes on a disequilibrium. No definitive conclusion is possible because a triumphant deceiver presupposes a frustrated and potentially disruptive victim. Despite the fact that Thibault is no longer held accountable before the law, nothing would prevent an imaginative playwright from creating a sequel in which the ultimate frustration of Pathelin prompts a new deceptive strategy to get the better of the shepherd. It is precisely the final proverbial utterance which disguises this disequilibrium and potential "openness" of the story type. The proverb is a form of anonymous, conventional wisdom that supplies a generalized paradox—that of the clever being deceived by the supposedly inexperienced—to sanction this specific case in which the shepherd deceives the lawyer. The gnomic insight spoken by Pathelin provides the essentially "open" story type with a kind of pseudoequilibrium, and the play may now close because it has validated anew, and is validated by, a proverbial truth.

Conspicuous use of a proverb to complement an essential element of the play is hardly surprising, for proverbs were widely employed throughout the Middle Ages. If the countless collections of medieval European proverbial expressions would seem to reflect their extensive use in popular culture, there is no dearth of evidence that they were highly esteemed and cultivated among the learned as well. They were put to sophisticated use in sermons no less than in collections of lyric poetry, *chansons de geste*, courtly romance, and religious and secular drama.[3] Their judicious use to achieve special sententious and stylistic effects was prescribed by rhetoricians from the twelfth century on, and as late as the sixteenth century, Henri Estienne observes that "good proverbs, appropriately applied, adorn the language of those who generally express themselves well."[4] According to Grace Frank, the literature of the earlier Middle Ages would seem to reflect a tendency to rely on proverbs for straightforward expressions of "uncontested wisdom . . . to facilitate the tasks of preaching, teaching and entertaining the commonality," while late medieval proverbial usage reflects "a shift from respect for tradition . . . to emphasis for various reasons, upon creative originality of thought and novelty of form."[5] This is particularly true of their abundant use in fifteenth-century French poetry.[6]

The clever insertion of a proverb to close *Maistre Pathelin* is typical of such late medieval innovative use of sententious expressions to ornament more than to instruct. Nor is this the only colorful proverb in the play, which from beginning to end is suffused with terse, incisive bits of gnomic wisdom. Le Roux de Lincy was able to locate no less than twenty-two proverbs in *Pathelin,* and it is likely that he, like most paremiologists, set aside a handful of additional proverbial expressions in current fifteenth-century usage but unrecognizable because not recorded in any surviving inventory.[7] While it may frequently be the case that a literary text is the ultimate destination in the itinerary of an orally transmitted proverb, it has been persuasively argued that in some instances a literary text may be the point of origin for an expression that subsequently acquires the status of common coin. Inasmuch as proverbs often display the same distinctive features, such as binary semantic and rhythmic oppositions, metaphor, connotation, archaic syntactic structures, anonymity, recurrent structural armatures, and so forth, proverbial expressions may be generated in a given text by analogy with extant models.[8] It has been suggested that the character-type represented by Pathelin may be at the origin of later proverbial use of the verb *pateliner* to designate a certain type of deceptive behavior involving the clever use of language.[9] Likewise, "revenons à ces moutons" (v. 1291; Come now, let's get back to those sheep), "à rendre au jour du jugement" (vv. 86, 1591; with payment due on Judgment Day), and "tu fais le rimeur en prose" (v. 1569; literally: You're rhyming in prose, i.e.: You're running this into the ground) are among expressions that may have become proverbial as a result of the popularity of the play or, if already in common usage before the play, may have become more widely cited after their occurrence within the play. The fact that only the first of these three is cited by Le Roux de Lincy need not exclude the other two from consideration as proverbial elements on the basis of their intrinsic characteristics.

The majority of the proverbs identified by Le Roux de Lincy are used to express a given idea or situation in a new key, so to speak. For example, Pathelin assures his wife that he will quickly supply their lack of adequate clothing, for "en peu d'eure Dieu labeure" (v. 40; God does a deed with all due speed), while she reminds him that "qui emprunte ne choisit mye" (v. 79; Beggars can't be choosers), which conveys her skepticism about his alleged ability to afford cloth of superior quality. The physicians attending Pathelin "en oeuvrent comme de cire" (v. 627; We're like putty in their hands.), that is, without difficulty and masterfully, as if they were working with malleable wax. The proverbial "main sur le pot" (v. 396; i.e.: If I had asked him to drink on it . . .) is in effect an evocation of ritual imbibing to validate a commercial transaction. Before the bench, Guillaume must "avaler sans mascher" (vv. 1319–20; Right now I'll just have to swallow it), that is, accept against his will the ultimatum of the judge to refrain from discussing irrelevant matters. Several proverbs, including the closing evocation of geese and goslings, are figurative expressions of deceit. Thus, to deceive may be to "vendre coquilles" (v. 1570; i.e., to deceive by selling shells that are empty) or "faire entendant / De vecies que sont lanternes" (vv. 800–801; to imply that bladders are lanterns; cf. in English: the moon is made of green cheese), while the naïve victim of deceit may be a gullible "Guillaume" (v. 772) or a "becjaune" (vv. 349, 263; i.e., one having the "yellow beak" of a young, and therefore naïve, bird).

In general, the proverb in *Pathelin* functions as a *paratext*—a minimal, closed textual entity introduced into the play at junctures where it behaves toward its host as a metaphoric parallel to replicate and, by generalizing the particular, to authorize some element of the dramatic discourse. To the extent that it mirrors the situations, events, and attitudes of the text into which it is inserted, the proverb becomes the locus of a *mise en abyme*, that is, a miniature replica of the text in which it occurs, and a device that adds reflexivity to important details in the play.[10]

This intimate and multifaceted interplay between the text of the proverb and the macrotext in which it is embedded necessitates that proverbs "grafted" onto larger texts not be studied in isolation, apart from their textual host. Ideally, a twofold approach is in order. Initially, intrinsic analysis of the proverb will yield valuable information concerning its narrative and discursive content. Numerous theoretical advances in this area have emerged from the recent work of Russian paremiologists.[11] Once intrinsic analysis is completed, it is necessary to identify the network of intertextual relations between the interpolated proverb and its host text.[12] This is especially important because meaning in either the proverb, the host, or both, may be greatly modified when the proverb is inserted.

Since the proverb which closes *Pathelin* is a miniature reflexive statement of the story type in the play and one whose position and imagery give it a special prominence, it seems to be a likely point at which *disposition* and *intention* conjoin. Ample reason, then, to subject it to a twofold, intrinsic and intertextual, analysis.

Interestingly enough, "les oisons mainnent les oes paistre" is not included in the inventory of proverbs in *Pathelin* compiled by Le Roux de Lincy. The distinguished paremiologist nonetheless cites two instances of it earlier in his study, both from the relatively late *Curiositez françoises* by Antoine Oudin (1640):

> —L'oison mène l'oye paistre,
> Et le béjaune précède le maistre.

(The gosling leads the goose to graze, and the novice precedes the master.)

> —Les oisons veulent mener paistre leur mère.[13]

(The goslings want to lead their mother to graze.)

The second verse of the couplet glosses the paradox of the gosling leading the goose, thus creating a metaphor *in praesentia*. According to M. de la Mésangère, "béjaune"—or "bec jaune"—refers to an inexperienced individual, one who still has the "yellow beak" of a young fowl.[14] The modal auxiliary verb of volition *(veulent)* in the second citation renders it more tentative and less emphatic, yet both variants are unmistakably in the same figurative lineage as the closing proverb uttered by Pathelin.

Intrinsic analysis of "les oisons mainnent les oes paistre" discloses clearly identifiable narrative and discoursive features. The statement tells a story in which an agent, or performer of action, designated collectively as "oisons," acts upon a collectively designated recipient of action, or patient: "les oes." Paradox is the chief quality of the discoursive coherence, for the roles of patient and agent are reversed and contradict the natural order: Mother Goose has become a follower. Be it noted that the denotative content of the statement expresses an unnatural relation between novice and master but that, intrinsically, there is no apparent denotation of deceit. Either a cultural background or a broader discoursive context furnished by the host must provide the semantic data that enable the statement to acquire the connotative force of deceit. We shall return to this presently.

Further intrinsic analysis of the proverb reveals a discoursive configuration made up of two classemes. Agents and patients are familiar barnyard fowl, whence the classeme /animality/. The activity they engage in involves the consumption of nourishment by animals ("paistre"), whence /alimentation/.

The most interesting observation that can be made as a result of examining this statement apart from its host is that it lacks the most important single distinctive trait of the proverb, which is metaphor. Divorced from all referentiality to a specific situation in the play, it does not even display the qualities of a metaphor *in absentia.* It merely makes a rather flat assertion regarding an instance of unnatural behavior in the animal kingdom.

These circumstances immediately change as we reinsert the statement into the context of the host text. The broader discoursive context reflexively enriches the connotative aspects of the statement, thus ensuring its value and function as a metaphor of the type found in proverbs. Consider the immediate discoursive environment:

	PATHELIN
	Par Saint Jehan, tu as raison:
Conclusion:	les oisons mainnent les oes paistre!
	à part
Major:	Or cuidoye estre sur tous maistre,
	des trompeurs d'icy et d'ailleurs,
	des fort coureux et des bailleurs
	de parolles en payement,
	a rendre au jour du jugement,
Minor:	et ung bergier des champs me passe!

(vv. 1585–92)

(By Saint John, you're right: the goslings lead the geese to pasture. [*To himself.*] I thought I was the master in these parts of all the cheaters and swindlers and those who give their word in payment, collectible on Judgment Day; and now a shepherd of the fields outwits me.)

Several things happen to the statement in this context. Chief among these is the fact that Pathelin provides his own explicative gloss. As we learn that Pathelin thought himself to be the "master" of deceit and the shepherd but a novice, we become aware of a coherent specific situation that is retrospectively analogous to the gosling-geese paradox. The latter now becomes a metaphor *in praesentia*. Moreover, like a proverb, it serves as a metaphoric generalization whose referentiality moves from textual circumstances to some extratextual pseudolaw that is nonspecific to a given situation in a definite time or place. It now has "the look and the feel" of a bit of proverbial, conventional wisdom, with that quality of timeless, anonymous generality that will serve as an appropriate citation to characterize some specific discoursive coherence in the host text. The manner in which Pathelin makes the statement to achieve such a generalization of his situation is characteristic of the situation of enunciation normally found when proverbs occur in literary texts.

In addition to providing an analogy between a situation and a generality, the proverbial expression assumes the function of conclusion in a syllogistic structure. As indicated in the margin above, the *major premise* consists of what Pathelin formerly held to be true, the *minor premise* is an instance that contradicts this belief, while the proverb presents the logical *conclusion* resulting from this contradiction. A similar structure, with the conclusion preceding major and minor premises, has been noted in the use of *sententiae*.[15] In this example, the structure further casts into relief the proverbial statement by making it serve as a conclusion.

If this image of goslings and geese acquires the earmarks of a proverb as it becomes embedded in an immediate discoursive environment, is it truly a proverb? It has been demonstrated that recourse to a paremiological inventory such as the copious compilation of a Le Roux de Lincy or of a Morawski is not necessarily an infallible guide, since many proverbs current long ago may easily escape notice, while the arbitrary criteria of the analyst may unduly exclude or include cetain expressions.[16] If the discoursive context that follows upon the geese-goslings expression indicates that it is indeed proverbial, was it in fact a proverb in fifteenth-century usage prior to the play? The play itself furnishes at least partial evidence that it was. Earlier, the verb *paistre* is used figuratively, meaning "to deceive: "chascun me *paist* de lobes," says the clothier (v. 1007; Everybody feeds me lies). It is also used to denote a deceptive comportment in the verbal agglomerative "faire paistre" when Pathelin says, "Il vous fait paistre" (v. 1295; i.e., He's trying to make an ass of you!), in order to convince the judge that Guillaume is really attempting to deceive the court instead of merely confusing one grievance with another. Moreover, "mener paistre" itself appears in a connotation of deceit in verse 1085. These instances confirm the figurative value of the agglomerative "mener paistre" in the proverb, thus revealing that, by current usage, "les oisons mainnent les oes paistre" was *already* a statement with metaphoric value independent of the discoursive context created by the conclusion of the play. The syntactic postponement of *paistre* results from the need to create a rhyme for *maistre* in the following line. Occurrence of this expression in a couplet based on the rhyming of *paistre / maistre,* as in the version cited from Oudin by Le Roux de Lincy, further indicates that the playwright consciously inserted the geese-goslings expression as a previously current proverb and not as an original creation.

Identification of "mener paistre" as a figure of deceit in current usage demonstrates that, even apart from context, the public would have received "les oisons mainnent les oes paistre" as a proverb, and not as a mere statement of paradox. Having restored the expression to its fifteenth-century cultural context, we must modify our evaluation of its classematic content. Given the metaphoric value of "mener paistre," we can now see that there are not two but *four* basic classemes in the expression. In addition to /animality/ and /alimentation/, we recognize /nonalimentation/, since "mener paistre" is understood figuratively. Moreover, the classeme /deceit/ is produced by this figurative usage. Mother Goose may lead her goslings out to graze, but if permitted, they would merely lead her astray. Reception of the statement as a proverb relies on the mechanism of connotative semiosis whereby the literal classeme /alimentation/ is displaced by its figurative counterpart, /nonalimentation/. When this displacement occurs, /deceit/ is understood:

Literal Classemes   *Figurative Classeme*
/animality/
/alimentation/ } + /nonalimentation/ = /deception/

The narrative development of the deceiver-deceived story type thus culminates in a proverb whose narrative structure is a reflexive miniaturization of the story type and whose chief discoursive elements constitute a figure of deceit as well.

If this proverb reflects the main narrative development in *Pathelin,* does it also reflect other levels of discourse as well? To what extent do these four classemes occur in earlier segments of the play?

In fact, the same discoursive configuration of four classemes *does* appear elsewhere. Consider the figure of deceit prominently developed in the first half of the play: "manger l'oe" (to eat goose).

In 1931, Mario Roques classified occurrences of this expression and its variants according to three categories:

I. Literal sense, to dine on roast goose:

    1. vv. 300–301:   Et si mangerez de mon oye,
                            par Dieu, que ma femme rotist. (Pathelin)

(By God, we'll even eat the goose that my wife is roasting.)

2. vv. 500–502:   Je doy boire et si mangeray
　　　　　　　　　de l'oye, par saint Mathelin
　　　　　　　　　chiez maistre Pierre Pathelin.

(Clothier: I'll soon be drinking and eating goose at Master Pierre Pathelin's house.)

3. vv. 698–99:   Et n'avez vous point d'oye
　　　　　　　　　au feu?

(Clothier: And don't you have a goose cooking?)

II. Figurative use, the idea expressed being "deceit":

1. v. 1577:　　　　　　LE BERGIER
　　　　　　Bee!
　　　　　　　　　　　　PATHELIN
　　　　　　　　　　　Me fais tu mengier de l'oe?

(Shepherd: Baa! Pathelin: Are you trying to pull the wool over my eyes?)

III. Either literal use, as in I, or figurative, as in II, or a play on both:

1. v. 460:   Il doit venir manger de l'oe.

(Pathelin: He's supposed to come eat goose with us.)

2. vv. 700–702:   Ha, sire, ce n'est pas viande
　　　　　　　　　pour malades; mangez vos oes
　　　　　　　　　sans nous venir jouer des moes.

(Guillemette: Sir, that's not a dish for sick people. Go chase your own goose and don't come here making fun of us.)

Roques pointed out that the clothier's literal understanding of the expression contrasts with the figurative sense in which it is meant by the other actors in the play, maintaining that this is possible by the use of *oye*, as in the examples in Section I above, when it is a question of creating in the mind of the clothier the image of a literal goose roasting in the oven, in contrast with the use of *oe* when deceit is meant, as in Sections II and III. The clothier thus fails to recognize the malicious implications of an expression that was—as Roques also maintains—popular before the play was written.[17] For the clothier, the term *oye* combines the classemes of /animality/ and /alimentation/:

Clothier:　　　　　OYE
　/animality/　 ⎫
　　　　　　　　 ⎬　≠　　/deception/
　/alimentation/⎭

His inability to seize the metaphoric import reflects a truncated paremiological competence. By contrast, the couple figuratively understood *oe*, as is apparent when Pathelin returns home with the news that the clothier "doit venir manger de l'*oe*" (v. 460: He's supposed to come eat goose with us). This elicits no query from Guillemette as to *what* goose is meant, whereas it might have, had she taken the expression literally. Furthermore, near the end of the play, Pathelin asks the shepherd rhetorically, "Me fais tu mengier de l'oe?" (i.e., Are you trying to pull the wool over my eyes?), in which context it could not be meant literally but only as a figure of deceit. Thus, like "les oisons mainnent les oes paistre," the use of "manger l'oe" to designate a delusive comportment includes all four classemes:

Pathelin, Guillemette: OE
/animality/   } +   /nonalimentation/ = /deception/
/alimentation/

Unlike the geese-gosling proverb, where /animality/ is the classeme of the agents and patients, /animality/ in "manger l'oe" is the classeme of the object of value. Yet in both cases, /deception/ results from the negation of /alimentation/ and the literalization of /nonalimentation/. Just as the goslings will not lead the goose to graze in greener pastures, so the clothier eagerly anticipating a dinner of roast goose will ultimately be left "sur sa faim." (Something is indeed "roasted" in the first half of the play, but it is certainly not a goose.)

Like "les oisons mainnent les oes paistre," "manger l'oe" is descriptive of a deceptive narrative strategy. It is narrativized in the first half of the play in terms of a quest by Pathelin followed by the counter-quest undertaken by the clothier. Again like the later expression, it functions in a special kind of figurative network which could be called a *proverbial marker of closure*. The closure of the first half of the play is predicated on the strategy by which Pathelin will definitively keep the bolt of cloth. To make this possible, it is necessary to ensure, in the figurative sense of /nonalimentation/, that the clothier "mange l'oe." The success of this ruse, as well as the closure of the first half of the play, is made explicit in the first line of the second half of the play, when the clothier says, "Quoy dea! chascun me *paist* de lobes" (v. 1007; Everybody feeds me lies!). Here he voices the nonalimentary nature of his alimentation.

The link between the closing proverb of the second half of the play and earlier developments is further emphasized by the recurrence of *paistre*. This verb, like Modern French *paître*, means "to feed (an animal) . . . [or] lead (animals) to the fields (so that they may nourish themselves)," according to Robert. Yet it may also designate human consumption of food, as when Pathelin asks the clothier if he is doing well enough in business to "se paistre" (v. 115, buy food). This figurative usage, followed by later occurrences in figures of deceit ("chascun me paist de lobes," v. 1007; "il vous fait paistre," v. 1295), all of which apply to humans rather than to animals, prepares the way for assimilation of the classeme /humanity/ to that of /animality/ in the closing proverb.

In two sets of varying combinations, the same four classemes serve to effect a transition between the two major segments of the play. The figure:

$$/\text{alimentation}/ + /\text{nonalimentation}/ = /\text{deception}/$$

in the clothier's "chascun me paist de lobes" is immediately followed by his lawsuit against the shepherd, who has been stealing his sheep for his own /alimentation/, whence the figure:

$$\left.\begin{array}{l}/\text{animality}/\\/\text{alimentation}/\end{array}\right\} = /\text{deception}/$$

In addition to reflecting the two main narrative strategies of deceit, marking closure in these schemes, and effecting a transition between them, the same four-element discoursive configuration determines the figure of deceit in one of the most arresting, lively, and reflexively significant passages in the entire play, that in which the fable of the fox and the crow is retold by Guillemette. As Pathelin details to his spouse the manner in which he obtained cloth on credit, she recalls the fable as an analogous episode:

> Il m'est souvenu de la fable
> du corbiau qui estoit assis
> sur une croix de cinq a six
> toises de hault, le quel tenoit
> ung fromage au bec; la venoit
> ung renard qui vit ce froumaige;
> pença a luy: "Comment l'aurai ge?"
> Lors se mist dessoubz le corbeau.
> "Ha!" fist il, "tant as le corps beau,
> et ton chant plain de melodie!"
> Le corbeau, par sa cornardie,
> oyant son chant ainsi vanter,
> si ouvrist le bec pour chanter
> et son fromaige chet a terre
> et maistre Renard le vous serre
> a bonnes dens, et si l'emporte;
> ainsi est il, je m'en fais forte,
> de ce drap: vous l'avez happé
> par blasonner, et attrappé
> en luy usant de beau langaige,
> comme fist Renard du froumaige;
> vous l'en avez prins par la moe.

(vv. 438–59)

(That reminds me of the fable of the crow, who was sitting up on a high cross with a piece of cheese in his beak. A fox came by and, seeing the cheese, thought to himself, "How can I get that?" Then he sat directly beneath the crow and said, "Ah, you have such splendid feathers and your song is so melodious." The vain and foolish crow, hearing his song praised like that, opened his beak to sing. His cheese fell to the ground and Master Fox grabbed it in his teeth and ran. That's just the way it was, I'm sure, with this cloth. You got it by flattery and sweet-talk, the same way the fox got the cheese. You really put one over on him.)

Clearly, the fable and the play are linked by resemblances in narrative structure. In each we find an object of value (cheese/cloth), an agent (fox/Pathelin), a patient (crow/clothier) and, with the aid of flattery, a transfer of the object of value from patient to agent. The fable as told by Guillemette replicates the narrative structure of the first sequence of the *Pathelin*. One might also legitimately identify this insertion of the fable as another instance of *mise en abyme,* whereby the strategy of deceit in the encased story mirrors part of the dramatic action.

Yet an even closer affinity between fable and play is created by the presence of the same four major classemes found in the closing proverb. The fable is an account of delusive persuasion (/deception/). The matter of food is introduced with the object of value (/alimentation/), and effective deceit is consequent upon denial of food to the victim (/nonalimentation/). Finally, the actors belong to the kingdom of beast and fowl (/animality/). As in both "manger l'oe" and "les oisons mainnent les oes paistre," /alimentation/ is supplanted by its negative counterpart, and it is this classematic occultation at the expense of the victim which characterizes the semanticization of deceit. In contrast with the two proverbial expressions in the play, however, /nonalimentation/ in the fable is an *event*. In "manger l'oe" it is both an event and a figure of deceit understood at a nonliteral level. In the closing proverb, its pertinence has become exclusively figurative with regard to the final reversal to which it is applied. This progressively figural development of the discursive configuration reveals to what a great extent the metaphoric synthesizing power of proverbs is operant in the proverbial expression that closes the play. Moreover, the fable and the two proverbial figures of deceit all tend to suggest that the primary locus of affinity between the narrative infrastructure and other levels of discourse consists of this particular discursive configuration.

Further consideration would suggest that, in addition to these moments in the play when the configuration synthetically manifests the close bond of *disposition* and *intention,* virtually every one of the six instances of the narrative function "deceit," D^1 through D^6, relies in some significant way on at least two—and frequently more than two—of the four classemes that make up the configuration.

In D^1, Pathelin insincerely promises to pay for the cloth, successfully postponing payment by inviting the clothier to a dinner at which he will settle the account. As Larry S. Crist has noted, "the 'promise of dinner' causes Pathelin's side to 'outweigh' the clothier's," for the latter waives his policy against credit at least partly on the basis of the promised meal.[18] At this point, Guillaume and Pathelin reach an accord on the basis of mutual understanding of the classemes /animality/ and /alimentation/ evoked by the roast goose. When Pathelin later explains to this wife that, because the clothier is coming to "mengier l'oe," they must therefore pretend that Pathelin is mortally ill, the delusive figurative register of "manger l'oe" is, as we have seen, created by the two additional classemes, /nonalimentation/ and /deception/.

Concurrent with D^1, D^2 is the clothier's (ultimately abortive) effort to persuade Pathelin that his merchandise is worth more than it truly is. To support this strategy, Guillaume attributes high prices of cloth to the fact that "Trestout le bestail est peri / cest yver par la grant froidure" (vv. 244–45; All the sheep died last winter in the great freeze.). Here, allusion to a disaster evoking the classeme of /animality/ creates an anterior circumstance to facilitate delusive persuasion. Moreover, /nonalimentation/ of cattle, as a result of the severe winter, is a likely conclusion to be drawn from this laconic account: either there was no feed available, in which case the animals died from malnutrition, or else they were frozen to death, and could thus not be fed and conditioned for spring shearing. In short, the cloth trade appears to have fallen on hard times, if we take seriously what the clothier says. Even Pathelin wonders aloud if Guillaume can earn enough to put food on the table: "Comment se porte marchandise? / s'en peult on ne soigner ne *paistre*?" (vv. 114–15; And how's business? Are you able to keep the wolf from the door?).

In D^3, where Pathelin and Guillemette play the "death scene," eventually convincing the clothier that he errs in his identification of Pathelin as his debtor, a cognitive ruse completes the pragmatic swindle initiated in D^1. The /deception/ involves literal /nonalimentation/ of the clothier, with considerable play on the image of the goose, either as a culinary object—"Et n'avez vous point d'oye / au feu?" (vv. 698–99; And don't you have a goose cooking?)—or as a figure of deceit—". . . mangez vos oes / sans nous venir jouer des moes" (vv. 701–2; Go chase your own goose and don't come here making fun of us). The clothier is forced to acknowledge that something other than food is being served: "Je n'ay point aprins qu'on me *serve* / de telz motz en mon drap vendant" (vv. 798–99; I'm not used to being paid [literally, "served"] with words when I sell my cloth.). One of the masterful touches in the play is the series of dialects in which Pathelin raves, culminating in this passage of kitchen Latin that manifests all of the essential classemes:

Paremiopathelin the Sententious

>   quid petit ille mercator?
>   Dicat sibi quod *trufator*,   /deception/
>   ille qui in lecto jacet,
>   vult ei dare, si placet,
>   de *oca* ad *comedendum*.   /animality/   /alimentation/
>   Si sit bona ad edendum,
>   pete tibi sine mora.
>
>   (vv. 962–68)

(What does that merchant want? Let him say to himself that the swindler, the one lying in bed, wants to give if he will, some goose to eat. If it's good, ask for some without delay.)

In addition to the three explicit classemes in the passage, that of /nonalimentation/ is clear from Pathelin's recumbent situation, which is hardly pertinent to culinary matters.

D⁴ has taken place before the events in the play and thus serves as an extra-diegetic catalyst for the second half of the play, featuring the shepherd. From the outset, he cleverly plays on the ambiguity of /alimentation/ and /nonalimentation/ in the verbal agglomerative "mener paistre," as is evident in the following enjambment:

>   LE BERGIER
>   J'ay a faire a ung entendeur,
>   entendez vous bien, mon doulx maistre,
>   a qui *j'ay long temps mené paistre
>   ses brebis*, et les y gardoye.
>
>   (vv. 1083–86)

(I work for a certain merchant, you know, and for a long time I've taken his sheep out to graze and I guard 'em. . . .)

We learn that he has himself been feeding on these creatures. In describing his deceit to Pathelin, the shepherd broaches /alimentation/ with an explicit reference to the digestive tract. When the clothier would tell him to get rid of the dead sheep, " 'Voulentiers,' fais je; mais cela / se faisoit par une aultre voye, / car, par saint Jehan, je les mengeoye, / qui savois bien la maladie" (vv. 1101–4; "I'll be glad to," I'd say; and I'd get rid of it all right, but not the way he thought, for, by St. John, I ate every one of 'em, 'cause I knowed what they really died of). The obvious humor of /animality/, whereby the shepherd's unorthodox relation to the sheep he has consumed is one of englober to englobed, is emphasized onomastically by his name Thibault Aignelet, and deconstructively by the lawyer: "L'Aignelet, maint aigneau de let / luy as cabassé a ton maistre?" (vv. 1139–40; Aignelet, did you appropriate many lambs from your master?). (An *agneau de lait* is an unweaned lamb, and thus a figure of innocence.) Literally, /deception/ involved /nonalimentation/ of the livestock, which ceased when they were slaughtered, while paradoxically, the /alimentation/ of the shepherd was thereby assured.

In D^5, the courtroom scene, the clothier tries to demonstrate deceptive comportment on the part of the shepherd, while Pathelin, in the role of defender of the innocent, uses the vocal /animality/ of Thibault to attempt deceptively to prove his client's /nonalimentation/. After Thibault is absolved, the judge offers /alimentation/ to Pathelin (vv. 1499–1500). One wonders if at this point the judge, who is not only deceived but an unwitting deceiver, is not paradigmatically associated with Pathelin by the role of "donor of repast" with its overtones of deceit. Such an implicit reception of this detail is indeed possible on the classeme /alimentation/. In response to this offer, Pathelin elects to forgo /alimentation/ in order to reap the benefits of deceit. The four classemes also come into this scene by way of the garbled account Guillaume makes of his grievance against the shepherd. Pathelin turns this confusion to the advantage of the shepherd by implying that Guillaume is deliberately attempting to confuse the judge: "Par le sang bieu, *il vous fait paistre*" (v. 1295). While Pathelin maintains that Guillaume is "feeding" the judge a line, Guillaume concedes that he must "swallow" his venom over being hoodwinked by Pathelin: "il le me couvient *avaler / sans mascher*," i.e., I must give up pursuit of Pathelin for larceny on this occasion (vv. 1319–20).

Finally, in D^6, Pathelin, having foregone /alimentation/ with the judge, sets about to collect his fee from the shepherd, who dupes his lawyer by continuing his vocal /animality/ prior to fleeing.

We can readily see, then, that the classemes organized by the discursive configuration of the closing proverb are diffused throughout the play, creating a scattered array that progressively reinforces the synthesizing energy of the closure.

Attribution of so much importance to the proverb is in no way meant to suggest that it contains the only discursive configuration of any importance to the play. One might with equally significant results study the classemes in the figures of exchange, for example, and we have already begun to see to what a great extent the figures of deceit participate in an astonishing variety of tributary discursive configurations. Obviously an exhaustive inventory of classemes in a text of the complexity of *Pathelin*, were it in fact possible, would fill tomes without even beginning to exhaust what is a potentially infinite process of semiosis. Yet by tracing this one relatively simple, though prominent, set of classemes through the play, we can nonetheless begin to see to what a great extent the "intention gentile" praised by Estienne is "conjointe" with the "bonne disposition."

There may yet remain some question as to why the final proverb, rather than the classematically related fable, is identified as the primary locus of narrative and discursive conflation. If the same discoursive configuration subtends both fable and proverb, why not attribute a greater synthesizing value to the former?

In point of fact, it is not at all surprising to discover a particular affinity between the fable and the final proverb, for both provide a similar reflexive metacommentary on the deceit in the play, whence their similarity of function with regard to the host. It is well known that fables as well as proverbs belong to that vast body of sententious literature which harks back to remote ages. In some cultures "fable" and "proverb" are in fact designated by the same term.[19] Moreover, the fable may in some instances close on a proverbial utterance. Under these circumstances, the fabular episode retrospectively illustrates the more general wisdom expressed in the proverb, almost as if the latter were the host of a fable amplified from it. Indeed, there are known instances of fables amplified from a proverb, though the reverse process is also documented, and in many cases it is simply impossible to determine which came first, the proverb or the fable.[20] All the more reason, then, to wonder why more importance should be accorded the closing proverb in *Pathelin* with regard to the establishment of a unifying configuration.

Part of the reason lies in the widespread usage of proverbs in late medieval farce. It is well known that many farces are simply dramatizations of proverbs (e.g., *Farce des femmes qui font acroire à leurs marys de vecies que ce sont lanternes*). If "manger l'oie" was indeed proverbial before *Pathelin* was written, the use made of this expression in the first half of the play may reflect the tendency apparent in some farces to concretize proverbial expressions.[21]

Yet this usage of proverbs in farce is not characteristically one that is postponed until closure. Such usage is nevertheless commonplace in other genres. Proverbs are likely to occur initially, as in exordia, terminally, or at any point within the late medieval text where their presence would effect a pause and intensify reflection.[22] Yet their occurrence at the end of a discoursive unit where, according to Jauss, they lead "to retrospective insight into the unavoidable course of things,"[23] is particularly common in medieval texts. One thinks of such collections as the *Proverbe au vilain*, the *Proverbe au conte de Bretaigne*, or the *Descrission des religions* of Li Rois de Cambrai, where each rhyming stanza closes with a proverb. Similarly in the fifteenth-century *Proverbes en rimes*, where 182 proverbs anchor 182 *huitains* and as many illustrations. Proverbs of closure serve as refrains in the ballad, as appropriate conclusions to fables, and as a means of closing argumentation in the *jeux-partis*.[24] As in *Pathelin*, the *Remede de Fortune* of Guillaume de Machaut culminates in a proverb which broadly synthesizes and unifies all that precedes.[25] Zumthor has noted a marked similarity between the widespread use of proverbs of closure in medieval texts and the use of *sententiae* to conclude a discourse. Prescribed by rhetoricians as *epiphonema,* this figure produces a synthesizing conclusion which "retrospectively nuances the entire discourse as the latter is nuanced by it." The "épiphonème proverbial" was "in vogue" during the fifteenth century, especially among the Rhétoriqueurs but, as we have seen, in other contexts as well.[26] The proverbial closure of *Pathelin* may thus be viewed as a reflection of current literary fashion, though it is perhaps more innovative in fact than the insertion of an illustrative fable within a host, inasmuch as the host in question is a dramatic work rather than a relatively brief lyric piece.

Apart from these examples of contemporary trends, the greater unifying value of the proverb as opposed to the fable may be determined on the basis of the relative appropriateness of each. The fable is an account of successful deceit by a quintessential figure of deceit, the fox, yet there is no anticipation of the deceiver deceived. This paradox is better captured in the proverb, with its ironic reversal of roles between the experienced and the relatively inexperienced. The fable is consequently applicable to the first half of the play, while only the proverb applies reflexively to the action of the play as a whole. It is a more comprehensive figure of deceit, synthesizing the fundamental story type as well as a key discoursive configuration which manifests its classemes throughout the play.

Given evidence of late medieval amplification from proverbs that function in closure, the question may arise as to which came first in the creative process of the playwright, the proverb or the play? On the basis of the foregoing narrative and discoursive analysis, the question must surely remain unanswered for lack of the kind of substantial evidence that is normally impossible to produce. One might be tempted to hypothesize that the play came about as the result of an effort to amplify the proverb which Pathelin utters in the final lines. Yet we must immediately concur with those skeptics who would argue that to accept such simple answers to unanswerable questions concerning the genesis of this dramatic masterpiece would be to put the cart before the horse and the gosling before the goose.

Excursus: The Three Faces of Logopathelin

Long after Guillemette had pointed out that the fox in the fable is a prototype of Pathelin, since both are competent cozeners of cheese or cloth, Robert Louis Stevenson wrote that "there can be no fairer ambition than to excel in talk; to be affable [and] gay . . . to have a fact, a thought, or an illustration pat to every subject. . . ."[1] Pathelin the cagey fox had surely realized such an ambition:

> Mais, au fort, ay je tant bretté
> et parlé qu'il m'en a presté
> six aulnes. . . .
> (vv. 433–35)

(Anyway, I talked so fast that he finally gave me six yards on credit.)

Guillemette likewise attributes the guile of her talkative spouse to his way with words. Like the fox, Pathelin produces discourse with sharp teeth: ". . . vous l'avez *happé* / par blasonner, et *attrappé* / en luy usant de beau langaige, / comme fist Renard du froumaige . . ." (vv. 455–59; You got it [literally: snapped it up] by flattery and sweet-talk, the same way the fox got the cheese). Words are the teeth of deceit, and in the mouth of Pathelin they create a medium of exchange that takes the place of transactions in currency. Above all else, Pathelin styles himself as a master of the art of conning by the substitution of a smooth tongue for hard cash, as he reveals in his closing lament:

> Or cuidoye estre sur tous maistre,
> des trompeurs d'icy et d'ailleurs,
> des fort coureux et *des bailleurs*
> *de parolles en payement,*
> a rendre au jour du jugement . . .
> (vv. 1587–91)

(I thought I was the master in these parts of all the cheaters and swindlers and those who give their word in payment, collectible on Judgment Day . . .).

This glum recognition that his supposedly unrivaled capactiy to do dastardly things with words has at last been bettered by the likes of a lowly shepherd is unduly disconsolate. Was it not the lawyer himself, this late fifteenth-century W. C. Fields, who conceived the ruse of the *paroles bêlées*? That it was finally turned against its creator is of no consequence to his reputation as a trader of words for things. On the contrary, his defeat by the bleating *berger* is itself further testimony to his talents, for we see that even the one who conceives such a clever ruse is not impervious to its consequences. Whence in the ultimate reversal an additional tribute to his verbal virtuosity.

It is no doubt true that this quality is apparent in the other characters who verbally manipulate the system of exchange, such as by depicting a hard winter that has driven up the price of wool, or, on the opposite end of the scale of coherence, by emitting an onomatopoetic anaphora, thus avoiding legal fees by verbal "fleecing." Yet the delusive discursive doings of Pathelin are featured much more prominently than those of the other characters. To see that this is the case, we need only consider the *alternating rhythm* with which Pathelin is in the spotlight. The even-numbered deceptions are given far less prominence. In D^2, deceptive price fixing by the clothier is both abortive and incidental. So, eventually, in D^4 is the "muttonous" behavior of the shepherd which, after all, occurred well before the action of the play. D^6 is a brief ironic coda. Contrast the odd-numbered, Pathelinian scenes: In D^1, Pathelin, who is simultaneously subject, addressor, and addressee of his own narrative program, carries the cloth away without having to bolt with it; in D^3, again as subject and addressor, he dies a two-part, double-dealing death by counterfeiting multilingual madness; and in D^5, posing before the bench as the voluntary advocate of a "destitute" client, he wins his case while assuring that justice remains ambiguously and precariously suspended. In all three of these major productions, Pathelin not only uses language to accomplish his ends. Pathelin *is* language, wrenched from its conventional usage in a playful assault on the institutional contexts from which it sprang. Although uttered to delude and thus accessories to material objectives, the languages of Pathelin are also a tribute to the infinitely flexible vitality and potential of words. The narrative skein unwound from beginning to end is merely a framework to be repeatedly, elaborately overlaid with the tangled webs of words in which Pathelin entraps his prey.

In all three deception sequences featuring Pathelin, it is of more than casual interest that the opposition between recognition and nonrecognition is the foundation upon which the verbal edifice of deceit is constructed. In D^1, Pathelin pretends to recognize the lineal heritage of Guillaume in his physical features in order to win the confidence of the clothier and pave the way to long-term credit. Obversely, the success of D^3 requires that Guillaume not recognize Pathelin as his client, and this necessitates that he be convinced that there may in fact be a certain lanternlike quality about bladders, that is, that his initial recognition is erroneous and that this wretched sufferer is indeed at death's doorstep. In D^5, Pathelin strives to remain incognito, but the clothier recognizes his debtor, consequently losing control of his discourse as Pathelin gains full control of the situation with his.

The recurrent play with aspects of identity and recognition is not by any means original with this particular French farce. In fact, it occurs in the very earliest of those that have survived, *Le Garçon et l'aveugle* (late thirteenth century), where its effectiveness as a means of deceit stems from the use of mechanical rudiments of intonation, gestures, and proxemics, or spatial semantics. What is remarkable about *Pathelin* is the way in which identity and recognition, as well as their antitheses, transcend the values of elementary farcical strategies and serve as the means of producing and highlighting language.

The concomitant opacity of language in the play has been the object of comment for centuries. The abundance of collected notes on colorful, unusual, or obscure linguistic features attests to the richness and subtlety of language in the play.[2] All the more reason, then, to focus our discussion on those three linguistically "dense" sequences involving, respectively, portraiture, death, and litigation, in which Pathelin excels in talk by doing his manipulative thing with words, sometimes affably and gaily, but always with an illustration pat to every subject.

4
Pathegyrics, or the Subversive Encomium

Although Pathelin clearly excels in talk, it is not random talk—of good health or the way business is going (vv. 101–15)—that helps him achieve his goals. In each of his three verbal masterpieces, it is largely a question of using language in a context created by a particular institution, whether it be death, law, or portraiture, and of adopting a role suggested by this institutional context. Before the bench, Pathelin reverts to the strategies of legal disputation as practiced in his day, while at home on his deathbed, he first adopts the attitude of a patient anxious and bewildered by the diagnoses and remedies of his physician, then switches to the idioms of madness *in extremis*. As we shall see in the next chapter, the latter role also has an institutional context, created by the *artes moriendi* which were widely read in the late Middle Ages. In DS[1], he pays homage to the lineage of the clothier in a manner calculated to provoke sympathetic reception of a long-standing client. To accomplish this, he relies on the literary conventions of portraiture.

Returning home with his newly acquired cloth, Pathelin recounts to his wife how he ingratiated himself with Guillaume. This was achieved primarily by praising the valor and lineage of the clothier's late father, emphasizing the filial resemblance and slipping in a reminder of how the elder would courteously extend credit. The account immediately reminds Guillemette of the fable. Indeed, the masterful use of language is the key to success for Maître Pathelin as for Maître Renard, and in both cases the strategy of the deceiver is realized by flattery of familial characteristics. Just as the fox pays tribute to the inherited beauty and vocal talents of the crow, so Pathelin has regaled the clothier with adulation of the handsome appearance and generosity of the late elder Joceaulme, whose merits, he insists, have been passed on to his son.

It is interesting that, in her somewhat elliptical retelling of the fable, Guillemette omits precisely that feature which best establishes the analogy between Renard and Pathelin, the one concerning the father of the crow. It is worthwhile to cite this detail from an independent version:

> "Ha, dit Renart, biau Tiercelin,
> Qui si estes enparentés,

Pathegyrics, or the Subversive Encomium

> Dommaiges iert que ne chantés
> Aussi bien com fist vostre pere.
> Se aussi chantissiez, par saint Pere,
> Je cuit qu'en tout le bois n'eüst
> Oisel qui tant a tous pleüst."[1]

(Says Renart, "Ah, 'tis a shame, Tiercelin, my handsome friend, that you, who are of such fine stock, do not sing as well as did your father. If you were to sing like that, I daresay, by the Holy Father, that there's not a bird in these woods who'd seem as pleasing to us all.")

These lines are highly anticipative of what Pathelin himself says in praise of Guillaume's father:

> "vez vous la: vëez vostre pere;
> vous luy resemblez mieulx que goute
> d'eaue, je n'en fais nulle doubte.
> Quel vaillant bachelier c'estoit!
> le bon preudomme, et si prestoit
> ses denrees qui les vouloit.
> Dieu luy pardoint! Il me soulloit
> tousjours de si tresbon cueur rire.
> Pleust a Jhesucrist que le pire
> de ce monde luy resemblast!
> on ne tollist pas ne n'emblast
> l'ung a l'aultre comme l'en fait.
>
> (vv. 168–79)

(By God, the more I look at you, the more I see your father. You're more alike than two drops of water, without a doubt. What a gentleman he was, what an honest man, who would sell his goods on credit to anyone who asked. May God have mercy on him. He always used to give me a hearty laugh. Would to Christ the worst in the world were like him; then people wouldn't rob and steal from each another the way they do.)

In both cases, it is a question of manipulative evocation of the father in a context of panegyric, whether in terms of vocal talent or generosity with credit. The object is to imply that the same conduct would be commendable in the son and that the environment, either the woods or the world in general, would be thereby enhanced. The intertext between fable and play would thus seem to surpass the details in the account by Guillemette. Her omission of the matter of lineage is perhaps attributable to the widespread popularity of the fable, which obviated the need to mention one of its most important aspects.[2]

The key descriptive term for the delusive tactics of Pathelin in DS[1] is "blasonner," which in this context describes a particular kind of affable and gay talk akin to flattery:

> ainsi est il, je m'en fais forte,
> de ce drap: vous l'avez happé

> par *blasonner*, et attrappé
> en luy usant de beau langaige,
> comme fist Renard du froumaige:
> vous l'en avez prins par la moe.
>
> (vv. 454–59)

(That's just the way it was, I'm sure, with this cloth. You got it by flattery and sweet-talk, the same way the fox got the cheese: you really put one over on him.)

Guillemette uses the term quite generally here, reflecting the same sense of excessive praise found in late medieval figurative usage of *blason*, as in this example from Gringore:

> Princes, oyez des saiges les raisons
> Et de flateurs evitez les *blasons*.[3]

(Princes, heed the counsel of wise men and shun the blazonry of flatterers.)

In fact, the use of "blasonner" by Guillemette betrays an awareness that, in the fable as with Pathelin, it is a question of flattering the lineage, as one might "redorer le blason," so to speak. This emphasis on the familial sense of "blasonner" is anticipated in the earlier description Pathelin gives of his demeanor with the clothier:

> Je l'ay *armé* et *blasonné*
> si qu'il le m'a presque donné.
>
> (vv. 407–8)

(By St. Mary, I flattered him and his whole family tree so much that he almost gave it to me.)

Juxtaposed with *armé*, *blasonné* is evocative of the traditional, heraldic sense of *blason* as "an ensemble of distinctive signs and emblems of a noble family" (Robert). Thus, both Pathelin and his spouse view his flattery as especially noteworthy in terms of its familial emphasis.

In the encomium lavished upon the Joceaulme family by Pathelin, we find a masterpiece of pathegyric—or pejorative panegyric—which freely exploits devices of portraiture inherited from literary tradition.

Guillaume resembles his father "comme droitte painctures" (v. 125; a "perfect picture"). This premise gives rise to amplification by enumerative detail:

> Ainsi m'aist Dieu que des oreilles,
> du nez, de la bouche et des yeulx,
> oncq enfant ne resembla mieulx
> a pere. Quel menton forché!
> vrayment c'estes vous tout poché!
>
> (vv. 142–46)

(Look at those eyes, those ears, that nose, that mouth! So help me God, never did a son more closely resemble his father! And look at that dimpled chin; you're really a chip off the old block.)

Specific mention of facial features—ears, nose, mouth, eyes, and chin—adumbrates the traditional catalogue of physical attributes that grace the typical portrait in earlier medieval narrative.[4] The physiognomy shared by father and son then evokes amazement that Nature could form two such identical faces (vv. 150–53). Moreover, the clothier bears a striking resemblance to his Aunt Laurence (vv. 158–64). This is clearly a family portrait, and Pathelin can only conclude that family resemblance is the one quality which sets this family apart from all others in the realm (vv. 165–66).

Yet like a lovely cake left overlong in the rain, the veneer of the description is streaked and blurred. If for the supposedly myopic merchant the frosting is meant to seem glossy, it is otherwise for the spectator who cannot fail to remark the way Pathelin highlights his encomium with blemishes and flaws.

Consider the Nature topos as he adapts it to the purpose of a father-son comparison. We recall that in medieval romance Nature is personified as the chief adjuvant of God in the creation of mortals. She is known for her realization of an individual who is *sui generis* and superlative in both physical and moral qualities. Such perfection could not be achieved again.[5] In octosyllabic couplets, Pathelin echoes the convention so well that one can only accept as true his earlier boast that he has had some education (see vv. 14–27). Here, his ideolect is that of the narrator in romance:

> Sans faulte, *je ne puis pencer*
> *comment Nature en ses ouvraiges*
> *forma* deux si pareilz visaiges,
> et l'ung comme l'aultre tachié . . .
>
> (vv. 150–53)

(Truly I can't imagine how nature in all her works formed two faces so much alike that one is blemished exactly like the other.)

The italics have been added to designate phrasing that could fit harmoniously into the context of a twelfth-century portrait, so deliberate is the parody. The irony comes into play with the word *deux*, for the topos traditionally expresses amazement that Nature could form *one* incomparable, unequivocally perfect creature, not two who are equally "blemished" *(tachiés)*. The pejoration carries undertones of the scars of acne or, worse, of the ravages of congenital syphilis. Also implied is that, in this unparalleled instance of apparently careless "cloning," Nature had her mind on other matters. Read retroactively, what initially awakened anticipation of a straightforward use of tradition now says something akin to: "How on earth could Nature have committed such a blunder twice?"

This malicious bit of intertextuality is reinforced here and there by a series of negative depictions of resemblance, procreation, and lineage. The cleft chin—"c'estes vous tout poché!"—is a distinctive yet unflattering feature, evocative of the well-chiseled prominence of a scar, or of a face framed by the type of pouch characteristic of the double chin. Whence also, perhaps, an emblem of the corpulent, and therefore prosperous, merchant. Guillaume favors his father "mieulx que goute / d'eaue" (vv. 169–70; ... more alike than two drops of water), regardless of whether this liquid be spittle,

> car quoy! qui vous aroit crachié
> tous deux encontre la paroy,
> d'une maniere et d'ung arroy,
> si seriez vous sans difference.
>
> (vv. 154–57)

(Why, it's as if somebody had spit you both out in the same way, like two gobs against a wall. You're the very spit and image of your father)

or urine, as in the following pun:[6]

> Enhen, quel mesnaiger vous estes!
> Vous n'en ystriez pas de l'orine
> du pere ...
>
> (vv. 184–86)

(Ah, what a good businessman you are! But you wouldn't be your father's son, if you weren't.) [The pun on *orine*, meaning either "lineage" or "urine," is lost in translation.]

Facially the "spit and image" of his father, endowed with the characteristics of his paternal origin, and metaphorically of the same urological composite, Guillaume nonetheless from the neck down is bodily the image of his Aunt Laurence. Note the descending descriptive order said by Faral to be prescribed by Latin rhetoricians.[7] It is as if aunt and nephew were two equally rotund snowmen: "vous luy resemblez de corsaige / comme qui vous eust fait de naige" (vv. 163–64; You resemble her in shape as if someone had made you both of snow). Follows the observation that "en ce païs n'a, ce me semble, / lignaige qui mieulx se resemble" (vv. 165–66; I think there's not a family in the whole region whose members look so much alike), that is, all are plump.

The cumulative effect of these watery images is, at least from the vantage point of the spectator, to "liquidate" the lineage of Guillaume. Is the clothier in fact the son of his father, as Pathelin repeatedly asserts? (e.g., "vez vous la: veëz vostre pere," v. 168). The answer is tautegorically yes:

> et qui diroit a vostre mere
> que ne feussiez filz vostre pere,
> il auroit grant fain de tancer.
>   (vv. 147–49)

(If anyone should say to your mother that you're not your father's son, he'd just be itching for a quarrel.)

Yet, as we have seen, there is the recurrent counterimplication that, instead of by normal bisexual reproduction, within the institution of wedlock, Guillaume was procreated illegitimately, and that his heritage is chiefly one of venereal affliction. Or else he is the flawed product of Nature's handiwork, or perhaps expectorated, micturated, or even rolled out of snow, but in any case an anomaly which contradicts the notion of normal lineal ascendancy.

Lest this repetitive pejoration on the basis of shared physical attributes become too obvious, Pathelin laces his impromptu oration with phrases that *seem* to extol moral qualities.[8] Elements of the eulogy creep in, and eloquence occasionally aspires to the solemnity of funeral oratory.

> Ha, qu'estoit ung homme sçavant
> (je requier Dieu qu'il en ait l'ame),
> de vostre pere!
>   (vv. 118–20)
>   * * *
> Se Dieu eust oncq de creature
> mercy, Dieu vray pardon luy face,
> a l'amë.
>   (vv. 126–28)

(Ah, what a wise man your father was! God rest his soul. . . . If God ever had mercy on one of his creatures, may he grant true pardon to his soul.)

He was endowed with the foresight to predict the current state of world affairs and was in his own time held to be among the righteous (vv. 130–35). His qualities were truly nobiliary:

> Quel vaillant *bachelier* c'estoit!
> Le bon *preudomme*, et si prestoit
> ses denrees qui les vouloit.
>   (vv. 171–73)

(What a gentleman he was, what an honest man, who would sell his goods on credit to anyone who asked.)

(*Largesse* is indeed foremost among the virtues of feudal aristocracy as depicted in courtly romance, but it was achieved by giving the unsolicited boon, or *don,* and not by serving as lender or creditor.)[9] Yet he tendered his generosity with a hearty laugh and was exemplary in all his dealings.

Would that the dregs of this world were like him; people would not purloin and pilfer the way they do nowadays (vv. 174–79). Thus are stereotypical bourgeois sentiments and values elevated to the sublime dignity worthy of a great statesman of antiquity, merely by means of a few epideictic conceits. The deliberately uncomplimentary thorns are disguised in these bushy passages of hyperbole spaced at timely intervals throughout the portrait. Rather than damn with faint praise, Pathelin has chosen to damn with *feigned* praise.

It is quite another matter in the devastating portrait that Pathelin later presents before his wife. Equivocal praise has given way entirely to the most vicious sort of vituperation. Pathelin obviously abhors the thought of having been compelled to utter noble sentiments about a family which is clearly *roturier*. At last we see to what extent the Joceaulme coat of arms is tarnished on its underside. As Pathelin tells Guillemette what he truly thinks of the clothier and his relatives, the term *blasonner* is now realized in the ironic sense of "derision and mockery" (Robert). The family is neither a praiseworthy lot,

> Je luy disois que son feu pere
> fut si vaillant. "Ha!" fais je, "frere,
> qu'estes vous de bon parentaige!
> Vous estes," fais je, "du lignaige
> d'icy entour plus a louer."
> Mais je puisse Dieu avouer
> s'il n'est attrait d'une peaultraille!
> la plus rebelle villenaille
> qui soit, ce croy je, en ce royaulme.
>
> (vv. 409–17)

nor generous in their dealings with others:

> "Et puis," fais je, "saincte Marie!
> comment prestoit il doulcement
> ses denrees!—si humblement!
> C'estes vous", fais je, "tout crachié!"
> Toutes fois, on eust arrachié
> les dens du villain marsouyn
> son feu pere, et du babouyn
> le filz, avant qu'il en prestassent
> cecy, ne qu'ung beau mot parlassent.
>
> (vv. 424–32)

(I told him that his late father was such a worthy man. "Oh, my friend," says I, "what good stock you come from! Your lineage," says I, "is the purest in the whole district." But I swear to God that guy comes from the scurviest lot of scoundrels and the vilest riff-raff in the country.... "Holy Mary," says I, "how easily he gave his merchandise on credit, and without pretense! I can see," says I, "that you're his spit and image." But you could pull all the teeth of that sea-hog of a father and that baboon of a son before they'd give you anything on credit or even give you the time of day.)

It is interesting to note that, once again, the classeme /animality/ appears in this dramatic-ironic defamation of the family of Guillaume Joceaulme. In other occurrences of the classeme, however, the inventory is confined either to wild animals, as with the two types of predators so appropriately set at odds in the fable, or else to barnyard animals (sheep, geese, etc), as in the closing proverb. Although the clothier is identified with the barnyard category—"Je suis certain qu'il viendra *braire*" (whining, braying), says Pathelin (v. 462)—the negative identification of father and son as, respectively, sea-hog and baboon introduces a new category, the exotic beast not seen under normal circumstances in northern Europe. One is reminded here of how Edmund Leach has arranged animal categories in terms of proximity to humans: Self... Pets... Livestock... Game... Wild Animal, the latter category being equivalent to "Stranger" on the human scale.[10] In the play, the Wild Animal category produces the effect of extreme distancing in the negative portrayal of Guillaume and his father; though merchants, they are depicted as creatures with which humans do not have any exchanges whatsoever.

Yet even this negative description is reminiscent of antecedent types of portraiture. It will be recalled that epideictic oratory was traditionally the domain of censure no less than of praise. The mention of "peaultraille" and "rebelle vilenaille," as well as the accusation of greed and stinginess are clearly meant to vilify family background and character. As in the rhetorical tradition of *laus* and *vituperatio*, positive qualities like generosity and high birth are supplanted by their negative antithetical counterparts to effect the censure.[11] Closer in time to the play are the many portraits of ugly, physically deformed characters in medieval narrative. Memorable examples include the Giant Herdsman in *Yvain* and his counterpart in *Aucassin et Nicolette*. On the distaff side, the Loathly Damsel in the *Conte del graal* and Maroie in *Le Jeu de la feuillée* come to mind. Among the features that typify the "ideally ugly person" in this tradition, Colby lists "a large head, bristly black hair, an extremely wide forehead, big, shaggy eyebrows, abnormally large, fiery red eyes; a thin face, a flat nose, a cavernous mouth ..., huge teeth, a mustache, a beard, big ears, a deformed back, an immense belly, an excessive amount of hair..., black skin, and gigantic size."[12] Many of these details would adequately describe a simian primate, like the "baboon" to which Guillaume is equated by Pathelin. Unlike oratorical vituperation, however, these ugly creatures in medieval vernacular tradition normally fulfill a positive function, by indicating, explicitly or implicitly, some defect of behavior, understanding, or values in the protagonist. This lambasting of the Joceaulme family is thus something of a *hybrid* with regard to these two earlier traditions, combining elements of moral censure with attributes of ugliness, so that, in effect, the latter serve as indices of the former: Ugly does as ugly is, so to speak.

It is apparent that the method of portraiture candidly used by Pathelin in the company of his wife differs radically from the encomiastic strategy deployed to deceive the clothier. In the former instance, insults are used quite liberally to gloss insincerely flattering details, whereas in the presence of the clothier, Pathelin loses no opportunity to synthesize flattery and insult. While the vehicle is made up of clichés normally used to praise, they are consistently undercut by the tenor of insulting implications. This simultaneous practice of *laus* and *vituperatio* constitutes a parody of epideictic oratory, whose rules permitted either praise or censure, but proscribed the use of both at one and the same time.[13] Parody notwithstanding, Pathelin takes his cue directly from this oratorical tradition rather than from the norms of medieval vernacular composition, in which devices of portraiture were used more for esthetic ornamentation than to support a point in persuasive discourse.[14] It is almost as if Pathelin had prepared his pathegyric in advance by dusting off some neglected descendant of the *Rhetorica ad Herennium,* or of Cicero, Quintilian, or Priscian, borrowing therefrom the recommended topoi of citizenship, family, profession, deeds, and physical attributes, plus a few touches from medieval vernacular tradition, and loaded his discourse with carefully chosen barbs before setting out for the mercantile fair. Thanks to Pathelin, oratory once again makes its way into the public domain, centuries after Tacitus had sounded the knell of persuasive discourse.[15] Even in this shameless transgression of fundamental precepts of the encomium, we can see that, for a few moments at least, rhetoric is alive and well and living in Paris.[16]

One may ask whether Guillaume fails to recognize the negative implications in the portrait or simply chooses to ignore them. Although he occasionally betrays a certain lack of perspicacity, the clothier aspires to shrewdness, particularly where matters of business are concerned. Albeit without good reason, he does congratulate himself on having sold overpriced merchandise (vv. 349–51). It may well be that he decides to overlook the insults and to exact his revenge on the pocketbook of his client. This is to some extent a matter of how the director represents the scene, either by having Pathelin "play to the house" at the expense of Guillaume, or else by showing in the expressions and gestures of Guillaume that the latent implications in the portrait have not gone unnoticed. It is noteworthy that any residual flattery in the portrait is apparently not sufficient on its own to persuade the clothier to allow his merchandise to leave the stall on credit. Nonetheless, the clothier later recognizes that this flattery had been in some way efficacious: "Vous m'avez trompé faulsement, / et emporté furtivement / mon drap, par vostre beau langaige" (vv. 1480–82; You tricked me with your eloquent speeches and carried my cloth away like a thief.).

Yet to accomplish the degree of persuasion needed for credit, it is eventually necessary that Pathelin promise gold and a goose (vv. 298–301), thereby setting the stage for another verbal *tour de force* when the clothier comes to collect.

5
Thanatopathelin and the Art of Dying

In his pseudocelebration of Guillaume's father in Guillaume, Pathelin demonstrated his own acceptance of the premise that recognition of physical features, both of physiognomy and of morphotype, is a sufficient condition for attribution of an individual's identity. Language served in that instance to affirm the reliability of naïve perceptions. Now, when Guillaume arrives to take advantage of the benefits that having been recognized apparently acquired for him, Pathelin sets about to demonstrate the naïveté and total unreliability of perceptions, so that physical resemblance is in reality a difference.

To achieve this effect with verisimilitude, Pathelin divests himself of his affable, upright, magisterial facade, much as the fox casts aside one sheepskin cloak for another, in order to adopt the wan, horizontal, sepulchral attitudes of the doomed and bedridden invalid, carefully spreading the shroud around his moribund members. Whereas before, Pathelin's language had been the means of communicating a recognition of the survival of the dead among the living, it is now the means of ensuring the failure to distinguish between those who are truly dying and those who, in both the physical and moral sense, are merely lying. To a considerable extent, the success of this illusion, consisting of eccentric languages and an appropriate context of enunciation, is assured by the playwright's reliance on the discourse of death as it was institutionalized in contemporaneous popular devotion.

Around the middle of the fifteenth century, not long before the creation of *Maistre Pierre Pathelin*, there appeared a Latin work which has come to be known generally as the *Ars moriendi*. It was a treatise destined to serve the needs of popular devotion and most likely originated within a clerical milieu.[1] The text was disseminated in many forms during the second half of the century, yet it invariably dealt with the same fundamental situation. At the bedside of the dying man there occurs a cosmic struggle between the devil and his grotesque fiends on the one hand and the good angel flanked by numerous heavenly agents on the other. The gaunt and beleaguered invalid looks on in alternate states of dysphoria and euphoria as each party repeatedly challenges the other for possession of the soul that is about to take leave of its mortal abode. So that the devout Christian "might know in advance the temptations and the anguishes attendant upon these darkest of life's hours and thus surmount them,"[2] the *Ars moriendi* was written in a heavily didactic vein. There were two standard versions. The longer, consisting of six parts, includes practical counsel on the art of a Christian death, a discussion of the five temptations to which the dying are vulnerable, two series of questions which, if properly answered, will assure salvation, meditations on the life of Christ and prayers to be uttered *in extremis*, advice to those in attendance, and the prayers that they should recite. The shorter version develops the second section of the longer, detailing the temptations consequent upon the struggle of good and evil.[3]

It would seem that a handbook devoted to such a dismal subject would very quickly have been consigned to obscurity. On the contrary, it enjoyed an extraordinary success. Representations of the ravages of death, especially from warfare and pestilence, abound in European art and literature of the later Middle Ages, and they alone would have assured the *Ars moriendi* a public emotionally and psychologically attuned to its subject matter.[4] Yet there had also been a profoundly significant change in the conceptualization of a Christian's accountability at the moment of death: the earlier medieval belief that on Judgment Day a final reckoning would separate the blessed souls from those eternally damned had given way during the fourteenth century to greater emphasis on the moment of death as the crucial determinant of the ultimate fate of the soul. It was now thought that a sufficiently contrite and penitent attitude at death could eradicate a lifetime of sin. Whence the personal importance of making a salutary exit from this life into the hereafter.[5] A handbook dealing with the art of dying devoutly thus became an important item in the Christian household.

That it was widely appreciated is evident from the 234 known manuscripts that remain, in German, English, French, Provençal, and Catalan, as well as in Latin. Prior to 1500, over 100 printed editions were made from either xylographs, where text and illustrations are both produced in woodcuts, or from movable type,[6] and though its popularity had begun to wane by the mid-sixteenth century, it was still edited beyond 1600.[7] In catalogues of incunabula, it figures among the books most reedited in France and Germany and, especially in France, it is among the most frequently printed works, along with courtly and popular narrative. According to Febre and Martin, an early shelf of printed books might typically have contained "the *Faintes du Monde* attributed to Guillaume Alexis, farces such as *Pathelin*, the *Ars moriendi*, the *Shepherds' Calendars*, almanachs," and so forth.[8]

Though undoubtedly the result of a random sampling, this juxtaposition of *Pathelin* with the *Ars moriendi* is significant, for each in its own way develops the theme of death in terms of a personal confrontation with temptations.[9] In fact, one recent article has, though somewhat awkwardly, proposed that the episode of the "feigned death" in *Pathelin* is a parody of the *Ars moriendi*.[10] If from a modern perspective we might find little common ground between a sober religious handbook and a farce, a fifteenth-century audience for whom the *Ars moriendi* was popular—shall we say "bedside"—reading, might well have found the rapprochement quite apposite. Would not the dramatic representation of a domestic scene of dying have evoked in some contemporary minds the agonies of the bedchamber depicted in the *artes moriendi*? The question bears closer scrutiny than it has heretofore received.

As we shall see presently, the play contains passages that owe their coherence to the series of eleven woodcuts that illustrate the shorter version of the treatise. These vividly depict the five diabolical temptations of the dying man, the five corresponding scenes of angelic inspiration to counteract their effect, and a final scene in which the dead man's soul leaves his body accompanied by a heavenly host. It has been suggested that the widespread popularity of the *Ars moriendi* was due largely to these illustrations in the xylographic and typographic editions, for they appealed directly to the imagination of the unlettered as the Latin or even the vernacular text could not.[11] If there is an intertextual relation between treatise and play, it is clearly a result of the powerful pictorial medium of the former.

The likelihood of influence is increased by the relative chronology of the two. The years between 1465 and 1470 are generally regarded as the period of greatest production of xylographic incunabula,[12] and this is also the period usually cited as the most likely to have witnessed the creation of the farce. Holbrook maintained that *Pathelin* was composed in 1464, while other estimates fall between 1468 and 1474.[13] Precise dating of early xylographs of the treatise is inconclusive at best, though a French translation, in its first xylographic edition, known as *L'Art au morier*, has confidently been put at ca. 1465.[14] The woodcuts used for this edition and its Latin counterpart were perhaps made as early as 1450.[15] Inasmuch as the *Art au morier* is the first known book printed in French,[16] its novelty may have garnered considerable popular attention and thus have heightened the potential success of a dramatic parody based on its woodcuts. Whatever the case, reasons of chronology dictate that subsequent comparison of treatise and play be based on the illustrations of this edition.[17]

To create the scene in which the clothier twice appears to collect for the cloth Pathelin has obtained on credit, the playwright seems to have relied on the discourse of death in the treatise on dying. From this handbook, he devises a basic situation of enunciation. Pathelin is given the role of the dying man in the *Ars moriendi*, while his wife is made to alternate between the role of the pious Christian spouse and the good angel who repeatedly thwarts the strategies of the devil. The chief function of the devil and his cohorts is to tempt the sufferer by distracting him, and this is unwittingly accomplished by the credulous clothier. This play-within-a-play thus assumes the proportions of an animated *Ars moriendi*. It is therefore not surprising that several of the earlier printed editions of the *Pathelin* feature woodcuts evocative of those in the *Ars moriendi*. In these, we find Pathelin in his deathbed, attended by Guillemette and, occasionally, by Guillaume.[18]

Numerous details in the play serve to emphasize the resemblances between the actors and their counterparts in the treatise. Guillemette vividly evokes Pathelin's eleven-week moribund condition before ushering the clothier into the bedchamber:

> Il est bien taillé
> d'avoir drap! Helas! il ne hobe;
> il n'a nul mestier d'avoir robe;
> jamais robe ne vestira
> que de blanc, ne ne partira
> dont il est que les piés devant.
> (vv. 590–95)[19]

(He's in fine shape to buy cloth. Alas, he can't even move. He has no need for new clothes. He'll never get dressed again, except in grave-clothes; and he'll never leave his room again, except feet first.)

Like the dying man in the treatise, he is but a "povre chrestïen" (v. 676), "tant tormentez" (v. 672), and, as if mindful of the advice for those in attendance found in the handbook, Guillemette dutifully counsels this "poor tormented christian" to think not of his sins but of his spiritual well-being: "Helas! pensez a Dieu le pere" (v. 808; Alas, think about God the father . . .), and she frequently advises the clothier as to proper comportment in the presence of death:

> Ha, quel niceté!
> Seignez vous! Benedicité!
> Faictes le signe de la croix.
> (vv. 829–31)

(Oh, what madness! Cross yourself. *Benedicite*. Make the sign of the cross.)

She twice interprets the growing delirium of Pathelin as evidence that the end is near and that last rites are in order (vv. 856–57; 941–42), and at the end of the scene she attributes his babbling in Latin to his high esteem for the Divinity (vv. 970–72). In the role of the good angel, she attempts verbally to exorcise the "demonic" clothier:

> Alez vous en, de par les dyables,
> puis que de par Dieu ne peult estre!
> (vv. 652–53)

(Go away, by all the devils, since it can't be on God's part.)

Twice she accuses the clothier of "tormenting" Pathelin (vv. 672; 822), and expresses a desire to have the detractor bound (vv. 826–27), thus behaving toward him with an attitude of intolerant dominance characteristic of the angelic figure in the woodcuts. Guillaume is hardly a consciously demonic figure in this episode, and much of the comic effect stems from the manner in which the deceptive couple force him into this role. Yet his repeated interjections upon arrival—"Le dyable y avienne!" (v. 548; The Devil take your "speak low"!); "Le dyable y soit!" (v. 556; The Devil it has!)—as well as feigned suspicion of his motives on the part of Guillemette: "Dyable y ait part!" (v. 563; The Devil take it!)—all serve to associate the arrival of Guillaume with diabolical interference. Moreover, like the Devil in the *Ars moriendi,* Guillaume makes more than one assault on the "dying" man and each time is successfully repelled by Guillemette, who plays the vigilant guardian. Meanwhile, as Pathelin alternately invokes the Virgin and utters an oath of apostasy (vv. 833–36), or piously calls for his confessor by name (vv. 876–77), we are reminded of the sort of vacillation and paradoxical mental states said to be characteristic of the dying man.

These are merely sporadic and faint reminiscences of the treatise and its woodcuts. Together they do not add up to a strong case for intertextuality between treatise and play. As we turn to the woodcuts for the shorter version of the treatise, however, we find considerable evidence of direct influence of certain of the eleven engravings on the general structure and detail of the scene. In short, it would appear that the ideal Christian death, in which the five major diabolical temptations are overcome through five corresponding scenes of angelic inspiration, is displaced by a feigned death in which the temptations overwhelm the pseudosufferer. Whence a closer rapport between the agony of Pathelin and the five scenes of temptation. Interestingly, the five temptation woodcuts in the first French xylographic edition follow a progression which generally corresponds to the linear development of scene 5 in *Pathelin.*

Pl. I. *Temptation against Faith.*[20] In this picture, the emaciated and bedridden patient is surrounded by a variety of human, demonic, and heavenly figures that populate his grotesque visions. At his right, a devil is whispering to him and gesturing to three doctors in consultation among themselves, presumably concurring on the hopelessness of his condition. Above, a banner proclaims: "Infernus factus est," and a malevolent figure hovering in midair points downward. Beneath his index, a pagan king and queen kneel in adoration of an idol, and a second banner exhorts the sufferer: "Fac sicut pagani." Across the room, a third banner, held by a hideous creature, urges self-destruction: "interficias te ipsum," and we see a man preparing to cut his own throat. Alongside, a semiclad female scourges herself in a gesture of "indiscrete penitence."[21] Behind the dying man, a demon raises a veil to occult a vision of God, Christ, and the Virgin.

This scene corresponds to the first appearance of Pathelin in scene 5 (vv.

Plate I.

610–29). As Guillemette shows the clothier into the bedchamber, Pathelin chides her for having opened the windows and implies that as a result the room is full of grotesque creatures:

> Ha, meschante,
> viens sa: t'avois je fait ouvrir
> ces fenestres? Vien moy couvrir:
> oste ces gens noirs! Marmara,
> carimari, carimara.
> Amenez les moy, amenez!
>
> (vv. 610–15)

(Ah, wicked woman! Come here! Did I tell you to open these windows? Come cover me up. Get rid of these people in black! *Marmara carimari carimara!* Take them away from me, away!)

In reply to her question as to whether he is in his right mind (v. 617), Pathelin explains that he sees far more than she:

> Tu ne vois pas ce que je sens.
> Vela ung moisne noir qui vole!
> prens le, bailles luy une estolle;
> au chat, au chat! comment il monte!
>
> (vv. 618–21)

(You don't see what I see. There's a monk in black flying around the room. Catch him. Get a stole to exorcise him! The cat! Get the cat! Look how he rises up!)

As with the dying man, the agony of Pathelin is confined to the deathbed, yet this confinement is paradoxically unlimited by time and space, thanks to the rich visionary and hallucinatory images that drift through his consciousness. As in the woodcuts, the creatures are unmistakably demonic. Holbrook maintained that the call for a stole for the airborne black monk is in fact a request for exorcism which, according to evidence adduced in a second article, was normally conducted by a priest wearing a stole.[22] Accordingly, the incantatory formula, "Marmara, carimari, carimara" would be part of the ritual of exorcism as imaginatively rendered by Pathelin, who seeks to chase away the demons that he pretends are possessing him. The passage brings to mind the elfish nude figure hovering over the bed in the woodcut. If Pathelin is referring to this creature when he mentions a flying black monk, he may be calling for a stole simply to cover the unclad figure, or he may indeed be confusing the hovering demon with an exorcist. His reference to a rising cat in the following line would refer to the furry demon with the catlike ears raising a veil behind the bed. His next reference seems to be inspired by the three doctors at his right;

> Ces phisiciens m'ont tué
> de ces brouilliz qu'ilz m'ont fait boire;

> Et toutes fois les fault il croire,
> ilz en oeuvrent comme de cire.
>
> (vv. 624–27)

(Those doctors are killing me with all the vile potions they make me drink. And yet we have to believe them; we're like putty in their hands.)

Here Pathelin is expressing what is implied by the presence of the doctors in the Temptation against Faith: We must put our faith in these learned men of science regardless of their prognosis, for they are part of the visible, tangible world and not products of a delusive and imaginary eternal realm. At this point, Guillaume is identified mistakenly as a physician by Pathelin, and the balance of the first visit of the clothier is played out in this mode (vv. 628–706).

Pl. II. *Temptation to Despair.*[23] The dying man is again surrounded by demons, each memorably grotesque in his own way. One holds a list of the sins committed by the dying man: "Ecce peccata tua," reads the banner. Others gesture to visions of his past transgressions. There is the woman with whom he sinned ("Fornicatus est"); the man to whom he lied ("Perjurus est"); the man whom he stabbed ("Occidisti"); the beggar and the naked man to whom he denied food and clothing. In the accompanying text, the devil informs his victim that the past sins which he again sees before him are unworthy of pardon and damnable unto eternal fire (p. 22).

This illustration would seem to clarify two passages in the second part of scene 5, where the clothier, suspecting that he is being deluded, returns to the home of the lawyer. As Guillaume and Guillemette enter the bedchamber, Pathelin, now delirious, feigns recognition of a new feminine presence:

> PATHELIN, *délirant*
> Sus! tost! la royne des guiternes,
> a coup qu'el me soit aprouchee!
> Je sçay bien qu'elle est acouchee
> de vingt et quatre guiterneaux,
> enfans a l'abbé d'Iverneaux;
> il me fault estre son compere.
> GUILLEMETTE
> Helas! pensez a Dieu le pere,
> mon amy, non pas en guiternes.
>
> (vv. 802–9)

(PATHELIN [*delirious*]: Arise! Make way for the Queen of Guitars. Let her approach without delay. I know she gave birth to four and twenty guitarlings, sired by the Abbot of Iverneaux. I'll have to be the godfather. GUILLEMETTE: Alas! Think about God the father, my dear, not about guitars.)

This segment has not escaped commentary, but the commentary has largely been confined to the identity of Iverneaux, its abbey, and its abbot,

Plate II.

with fewer comments on its poetic appeal as a toponym.[24] Yet it is the broader context that compels attention. However *fantaisiste,* evocation of the illegitimate offspring of this unlikely union of the abbot and the Queen of Guitars calls Pathelin away from his spiritual preparation for death and rivets his memory to the things of this world. Indeed, the Queen of Guitars might well be the colorful appellative of one of the "sisters of the street" once frequented by Pathelin. Such names are familiar in Villon.[25] Whether by offering to serve as "compere" he is expressing a genuine desire to act as fellow sponsor to these children, making a veiled allusion to his own paternity by punning on the term, or, more likely, betraying a lecherous desire to be a "cofather" now that the winsome lady has approached him, he is clearly not behaving as one should according to the treatise. Instead of meditating on worldly sin, he should think of his heavenly Father, as Guillemette reminds him. She admirably fulfills the role prescribed in the preface to *L'Art au morier:* "Devant toutes choses doit on induire le morissant az choses necessairement requises a son salut." (Above all else, one must direct the sufferer to the things required for salvation.)[26] Accordingly, her admonition is a corrective to the aberrations of a consciousness tormented by a sordid past. Later in the scene, Pathelin again calls out to an imagined feminine presence, while staving off others:

> PATHELIN, *à Guillemette*
> Venez ens, doulce damiselle.
> Et que veult ceste crapaudaille?
> Alez en arriere, merdaille!
>
> (vv. 848–50)

(Come in, sweet damsel. What does that pack of scoundrels want? Get back, you shitten knaves.)

Both this passage and the earlier one evoke a prominent feature of the woodcut depicting the Temptation to Despair. A demon whispers "Fornicatus est" into the right ear of the sufferer while designating a shapely damsel at his immediate right. This iconographic detail would be the basis for the verbal metamorphosis of Guillemette, first into the mysteriously prolific Queen of Guitars and then, moments later, into the shapely "sweet damsel" to whom he beckons. His efforts to clear the room of the "crapaudaille" and "merdaille" so that he may privately carry out his designs with the damsel quite appropriately refer to the demonic mutants surrounding his bed.

Pl. III. *Temptation to Impatience.*[27] One of the more sparsely populated of the series, this woodcut features the dying man who, having overturned a table covered with his dining utensils, kicks a bare leg outward toward a recoiling man. At his side, a woman gestures with an air of resignation and the banner reads: "Ecce quantum penam patitur." In the foreground, a chambermaid holds a glass and a plate containing the leg of a fowl. From

Plate III.

under the bed, a demon congratulates the visitor: "Quam bene decepi eum." Commentary varies on this scene. Mâle indicates in his caption that the dying man is driving away his heirs, while O'Connor says that Moriens, the dying man, is kicking the doctor as the wife shows compassion.[28] I am inclined to take the visitor as a relative, because his simple garments do not correspond to the vestimentary iconography of the three professional men depicted in the Tempation of Faith.

Read either way, the scene is rich in intertextual resonances with the play. If the visitor is a doctor, the scene corresponds to the above-cited passage in which Pathelin pretends to confuse Guillaume with one of his physicians. On the other hand, if the visitor is identified as an heir, a different set of passages comes to mind. Pointing to the clothier, Pathelin exclaims:

> Çastuy ça rible et res ne done.
> Ne carrilaine! fuy ta none!
> Que de l'argent il ne me sone!
> *au drapier*
> Avez entendu, beau cousin?
>
> (vv. 838–41)

(That one there steals and gives nothing. Toll not the bell. Take your nap. Let him not speak to me of money. [*To the Clothier.*] Did you understand, cousin?)

In Limousin, he speaks of his guest as one who greedily takes (*rible*) yet gives nothing in return, then, in perfectly clear French, he avers that there is thus no need to raise the issue of money, asking his so-called "cousin" if he has made his point abundantly clear. By making it seem as if he is referring to a greedy relative, whom Guillemette immediately identifies as his Limousin uncle (vv. 842–45), rather than to his actual creditor, Pathelin manages to get away with the utterance in French because the context of enunciation is that of delirium.[29] As this demented state reaches its peak, Pathelin again addresses his "cousin":

> Alast! alast! cousin a moy,
> ilz le seront, en grant esmoy,
> le jour quant je ne te verré.
> Il couvient que je te herré,
> car tu m'as fait grant trichery;
> ton fait, il sont tout trompery.
>
> (vv. 913–18)

(Alas and alack, good cousin, they all shall bray in great sorrow the day that I see thee no more. And yet I must needs detest thee, for thou hast played false with me. Thy work is naught but deceit.)

Like the dying man besieged by his avaricious relative, Pathelin here justifies disinheriting his "cousin" who has deceived him. Although

Plate IV.

"cousin" is used in Middle French as a term of affection and not necessarily to designate familial relations, the hostile manner in which Pathelin addresses Guillaume and the fact that Guillemette consistently identifies invisible referents of his delirium as family members reinforces the connotation of kinship relations.

These passages would serve admirably as captions for the Impatience woodcut. The play also permits a humorous reflection on this scene: Rather than the leg of—what else?—roast goose on the plate carried by the maid, the visitor will get only a leg of the dying man, in the form of a swift kick![30]

Pl. IV. *Temptation to Vainglory*.[31] Moriens is now shown a vision of beatitude, in which the Deity is figured next to Christ, the Virgin, and saints. In the foreground, five demons tempt the sufferer by suggesting that his merit makes him worthy of joining this holy assembly. Holding crowns out to him, they utter exhortations to pride. "Gloriare," says one. "Tu es firmus in fide," adds another. Other banners read, "Coronam meruisti"; "In paciencia perseverasti"; "Exaltate ipsum." According to the text, temptation to spiritual pride is "aux devoz aux religieus et parfais plus infestes et molestant" (p. 26; more pernicious and harmful to the devout, religious, and righteous). Having resisted earlier temptations, the dying man is now threatened by the subtle conversion of his spiritual strength into a potential weakness.

This scene is perhaps the inspiration for a desire to convince the clothier that Pathelin wishes to become a man of the cloth:

> Sa! tost! je vueil devenir prestre.
> (v. 851)

(Quick, I want to become a priest!)

As if he had assented to the notion that exceptional spiritual merit now makes him worthy of a clerical vocation. However, the diabolical undertones of this wish are immediately apparent:

> Or sa! que le dyable y puist estre,
> en chelle vielle prestrerie!
> Et faut il que le prestre rie
> Quant il dëust chanter sa messe?
> (vv. 852–55)

(Now, may the Devil be part of that ancient priesthood! And must the priest laugh when he should be chanting his mass?)

Pathelin is more lucid than the dying man in the woodcut. Rather than accept a pious self-image, the lawyer acknowledges his wicked propensities and leagues with the Devil to subvert the image of the ecclesiastical cele-

Plate V.

Thanatopathelin and the Art of Dying 87

brant, who now laughs sardonically even as he officiates. Yet this very sacrilege is a product of the extreme "spirituel orgueil" and "complaissance" that the Devil would seek to induce in his victim (p. 26). The shocking irreverence of the lawyer is thus a demonstration of the possible consequences of succumbing to this temptation.

Pl. V. *Temptation to Avarice.*[32] In this scene, the bedchamber is filled with a constellation of memories. At the right of the sufferer, a demon points to his family and friends ("Provideas amicis"), while two others designate his lovely home with its wine cellar and stable ("Intendo thesauro"). A groom leads his horse into the stable, while a thief steals his wine. The strategy is to distract Moriens from thoughts of preparing himself to leave behind both the cares and the joys of this world. For this reason, the text admonishes those in attendance to avoid mentioning family, friends, and possessions (p. 28).

This theme from the temptation woodcuts is the one most fully developed in the play. The famous scene of the "divers langaiges" (v. 878) cultivates the psychological realism of a dying mind in an advanced state of regression, as it produces, willy-nilly, random scenes from the past of the victim. His dialects, explains Guillemette, are due to the fact that he had a Limousin uncle (v. 842), a mother from Picardy (v. 860), a Norman tutor (v. 902), and a paternal grandmother from Brittany (vv. 939–40). A memory gone haywire in the wake of dying cells: the languages of Pathelin create a palimpsest of *patois*.

The possibilities for verbal expression of past experiences and mental states are myriad. Pathelin frequently exploits the technique of multiple addressees, as if the room were overflowing with throngs of desirable and undesirable types. Occasionally, the effect approaches that of Joycean stream-of-consciousness, as in the following passage:

> Hé, par saint Gigon, tu te mens.
> Voit a Deu! couille de Lorraine!
> Dieu te mette en bote sepmaine!
> Tu ne vaulx mie une vielz nate;
> va, sanglante bote savate;
> va foutre! va, sanglant paillart!
> Tu me refais trop le gaillart.
> Par la mort bieu! Sa! vien t'en boire,
> et baille moy stan grain de poire,
> car vrayment je le mangera
> et, par saint George, je bura
> a ty. Que veulx tu que je die?
> Dy, viens tu nient de Picardie?
> Jaques nient se sont ebobis?
> Et bona dies sit vobis,
> magister amantissime,
> pater reverendissime.
> Quomodo brulis? Que nova?

Parisius non sunt ova;
quid petit ille mercator?
Dicat sibi quod trufator,
ille qui in lecto jacet,
vult ei dare, si placet,
de oca ad comedendum.
Si sit bona ad edendum,
pete tibi sine mora.

(vv. 943–68)

(Hey, by Saint Gengoux, you're lying! I swear to God! Great balls, may God send you misfortune! You're not worth an old doormat. Get out of here, you bloody old boot; fuck off! Leave, you low-life lecher! You're too malicious, by God! You there! Come have a drink and give me a peppercorn; I'll really eat it and, by Saint George, I'll drink to you. What do you expect me to say? Say, are you by chance from Picardy? The peasants there are dumbfounded. (Latin.) Good day to you, beloved master, most reverend father. How are you burning? What's new? There are no eggs in Paris. What does that merchant want? Let him say to himself that the swindler, the one lying in bed, wants to give him, if he will, some goose to eat. If it's good, ask for some without delay.)

Despite the lack of rapport with the immediate communicative context between Pathelin, his wife, and the clothier, this remarkable passage, like so much of his delirious raving, is laced with greetings to a supposed interlocutor. Other examples include: "Dont viens tu, caresme prenant? / Vuacarme, liefe gode man" (vv. 862–63; Where did you come from, carnival clown? . . . Awake, to arms, dear good man!); "Or cha! Renouart au tiné" (v. 886; Come here! Renouart au Tiné!); "Bé parlez a moy, Gabrïel" (v. 890; Hey, speak to me, Gabriel), and so forth. In the lengthy passage just quoted, Pathelin would first appear to address a hostile presence, one with whom he may have had unpleasant transactions (vv. 943–49). He then invites an acquaintance to quaff a few, and we catch fragments of their conversation, as Pathelin asks if he hails from Picardy, which is, after all, his maternal region (vv. 950–56). Switching to Latin, he addresses the cleric who was his tutor, echoing a phrase from composition class: "Parisius non sunt ova," if not thereby commenting on the dearth of eggs in Paris as he and his imaginary companion stroll through the marketplace, at which point he spots the merchant (v. 962). Hereafter, Pathelin uses his latinate culture to recall us to his bedside, as well as to remind us of the distinction between the *artificially* tortured cerebrations we have been following with difficulty and the truly delusive goose being served by the bedridden *trufator* (vv. 963–68). This surrealized monologue lends itself to the coherence of a visionary perspective that penetrates the walls of the tiny bedchamber and strolls, literally, down memory lane. Such temporal and spatial telescoping is in keeping with the popular belief that, at the time of death, the past is rehearsed in memory as vividly as if it had just taken place. This is a fundamental and explicitly acknowledged premise—and peril—in the *Ars moriendi* as well,[33] and it is most likely for this reason that memory is the last of the faculties to imperil the soul of Moriens before he expires. Throughout most of the second half of scene 5, right up to the moment of his feigned expiration, Pathelin seems to animate and, above all, to verbalize the visionary reminiscences suggested by the treatise and its engravings.

Pl. VI. *The Death of Moriens.*[34] In the last of the eleventh cuts, four angels behind the bed welcome the soul of Moriens, rising in the form of a small child. A priest places a long taper in the hands of the lifeless man, while a crucifix surrounded by saints appears at his left. On his right, six angry demons prepare to depart empty-handed, howling dejected cries displayed in the banners: "Confusi sumus"; "Heu insanio"; "Spes nobis nulla"; "Animam amisimus"; "Furore consumore." The text emphasizes at length the necessity for the dying man, if he is able to speak, to fill these last moments with prayers and other efficacious utterances that will save his soul. Moreover, the presence of a friend to assist in this final devotion is looked upon as indispensable.[35] Unfortunately, such companions are rare indeed, especially when the sufferer is reluctant to acknowledge his imminent demise.[36]

The entire death scene in *Pathelin* takes its cue from this depiction of the Christian death. Throughout, Guillemette is the faithful helpmate, tolerating the impatience of her spouse (vv. 628–29), commiserating (vv. 676–79), admonishing him to spiritual meditation (vv. 808–9), prescribing the sacraments (vv. 856–57; 941–42), even uttering a brief prayerful outcry for divine aid on behalf of her mate (v. 920). Her willingness to perform these functions despite his uncooperative behavior makes her exemplary in terms of the conditions to be met by the companion according to the treatise. At the moment of his feigned expiration, she interprets his uninterrupted prattle as the incontrovertible sign of a pious death:

> Par mon serment, il se mourra
> tout parlant. Comment il latime!
> Vëez vous pas comme il estime
> haultement la divinité?
>
> (vv. 969–72)

(I swear, he's going to die making speeches. My, how he Latinizes! Don't you see how highly he esteems the divinity?)

Indeed, his last moments are to some extent like those prescribed by the treatise. Like the dying man, he will not slip away in silence but rather in a torrent of words. Just before his last effusion (vv. 943–68), the clothier had asserted that "Il ne parle pas crestïen, / ne nul langaige qui apere" (vv. 937–38; It's no Christian tongue he's speaking, nor any that makes sense.). Pathelin disagrees: "Hé, par saint Gigon, tu te mens. . . . Dieu te mette en bote sepmaine! . . . Que veulx tu que je die?" (vv. 943; 945; 954: Hey, by

Plate VI.

Saint Gengoux, you're lying! . . . May God send you misfortune! . . . What do you expect me to say?). Like all of Pathelin's raving, this final passage exploits the rich ambiguity between the imagined interlocutors of a senile mind and the flesh-and-blood addressees to whom he may, because ostensibly deranged, say whatever he pleases with absolute impunity.

Appropriately, he will utter several verses in the Picard dialect of his mother before lapsing into one final paroxysm of kitchen Latin. Philipot was the first to suggest that, among the languages of Pathelin, Latin comes last to indicate that his death is at hand, whence the need for this sacramental idiom.[37] Frappier has suggested that these lines would most effectively have been intoned in solemn Gregorian chant.[38] The initial Latin greeting:

> Et bona dies sit vobis,
> magister amantissime,
> pater reverendissime.
>
> (vv. 957–59)

(Good day to you, beloved master, most reverend father.)

if not spoken to the schoolmaster of childhood days, is perhaps addressed to the priest, arriving to administer last rites. According to Chartier, this was the most terrifying of moments for the dying man and the one most likely to precipitate the end.[39]

Yet in the balance of this latinate pseudodemise, the *trufator* does not utter the traditional commendation of his spirit into the hands of the Almighty. What we hear is his last will and testament to the clothier, which is the promised "roast goose to eat": *de oca ad comedendum*. This is perhaps a ludic deconstruction of "Commendo te . . . ad deo" spoken by the priest in the *Commendatio animae*—the service of prayers for the dying—in the Roman Ritual.[40]

As a result of this empty bequest, the clothier will depart as dejected and empty-handed as are the demons in the eleventh woodcut, they without the soul, he without his cloth. Terrified and apologetic, he makes a hasty exit, reverently—and appropriately declaring "par ceste *ame*"—that he was mistaken, and begging the forgiveness that Guillemette is quick to grant him (vv. 975–86). It is he who now genuinely believes in the power of the Devil and recognizes his vulnerability to the Adversary:

> Par saincte Marie la gente!
> je me tiens plus esbaubely
> qu'oncques. Le dyable, en lieu de ly,
> a prins mon drap pour moy tenter.
> Benedicité! Atenter
> ne puist il ja a ma personne!
>
> (vv. 987–92)

(By the gracious Virgin, I'm more confused now than ever. The Devil, in his shape, took my cloth to tempt me. [*Crosses himself.*] *Benedicite*. May he leave me in peace.)

At last Pathelin, this Moriens Redivivus, relishes the thought of Guillaume tormented by nocturnal visions (vv. 999–1000), no doubt akin to those he has just enacted. Ironically, then, his bogus dramatization of the *Ars moriendi* has produced in the clothier the same sort of fear, reverence, and belief in the power of the Devil that its Christian counterpart was designed to do. *Par "divers langaiges," on arrive a pareille fin.*

In this intertextual reading of two contemporaneous documents, we have seen how thanatological discourse in the *Ars moriendi* provides both a situation of enunciation and a basis for improvisation in scene 5 of *Maistre Pathelin*. If we think of these two texts as noncongruent circles, as in a simplified Venn diagram employing only two circles, and of the intertext as the common area of overlap shared by each, we can see that this intertext is transgressive of the conservative (+) religious values in the textual circle of the treatise and conservative of the transgressive (−) values in the circle representing the text of the play.[41]

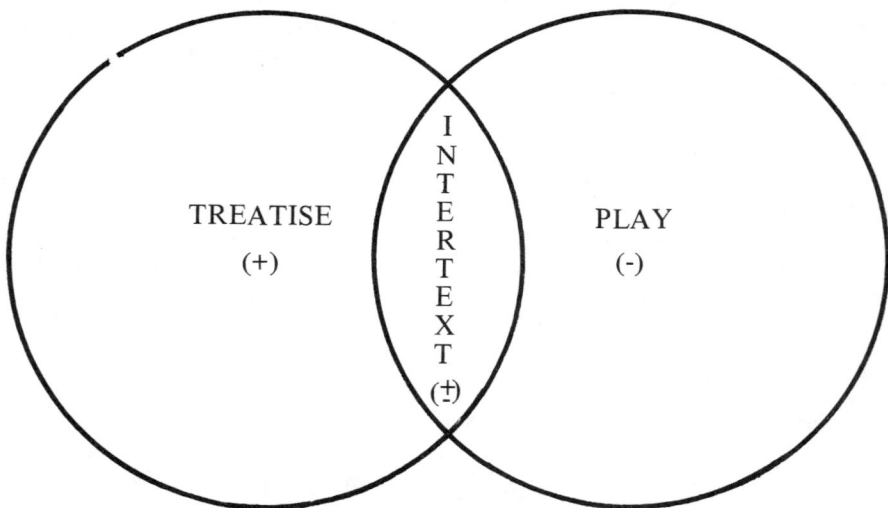

The result is a partially transgressive intertextuality which produces a kind of oscillation (±) between positive and negative valorization of the conventional context of the treatise. Such ambivalence toward cultural conventions is characteristic of much late medieval art and literature. One thinks readily of how conventions are both reproduced and emptied of their traditional content in the poetry of the Grands Rhétoriqueurs, the narrative of Antoine de la Sale, the *Testament* of Villon, certain spectacles in the Grands Mystères, and in Carnival. This oscillating intertext is descriptive of what Julia Kristeva has identified as a late medieval shift from a culture of symbol, conservative of cultural values, to a culture of sign, in which the liberation of traditional values from the plane of a transcendental signified becomes in itself a dominant cultural value.[42]

If the oscillating intertext produces negative feedback into the ideological context of the positively valorized text, in this case the treatise, the result is satire. Such is typically the case in the *sottie*.[43] If, however, the oscillating intertext reflects forward into the contestatory world of the transgressive text, as in our play, the result is parody. Satire and parody are not mutually exclusive terms, for satire is an ideational phenomenon while parody is a formal relation of textual resemblance. Satirical parody is thus not impossible and, indeed, is sufficiently common that the two terms *parody* and *satire* are sometimes, though incorrectly, used synonymously.

I cannot agree with J. L. de Altamira, who sees in *Maistre Pathelin*'s parody of the *Ars moriendi* a symptom of widespread desacralization in fifteenth-century culture.[44] A reading of the intertext does indeed disclose parody, as we have seen. Yet it is not satirical parody. Scene 5 neither advocates nor reinforces the fundamental values of the treatise, to be sure. But it never undermines or seriously questions them either. It is true that the demons and angels said to exist according to the treatise are revealed by Pathelin to be mere products of imagination, capable of convincing only the credulous clothier. Yet the context in which the noumenal, late medieval Christian cosmos is shown as unreal is itself unreal. We must not forget that this is a play embedded within a play, thus twice removed from the Christian household dealt with in the treatise. If there is any limited degree of satire in the play, it is assuredly aimed far less at religion than at mercantile values.[45] Rather than directing satirical negative feedback at the treatise, scene 5 parodies the Art of Dying in order to deceive the clothier, whose credulity is the ultimate focal point of ridicule. Far from satirically indicating a cultural trend toward desacralization, however, Pathelin's transgressive, parodic practice of the art of *thanatopathelinage* is in fact a sign of the extraordinary vitality of the treatise in late medieval popular devotion. Had it not been fixed in the contemporary mentality as a familiar and venerable religious model, the parody would not even have been recognizable by the public.

If the treatise and its woodcuts are neither faithfully reflected nor satirized in scene 5 but merely serve as the melodic line upon which Pathelin, like some gifted jazz artist, turns out a series of free improvisations, then what was the purpose in creating this intertextual dimension in the first place? It was most likely for no other reason than to produce that shocking esthetic pleasure of playing one medium into another, for the sheer delight of both eye and ear. In a period when playwrights normally adapted plays from the written medium to increase their impact on the public and when scenic designers of mystery plays took their cue from artists who in turn gleaned ideas from simultaneous staging, it is not at all surprising to find this type of intertextuality in *Pathelin*.[46]

The benefits of this discovery, it seems to me, should accrue to the modern stagecraft of the *Pathelin*. An enterprising set designer, versed in the pictorial tradition of the *Ars moriendi*, might well draw upon the intertext to enliven the staging of scene 5. In place of Hellmouth in earlier religious tradition, one might set an enormous open book, appropriately labeled and archaically adorned, out of which would step demons and angels, alternatively to torment and comfort the raving lawyer. Costuming, properties, and lighting might all be based to some extent on aspects of the woodcuts. The use of many actors in dumb show and *tableaux vivants* would greatly increase the coherence of this scene. Modern critics have spilled a great deal of ink attempting to identify the multiple addressees and the abrupt transitions in the lunacy of Pathelin. As we have seen, these are much more easily understood when we "read" them within the context of the *Ars moriendi*. Accordingly, their representational coherence would be far greater if the audience were able to see what Pathelin merely pretends to see. By resurrecting the intertext we might once more bring to life bright moments from a *memento mori*, moments when the signifying voice of the actor awakens from the graven images of death the ideolects of the quick and the dead.

6
Antipathiquelin and the Rhetoric of Torts

Thus far, we have seen two of the three faces of Logopathelin, both from the point of view of the clothier. First, there was the affable, gay Sympathiquelin, a long-standing family friend who seemed credibly creditable. Then we visited the wan and pale Pathétiquelin, who inspired feigned pity in his wife and genuine fear in his creditor. Now let us meet Antipathiquelin who, devoid of affability or gaiety but with a word *(bée)* and a phrase *(je l'assous)* pat to the subject at hand, will discredit his litigious adversary. For the first time, Guillaume begins, though belatedly and helplessly, to see how profoundly he is despised by Pathelin. To express his antipathy, the lawyer manipulates the judicial process, its language and technicalities, to show that if he was formerly unprepared to serve Guillaume the promised feast, he is now eager to help him cook his *own* goose.

It is not at all surprising that in *Maistre Pierre Pathelin,* a play featuring a lawyer in the titular role, the longest and most climactic scene should take place in a court of law. From its earliest textual incarnations, medieval French literature shows a keen affinity for the procedures and modes of thought embodied in contemporaneous legal institutions. It has been demonstrated to what a great extent problematic aspects of legal procedures are reflected in medieval French literary texts of the twelfth and thirteenth centuries.[1] Nor is this close relationship between medieval literature and law peculiar to France alone. Whether as a repository of words, phrases, images, metaphors, or situations, the law provided other medieval European literatures with an ample and ever-changing source of material.[2] In this regard, the drama is no exception. We find a clear-cut expression of divine and positive law in the earliest major French play, the *Mystère d'Adam,* in which the relation of God and man is couched in the terminology of feudal law.[3] In later medieval dramatic works, judicial procedures are seldom depicted mimetically, yet one occasionally finds scenes constructed around judicial themes. The court of the King of Heaven, theoretically the anagogical source of temporal or positive law since the time of Saint Augustine, is a prominent feature in the Grands Mystères and the English Mystery Cycles of the later Middle Ages.[4] Thematic treatment of transgression, guilt, justice, and judgment, as well as the formal structure of debate, occur in the miracle and morality play, as well as in the satirical *sottie* and the farce. Many French plays of the fifteenth and early sixteenth centuries bear the earmarks of the Basoche, whose membership, drawn from members of the legal fraternity, constituted one of the most important theatrical organizations in late medieval Paris and in more than a dozen provincial French cities.[5] These are some of the reasons why we might expect to find a sophisticated and nuanced treatment of court procedures even in a comic play whose thematic concerns are not confined to legal matters alone.

Legal themes in *Pathelin* have indeed been discussed at length in previous scholarship. Several articles have suggested the possible relations between the play and fifteenth-century legal institutions.[6] These studies prove beyond doubt that the playwright had an extensive familiarity with contemporary legal practice and that his competence is brought to bear in the creation of a trial scene whose details are frequently reminiscent of documented court procedures. Having observed that mockery is directed toward the inept plaintiff rather than toward either the counsel for the defense or the bench, H. G. Harvey has suggested that the play reflects the attitudes of the Basoche, whose law clerks would not have challenged the legal system in their exaggerated depictions of ignorant litigants. He observes that this aspect of the play might well appeal to an audience made up of members of the legal profession, even in our own day.[7] Indeed, lawyers might readily appreciate *Pathelin* as they would any exploitation of humorous elements latent in a mock trial staged by first-year students in a modern law school. Yet *Joceaulme versus Aignelet* is not an exemplary case in the annals of jurisprudence and hardly worthy of inclusion in a student casebook. What we do find in the scene is a willful and ludic distortion of jurisprudence to produce laughter at the expense of the law.

Studies of the play have frequently taken the tribunal scene very seriously, however. Discussion has focused on specific details that might faithfully reflect aspects of late medieval legal institutions. Questions concerning the professional status of Pathelin, the nature of the court, the jurisdiction of the judge, and even the geographic locale suggested by the play have led to elaborate hypotheses concerning the identity of the playwright and his social milieu.[8] The results have also included many valuable clarifications of difficult or obscure passages scattered throughout the play. Yet, perhaps without intending to, these studies have cumulatively fostered an impression that the genuine interest of the legal dimension in the play resides in its reflection of nondramatic matters. The risk involved in this sort of approach is obviously that the play may be appreciated primarily not for the comprehensive intrinsic coherence of the scene, but for certain constituent elements that might serve, however imprecisely, as secondary documentation for literary biography or for the history of institutions. In short, analysis of the tribunal scene has become a means to an extradiscoursive end, thereby diminishing its theatrological significance while exaggerating the import of an elusive historical reality.

In order to reorient discussion of this important scene in terms of its intrinsic coherence, it is worthwhile to consider an evaluation of the nature of juridical discourse itself, as characterized by A. J. Greimas and Eric Landowski in their illuminating analysis.[9]

Greimas and Landowski identify two complementary yet distinct aspects of juridical discourse, one involving the *production* of a legal edifice, the other having to do with its *verification*. Production is a *legislative* process, whereby elements of natural language—the idioms of quotidian discourse—are transferred from the referential to the legislative register of expression. The result is encoded law. Verification, on the other hand, is the actual *practice* of jurisprudence. As in the process of production, it is again a matter of proceeding from an "every-day," referential register to one which conforms to the language of the law. Yet in the process of verification, it is necessary to "translate" natural language into precisely that idiom which discloses its relationship to the legal edifice. Or, in the formal phrasing of the authors, the *practice* of jurisprudence proceeds by

> the translation of a non-juridical utterance into an utterance that conforms to the rules for constructing juridical utterances, and this in order to show that, among all utterances that juridical grammar is capable of generating, there exists at least one utterance that conforms to the one which stems from translation of the non-juridical utterance.[10]

Verification is therefore a process designed to measure a single episode of human conduct—a particular "life" situation—against a body of encoded law. At the end of the Middle Ages, the normal medium for this process was inquest.[11] As in legislation, verification by inquest, understood in its broadest sense, ostensibly produces coherent instances of juridical discourse.

The discourse of juridical verification is not always in total conformity with codified precedents, however. Greimas and Landowski emphasize that in the dynamic relationship between production and verification, the legal edifice itself is by no means static:

> If the juridical system, considered at its source . . . appears to be a solid and immobilized edifice, the very immutability of the law being one of its principal connotations, the system nevertheless evolves thanks precisely to constantly renewed juridical discourses that inform the underlying system with their innovations. In this sense, juridical practice is *production of law*. . . . But juridical practice is at the same time a *recurring procedure of verification* of the validity of instituted juridical language.[12]

Thus the end product of the legislative process becomes subject to modification by the discursive processes taking place before the tribunal.

The function of the inquisitory process as a mediator between the legislated code and its constituents is counterbalanced by its potential as a *creative* force in the continual reshaping of the law.[13] If the court is a locus of adherence to extant laws, it is no less a forum for the testing of these same laws, as well as for the discovery of their inadequacies and the means of correcting them.

This distinction between two different processes in juridical discourse, one involving production and the other verification, is illuminating when used to characterize the nature of previous scholarship on the legal themes in *Pathelin*. In these studies, there is a frequent tendency to consider the possible significance of isolated legal details within the historically documented edifice of law. Examination of this material is indeed necessary and justifiable, for without it numerous passages would remain impenetrable to the modern public. It has nevertheless taken undue precedence over analysis of the *process* of verification occurring *entirely within* the play. Rather than view elements of juridical discourse in the play chiefly in terms of a presumably immutable antecedent legislative product, as if the primary function of juridical signifiers were to signify the extratheatrical coherence of law, the task of criticism in this instance is to analyze the intrinsic development of strategies that may be either veridictory or productive, either reflective or transgressive of historical prototypes. However, inasmuch as this process is not represented as an authentic instance of jurisprudence, but rather as a literary and dramatic process of which jurisprudence is merely a verisimilar effect of meaning, we may legitimately expect to find a wide variety of deliberate contrasts between authentic legal procedures and their dramatic counterparts. The play, then, may be a locus of "play," in which juridical discourse, if not entirely transgressive of late medieval legal institutions, comes about as a result of indulgence in an imaginative exploration of possibilities latent in these institutions. It is the coherent *process* involved in this exploration which requires more attention than it has heretofore received.

To begin with, it should be observed that the foundation of the juridical process in *Pathelin* is a narrative structure upon which its coherent development depends. Of course, the very essence of legal verification is narrative. The modern cliché "courtroom drama" aptly captures the theatrical dimension of inquest, in which a story unfolds in words and actions before an audience composed of a judge and, often, a jury. Thus, "jurisprudence appears as a spectacle, in which the parties and the tribunal behave as *dramatis personae*.... The micro-stories in juridical discourse are descriptions of programs of comportments, organized according to logical and/or temporal relations [and depicting] *exemplary* developments of procedures...."[14] The narrativization of juridical discourse in the play involves two programs of comportment, one instituted by the clothier, the other by the shepherd and his counsel, Pathelin. Whence an opposition of strategy and antistrategy which ultimately brings the adverse parties before the tribunal, creating a spectacle in which the process of verification is ostensibly to take place according to the conventions of inquest.

Let us first examine the virtual program of comportment envisaged by the clothier. It will be recalled from our initial study of narrative syntax that Deception Sequences 1 and 2 culminate in the familiar disequilibrium of the "swindler" or "trickster" tale, whereby the victim of deceit remains unsatisfied and therefore the virtual subject of a counteroffensive. This is precisely the case at the beginning of the second half of the play. Having suffered the dupery dished out by Pathelin and Guillemette, Guillaume is reconstituted as a subject tormented by a performative desire. Frustrated in his yearning for gold and a goose, he turns his attention to the prosecution of his shepherd. He first expresses his grievance in the referential terms of natural language:

> Quoy dea! chascun me paist de lobes;
> chascun m'en porte mon avoir
> et prent ce qu'il en peult avoir;
> or suis je le roy des meschans:
> mesmement les bergiers des champs
> me cabusent. Ores le mien,
> a qui j'ay tousjours fait du bien,
> il ne m'a pas pour bien gabbé:
> il en viendra au pié l'abbé,
> par la benoiste couronnee!
>
> (vv. 1007–16)

(Damn it all! Everybody feeds me lies; everybody steals from me and takes all he can get. I feel like I'm the king of the wretched. Even the shepherds of the field defraud me. And my own shepherd, to whom I've always been generous, will not get away with cheating me. He'll be begging for mercy, by the Blessed Virgin!)

Here we find the essential elements of a grievance and a plan to seek redress before a judge. The pronominal "chascun" who carries off his possessions applies with equal force to both the lawyer and the shepherd, who occupy the same role of "deceiver." Aignelet, "the little lamb," is in effect a clever fox like Pathelin. Because of this paradigmatic relation, it is logical that the clothier will confuse the two grievances when he acts as his own counsel.

Moments later, as he lays out his case for the very shepherd he has just had served with a summons, he has already translated the details of his grievance into a legal strategy:

> Se je ne te sçay emboucler
> tout maintenant devant le juge,
> je prie Dieu que le deluge
> coure sur moy, et la tempeste!
> Jamais tu n'assomeras beste,
> par ma foy, qu'il ne t'en souviengne!

> *Tu me rendras,* quoy qu'il adviengne,
> six aulnes . . . dis je, *l'essomage*
> *de mes bestes, et le dommage*
> que tu m'as fait depuis dix ans.
>
> (vv. 1035–44)

(If I don't haul you before the judge in two shakes, I pray God to strike me with storm and flood. Never again will you get away with killing my sheep, I swear. And no matter what happens, you'll pay me for those six yards . . . I mean, for killing my sheep and for all the losses you've caused me in the last ten years.)

Rita Lejeune maintains that "emboucler" here means the same thing as modern slang "boucler" (to imprison).[15] This is untenable in context, for one does not "imprison" someone "before the judge" ("boucler . . . devant le juge"). More plausible is Holbrook's reading of "boucler" as "traîner, la boucle dans les naseaux,"[16] which captures the idea of "faire comparaître . . . devant le juge." Moreover, it is obvious from the italicized passage that the clothier seeks only to recover damages and not to imprison the shepherd. His sole objective is to exact compensation for the "carnage" *(essomage)* of his sheep, as he again states explicitly:

> *tu les rendras* au samedi,
> mes six aulnes de drap . . . je dy,
> *ce que tu as prins sur mes bestes.*
>
> (vv. 1048–50)

(. . . you'll pay me on Saturday for my six yards of cloth . . . I mean, for what you stole of my sheep.)

The fact that he already twice confuses restitution of the six yards of cloth with payment of damages is a subtle foreshadowing of the psychological effect to be more fully exploited at the time of the hearing. Yet there is never any hint in all of this that the clothier is determined to seek punitive measures.

Lemercier states with good reason that Guillaume is essentially involved in a *civil* procedure undertaken at his own initiative rather than at that of the judge: "Master Guillaume is scarcely concerned with inflicting penal servitude upon his shepherd."[17] Yet the same critic also points out that at this time there was only a nebulous distinction between civil and penal procedures and that, in inferior jurisdictions, a tribunal might prescribe punishment while at the same time awarding damages and restitutions. Pathelin would seem to be aware of this possibility, says Lemercier, for at the trial he says:

> Ha! Sire, le ferez vous pendre
> pour six ou sept bestes a laine?
>
> (vv. 1461–62)

(Oh, Sir, would you have hanged him for six or seven sheep?)

Particularly in cases of recidivism, like that of the shepherd, theft was indeed punished by death.[18]

The legal strategy initiated by the clothier may therefore have consequences of which even *he* is not fully aware. In any case, this strategy involves a civil procedure concerning a breach of contract. Whether this contract is one of mutual trust based on a verbal accord or formal written document will later become an issue in the inquest. We shall return to this later. Let it be noted, however, that apart from the possibly unanticipated penal procedure that could emerge from an inquest, the clothier makes explicit the main line of his strategy at the outset.

The same cannot be said of Pathelin, however. Although it eventually becomes clear that he was mindful of an antipathetic strategy all along, he never explicitly sets this forth, not even to the shepherd. Scholarship has not adequately appreciated the manipulative skill with which Pathelin prevents the case from being tried as a breach of contract. His chief objective is to assure that the inquest proceed on the basis of an offense not covered by the law of contracts, in other words, on the basis of what in current legal terminology would be considered a tort. Unlike a breach of contract, a tort brings before the law a plaintiff and a defendant who have not previously entered into mutual consent regarding the matter at issue.

Let us first consider the overt elements in the counterstrategy of Pathelin. He elicits the total candor of his client: "A son conseil doit on tout dire" (v. 1090: A client should hide nothing from his counsel). The facts could not be more discouraging to a potential counsel for the defense. In a confessional paroxysm, the shepherd recounts the gruesome details of violence and carnage that eventually led to his being caught, by numerous witnesses, in the act of killing the clothier's sheep for his own use (vv. 1091–114). Yet the case is not hopeless, according to the shepherd:

> Or ay je esté prins sur le fait,
> je ne le puis jamais nyer;
> si vous vouldroye bien prier
> (pour du mien, j'ay assés finance)
> que nous deux luy baillons l'avance.
> Je sçay bien qu'il ha bonne cause,
> mais vous me trouverez bien clause,
> se voulez, qu'i' l'aura mauvaise.
>
> (vv. 1113–20)

(So I was caught red-handed, I can never deny it, and now I come to ask if there ain't some way we can put the old hound off the scent, and don't worry about money, I got enough to pay you good. I know he's got a good case, but you can find some loophole, if you will, to make it worthless.)

The expression "bailler l'avance," glossed by Holbrook as "donner le change," "mystifier,"[19] is figurative of a program of delusive collusion. The shepherd is prepared to implore—nay, hire!—the lawyer to redeem his previously abortive deception. The admittedly guilty Aignelet knows that any normal inquest would find in favor of the plaintiff: "Pour ung il en trouvera dix / qui contre moy desposeront" (vv. 1151–52; . . . instead of one, he'll find ten to testify against me.). He therefore offers to pay Pathelin, in gold, of course, if he will find the "clause," or loophole, that would turn the verdict around in favor of his client.

Undaunted either by the bald truth about his guilty client or by his extraordinarily bold challenge, Pathelin immediately asks Thibault what he would pay him to fulfill his request:

> Que donras tu se je renverse
> le droit de ta partie adverse,
> *et se l'en t'en envoye assoubz?*
>
> (vv. 1122–24)

(What will you give me if I overturn the claim of your accuser and get you a full pardon?)

Rita Lejeune has accurately weighed the value of this proposal: in contrast with an acquittal, whereby the defendant is declared innocent of charges brought against him, the *absolved* party has already been recognized guilty as charged, but the infraction is qualified as not punishable by law.[20]

The outcome is well known, of course. In return for the promise of gold sovereigns, Pathelin finally achieves his objective when the judge places this interdiction upon the clothier:

> Je *l'assoulz* de vostre demande,
> et vous deffendz le proceder.
>
> (vv. 1471–72)

(I absolve him of your charges and forbid you to proceed.)

The reason why the judge reaches this verdict is also well known. Thanks to Pathelin, the shepherd is identified by the court as a "fol naturel" (v. 1394), and because he is therefore incompetent to stand trial, the litigation against him is moot. What is not so fully appreciated, however, is the covert counterstrategy—a narrative program of delusive comportment, if you will—which Pathelin never at any moment puts into words but which he manipulatively realizes throughout the court scene.

Perhaps already mindful that a civil case involving a recurrent breach of contract by theft might be treated with punitive measures, as in a genuine penal case, Pathelin must in any event prove that there was no valid contract, either written or verbal, between the plaintiff and the defendant. We know, of course, from the private confession of Thibault, that he had verbally agreed to work for the clothier as a shepherd, for which service he was remunerated (vv. 1083–88). There is no evidence of a written contract, and when evidence of a formal hiring contract is requested by the judge,

Pathelin diverts attention to another matter. More on this in a moment. On the basis of available information, we do find the necessary features of an express contract, or one in which the agreement is signified either by oral or written means. There was mutual assent between parties having the legal capacity to enter voluntarily into a contract, and the objective was not proscribed by law. Given the guilt of his client and the potentially ominous consequences if a breach of contract were to be demonstrated, the safest course for Pathelin to follow involves reducing the magnitude of the crime by removing it from the domain of the law of contracts. But how?

From the time of early common law, certain individuals have always been excluded from the privileges of contract. Current sketches of the prehistory of equal rights legislation have frequently pointed out that women were so excluded in some systems. More uniformly, children and *idiots* are held to be incapable of contracting. The insistence that Thibault adopt an idiotic ideolect in court is clearly motivated by a desire to show that he was incapable of contracting and therefore guilty of a tort, that is, of an infraction committed outside of contractual bounds. The tort in this instance is conversion of chattel, an offense that, if proven, would be greatly mitigated by the retarded mental state of the shepherd.

The crucial moment in determining whether this strategy will succeed or fail occurs precisely when the judge, having interrupted the clothier during the *libelle,* or opening statement, is about to find out if a hiring contract was ever effected:

> LE JUGE
> Or escoutons:
> Estoit il point vostre aloué?
> (vv. 1249–50)[21]

(Just a minute! Wasn't he hired by you?)

It is exactly at this moment that Pathelin, having previously remained silent and incognito, breaks conspicuously into the proceedings:

> Voire, car, s'il s'estoit joué
> a le tenir sans alouer. . . .
> (vv. 1251–52)

(That's a good point! Because if he had finagled to employ him without a contract . . .)

The clothier immediately recognizes Pathelin and launches into his confusion of cloth and sheep, so that we never learn what Pathelin was about to say. It is expressed in the syntax of a juridical utterance, however: "Yes, because if he had amused himself by keeping him without a proper hiring contact . . ." The open *if/then* structure, so characteristic of litigious grammar, cries out for completion, as if it were a question on a first-year law examination in torts.[22] Harvey maintains that Pathelin is seeking to get the case dismissed on a technicalty: "If there was no hiring agreement, if Aignelet was not the draper's hired man, [then] the judge may refuse jurisdiction, and, since this judge is in a hurry to get on to his next hearing, he may be persuaded easily to refuse the case on a technicality."[23] This is not a plausible interpretation, for Pathelin wishes to see that his client is absolved, not to have the case dismissed. Much more satisfactory is the view of Lemercier, that the judge merely wishes to clarify the nature of the juridical relations between the parties.[24] We must go a step further, however, and emphasize *why* this is so important. It is a matter of determining whether the dispute falls under the category of contracts or that of torts. If there was no hiring contract, then there is no question of a breach of contract.

There are several possible explanations of why Pathelin interrupts the proceedings precisely at this moment. He may have wished to imply that, by forgoing a formal hiring contract, the employer took unfair advantage of his employee. It is also conceivable that he merely wanted to remind the bench that the absence of a contract modifies the juridical relations between plaintiff and defendant. Pathelin could then proceed immediately as planned, by dramatizing his own feigned indignation to discover that this poor, harassed defendant was in fact mentally incompetent to enter into any sort of contract. We might also interpret the interruption as a calculated attempt to exploit the effects of an unanticipated "return from the dead." This would confuse Guillaume, draw attention away from the issue at hand, and remind him of the unpaid debt for the cloth. Such a tactic would enable Pathelin to discredit the clothier by showing that he is incapable of presenting a coherent argument. Above all, it would preclude the possibility of adducing evidence that a contract had been concluded.

However we may interpret this interruption, the effect is indeed to foreclose on the civil strategy of the clothier, who is never able to call witnesses or to present any evidence that the competence of the shepherd includes even the most rudimentary of fiduciary contracts. Had such evidence come forth, the ruse of the *paroles bêlées* would have been recognized as a sham, and the trial might have continued on the basis of a breach of contract with far more serious consequences for the shepherd. He would certainly have not been absolved on grounds of mental incompetence.

All things considered, it is doubtful that the interruption was calculated beforehand. As soon as he is recognized, Pathelin immediately attempts to hide his face and, when asked about this odd behavior by the judge, he pleads a toothache as cause (vv. 1255–60). We must therefore pay tribute to the way in which he turns a potentially awkward situation to his advantage, first by implying that the clothier had taken unfair advantage *(s'estoit joué)* of Guillame by retaining him illegally, then by asserting that the clothier has muddled his opening statement (vv. 1267–70), and finally by suggesting that he must somehow think the robe Pathelin is wearing was made from the wool of the purloined sheep (vv. 1273–81).

As soon as Pathelin launches into the fray with his attempt to prevent disclosure of any evidence of a contract, he seeks relentlessly to discredit the testimony of the clothier, and the scene becomes progressively more animated as it crescendoes toward the climactic verdict of the bench. As the harried judge expresses irritation with the verbal fumbling of Guillaume (vv. 1283–86), Pathelin chimes in with mockery of such ineptitude:

> il fault que nous luy reboutons.
>
> (v.1290)

"*We* must get back to the subject at hand"—by the "*nous*," subtly linking himself with the perspective of the judge. He then warns that the clothier is attempting to hoodwink the judge: "Par le sang bieu, il vous fait paistre!" (v. 1295; God's blood, he's trying to make an ass of you!) and proposes that the judge interrogate the "partie adverse" (v. 1298). Silent until now, Thibault answers each question put to him by the judge with a respectful bleat. After unsuccessfully attempting to question the defendant and then obtaining more confused discourse from the clothier, the judge urges the latter to conclude. Again to forestall the possible recognition of his ruse, Pathelin once more interrupts, proposing himself as the ideal advocate for the poor, dumb shepherd. The judge remarks that this would not be a lucrative case for Pathelin: ". . . c'est Peu d'Aquest!" (v. 1375). Losing no opportunity, the lawyer immediately presents himself as the altruistic advocate of the destitute:

> Moy je vous jure
> qu'aussi n'en vueil je riens avoir.
> Pour Dieu soit!
>
> (vv. 1375–77)

(I swear I have no thought of gain. Let it be for the love of God.)

Thus, from the role of innocent, impartial bystander, Pathelin gradually works himself into control of the situation. He accomplishes this not by the sustained verbiage of the lawyer but rather by provoking the speech of those around him. Between the surplus of signifiers emanating from the clothier and the shepherd, an acceptable opposition is established between the plaintiff and the defendant:

> *fin fol* (v. 1428) vs. *fol naturel* (v. 1394)
> (insidious   (natural-born
> fool)   fool)

Pathelin successfully imposes his word as the discourse of reason, moderation, charity, and even judgment, as he concludes for the judge with regard to both parties: "tous deux sont sans cervelle" (v. 1420; They're both brainless boneheads). Only the bewildered, frustrated clothier will see him as Antipathiquelin. To the rest of the court, he presents himself as the sort from whom one might very well purchase a second-hand car or a bolt of stolen cloth.

The rhetoric of torts in DS[5] is thus more a rhetoric of showing than one of telling. Pathelin shows that the shepherd can only be guilty on non-contractual grounds, and having shown why, he even proceeds quite brazenly to postulate the guilt of his client:

> Prenons qu'il en ait affolé
> six ou sept, ou une douzaine,
> et mangez . . .
>
> (vv. 1449–51)

(Let's say he did knock off six or seven sheep, or even a dozen, and ate them. . . .)

Likewise, he shows the stupidity of the clothier, not by forcing him to speak of irrelevancies, but by provoking him to multiply his own grievances into a verbal counterpoint of cloth and sheep. Thus, out of multiple instances of conversion of chattel Pathelin derives a single absolution, while delighting us with his free improvisations on the processes of juridical verification. Once again, he proves that he is unsurpassed at turning institutionalized discourse to his own best advantage, this time by showing that what at first appeared to be a litigious lantern was in fact nothing more than an atrabiliary bladder.

In terms of the juridical process of verification described earlier, we can see that the tribunal scene in *Maistre Pierre Pathelin* owes its dramatic effectiveness to the clever way in which it subverts the procedures of inquest. Although the situation of enunciation and the conventions are those normally associated with a court and its activities—so much so, in fact, that they resemble in detail features of fifteenth-century courts of law—the actual process depicted is one of mystification rather than one of verification. The triumph of appearances over reality is possible precisely because of this resemblance. No matter how dubious his credentials as a lawyer, Pathelin is sufficiently familiar with legal procedures to know that successful litigation is a matter of presenting evidence according to the ritualized patterns established by the juridical institution. Persuasion is largely a matter of form rather than of substance. The clothier actually blurts out the truth, but what is explicit in blurting is trivial compared to that which is implicit in bleating, because in this case bleating is a sign which is meaningful—and ultimately determinant—in the formalized system of inquest. It says one thing but means quite another to the judge, thanks to the way Pathelin creates an institutional context in which it may signify connotatively.

The scene thus suggests that, through artful manipulation of appearances, the juridical process of verification may discover an apparent truth which is antithetical to the Truth, whether the latter be a matter of known fact or a transcendental ideal. The scene illustrates that juridical discourse has no direct access to absolute verities and that the sole viable truth is the one which conforms to the laws of the discourse itself. The incontrovertible measure of its value as truth is created only from the criteria established by the discourse in which it signifies. There may thus be as many truths as there are discourses producing them.[25] The hypothetical consubstantiation of Verbum and Res, a frequent issue of speculation in earlier medieval theories of discourse, has given way to the alienation of words from things so that discourse is a matter, not of presentation, but of *representation*.

This dramatization of the relativity of truth and of the autonomy of juridical discourse with regard to the ostensible objective of its inquiry is not new to medieval literature. Consider two works of an earlier age. The late-eleventh-century *Chanson de Roland*, Oxford Version, presents the ordeal predicated upon an oath—a judicial duel between Pinabel and Thierry in this instance—as an adequate procedure for the discovery of truth concerning human culpability.[26] Here, ordeal is a process of verification which leads to the disclosure of Truth as an absolute value commensurate with divine law. The *Roland* implicitly ratifies a theological view expressed by Saint Augustine and frequently echoed thereafter, according to which human laws are sanctioned by divine law. Reason is the faculty which enables mankind to legislate in accordance with natural law, the chief determinant of right and wrong, as well as with eternal law, the will of God.[27] In matters that surpass human ability to determine right from wrong, the ordeal would lead to discovery of a transcendental signified occasioned by divine intervention in mundane affairs. Less than a century later, however, we find in the *Tristan* of Thomas an episode that seriously challenges this optimistic view of the ordeal. Iseut, guilty of adultery, is nevertheless unscathed in an ordeal of iron predicated on the oath she utters when charges are brought against her. This is because the oath asserts that she has lain in the arms of only two men, King Mark, her husband, and the pilgrim who lost his balance while assisting her descent from a boat.[28] The statement validated by ordeal signifies innocence to the court, but God and the reader know that the pilgrim in question was Tristan in disguise and thus recognize an exploitation of appearances through the clever use of language. The image of the ordeal as a reliable mediator of divine law and social order is seriously undermined. This fictive portrayal of a potential disparity between social justice and a process of legal verification conceived to discover it foreshadows what we find in the tribunal scene in *Pathelin*. Both show how juridical discourse is vulnerable to manipulation such that the apparent truths of its intrinsic coherence may not be commensurate with the need of society to discover truth and exercise justice. Implicit in both, then, is a critique of contemporaneous legal institutions. Just as the episode in the *Tristan* points out one of the serious deficiencies of the ordeal under oath in feudal law, the last scene in *Pathelin* shows that its replacement by inquest in postfeudal legal procedure by no means obviated the possibilities for abuse, manipulation, and error inherent in earlier practices.[29]

Indeed, as John Alford has shown, the displacement of custom by statutory law and the expansion of the court system precipitated a late medieval crisis that prefigured the birth of modern jurisprudence. A major consequence of increased legislative production was the proliferation of ephemeral or contradictory statutes within a hierarchy of widely different types of courts. Legality gradually ceases to be understood as a product of conformity with natural law in harmony with its ultimate source in divine law and becomes instead a matter of conformity with the legislated will of the state. The breach between theology and secular jurisprudence is widened by the gradual elaboration of a legal system in conformity with its own discursive logic but independent of metaphysical principles. A graphic record of the birth pangs that resulted from this transition remains in contemporaneous literature. "Most of the literary barbs," according to Alford, "were directed against the burgeoning new class of lawyers, clerks, notaries, and other legal technicians who—if we may believe half the satire of the age—were appropriating the law for themselves and whose livelihoods depended on making it as incomprehensible as possible."[30] Such figures were more than a mere convention; they betokened a profound epistemological upheaval whose tensions found expression in literary form.

Within this context of instability created by late medieval legal institutions in transition, *Pathelin* acquires satirical overtones which are reinforced rather than diminished by the evidence of contradictory influences from different juridical prototypes.[31] The foregoing analysis joins its predecessors in showing that Pathelin's delusive persuasive practice as a lawyer does not consist merely of the timeless devices of popular comedy, but that it reflects the coherence of juridical procedures peculiar to its age. Yet satire is by no means an end in itself in the play. Its import is considerably attenuated by the generalized context of delusion and deceit which extends to every institution represented and which ultimately engulfs even the titular character at the very apogee of his success as a legal acrobat. Far from imposing a somber metaphysical commentary on the action, the twice-evoked image of judgment—and consequently of justice—suspended until Judgment Day (vv. 86; 1591) merely serves to generalize the elements of satire into an observation about the norms of human interaction independent of time and place.[32] The potentially endless give-and-take of deceptive exchange becomes an image of the human condition to which no temporal institution, not even that of the law, is invulnerable. As in earlier transgressive play with epideictic and thanatopic discourse, the parody of law in *Pathelin* ultimately transcends satire in its self-reflexive fascination with the mechanisms and processes of deceit.

7
Manipathulin, the Delusive Persuader

Manipulation has an impressive etymological pedigree, stemming back through the apothecary's art, the Roman liturgy, even unto an emblematic value in the Roman legions.[1] As its root implies, it has to do with the hands and the work done therewith. Its early semantic field connotes the skillful blending of medicaments and the honest manual labor of the capable artisan. Subject and object were mediated by the hands, those dexterous extensions of the mind, so that mankind might modify the world and make it better. In the artisanal pursuit of clean objectives, dirty hands are a virtue. Eventually, manipulation also came to designate certain activities of mind, wherein the hands are simply metaphors for the processes by which ideas are conceived and toyed with mentally. Yet with excessive time on one's hands, one may turn inward upon the activities of the mind in its free play with the possibilities of the objective world. Like a house seldom cleaned by human hands, the mind tends to accumulate dirt brought in from outside, and it, too, gets caught up in the processes of cerebration. Idea: the delegation of one's mental projects, now somewhat linty and grimy, to the hands of others. Whence a different acceptation of manipulation: "Management with use of unfair, scheming, or underhanded methods especially for one's own advantage" (Webster). Management: manipulation becomes *gestionnaire*, a kind of control, not by manual but rather "submanual," underhanded means. In the manipulative pursuit of dirty objectives, clean hands are a must. "Just look at my hands. They're not dirty."—Jim Jones (in *Newsweek*, December 4, 1978).

Manipulation is a protean phenomenon likely to appear in any human activity. Its sophisticated use in advertising and the media is especially well documented though often unrecognized by the public.[2] It is also a staple of political campaigns and international relations, no less than of criminal activities and concentration camps. It is not uncommon even in organized religions. Manipulation may occur in relations between two individuals, or between an individual and a group, or among two or more groups. The consequences of manipulation may be as trivial as a household chore accomplished, or as ominous as biomedical experimentation and global warfare. Education relies on the positive effects of didactic manipulation, while history is largely an account of the good and evil consequences of manipulative tactics. The strategies of manipulation are abundantly detailed in games, fiction, film, and fantasies.

Although the term *manipulation,* in the sense of action delegated to achieve a selfish or covert objective, appears well after the fifteenth century, the type of conduct which it designates is already evident in the mischief of gods and tricksters in the earliest myths known to mankind.[3] The negative semanticization of this word was undoubtedly postponed by the proliferation of a wide variety of other figurative terms and expressions that participate in its semantic field. These may be words from standard usage [e.g., coax, coerce, flatter, force, incite, intimidate, provoke, seduce, tempt, terrorize, urge, etc.], words with particular metaphoric vigor [blackmail, bully, cozen, finagle, juggle, manhandle, rig, wheedle, etc.], or colorful—often ephemeral—expressions ["Make an offer one cannot refuse"; "Throw the game"; "Use the soft (hard) sell"; "Bait" someone, who may then "swallow—hook, line, and sinker," etc.]. Any word or expression concerning a "making to do" for a dubious or self-serving end could be examined as a possible expression of manipulation.

Analysis of the manipulative dimension in *Pathelin* must surely take into account such isolated words and expressions. Yet to account for the manipulative *processes* in the play, it is worthwhile to consider manipulation from a theoretical perspective. Apart from research in behavioral psychology involving aspects of deliberate or unconscious manipulation, formal study of the subject has frequently been sporadic and unsystematic.[4] One notable exception appears in the work of A. J. Greimas and his collaborators in the Ecole des Hautes Etudes en Sciences Sociales in Paris. Since 1976, their approach to the problematics of manipulation from a semiotic perspective has produced evidence that certain invariant properties inhere in the countless varieties of manipulation. Specific instances of intimidation, provocation, seduction, temptation, and other delegative activities are related through their common manipulative structures. While surface elements of manipulative actions may vary infinitely, they are organized and made operative by canonical forms. Such is the thrust of the Parisian hypothesis.[5]

This semiotic approach to manipulation proves to be most helpful in examining the manipulative dimension in a work like the *Pathelin.* It permits us to avoid mere cataloguing of words and expressions with manipulative overtones in order to see how these figure in a broader structural network. According to the Greimassian view, manipulation falls within a general structure of communication. There is an addressor, an addressee, and an object of knowledge transferred from the former to the latter. In manipulative communication, "the addressor-manipulator moves the manipulated addressee toward a position of lack of freedom: he cannot *not* accept the proposed contract."[6] In the play, such communicative processes convince the crow to sing, the clothier to confer credit then, later, to relinquish collection, and the court to absolve the culprit. In each of these situations, the addressee is manipulated toward a frame of mind from which the previously implausible if not unthinkable act now seems to be the appropriate, even compelling, thing to do.

This movement "toward a position of lack of freedom" is reflected repeatedly in certain of the proverbial expressions. One prominent phrase aptly captures the essential distinction between *action* and *manipulation*. If not already proverbial when the play was written, "manger de l'oie" acquires proverbial value within the play's discursive context, as we saw in Chapter 3. Figuratively, it conveys the notion of an *action* completed on the basis of a misapprehension of facts. To "eat goose" is to succumb to the effects of delusion or lying. Grammatically, it denotes an intransitive narrative program, or an "operation," in which a subject accomplishes his own strategy.[7] It produces humorous effects when a subject like Guillaume actually *believes* that he is about to fulfill his own strategy: "Et n'avez vous point d'oye/au feu?" (vv. 698–99; And don't you have a goose cooking?). Yet its true savor for Pathelin and for us stems from our recognition that this virtual action is really *transitive*, involving an independent operator who conceived the program for Guillaume in a very special way. With the introduction of a second subject into the program, the expression "manger de l'oie" acquires not only transitivity but its whole manipulative dimension and many latent connotations as well.

In a related proverbial expression near the end of the play, one which, as we have seen, is a variant of "manger de l'oie," the manipulative dimension is fully manifested: "les oisons mainnent les oes paistre!" (v. 1586). As the goslings lead the geese astray, we can see who the manipulative, operative addressor is, as well as his counterpart, the manipulated addressee of the delusive narrative program.

So can Guillaume, at least momentarily, as he suggests proverbially to Guillemette:

> Me voulez vous faire entendant
> de vecies que sont lanternes?
>
> (vv. 800–801)

Are Pathelin and Guillemette really attempting to dupe the clothier by substituting "bladders for lanterns," that is, sickness and death for repast and reimbursement? This expression features the causative structure "faire entendant": *to make to understand,* whence the "transfer of an object of knowledge" cited by Greimas as a basic ingredient in manipulative programs.[8] The causative cognitive transfer depicts Pathelin and his wife as the ostensible modifiers of the clothier's perception of the way things really are. This sort of *making to believe (faire croire)* is also descriptive of the basic process involved in each of Pathelin's three major deceptive strategies. His persuasive tactics involve a "making to believe" in his eligibility for a good credit rating, in his terminal illness, and in the shepherd's simple-mindedness as well as in his own linen-white, candid probity.

Manipulator and victim thus occupy the roles, respectively, of Persuader and Interpreter-of-Persuasion in this cognitive exchange. But more is at stake than knowledge. Consider the fable of the fox and the crow, for example, where a delusive transfer of information leads to the transfer of a tangible object, whence flattery for cheese. Likewise cozening for cloth. Manipulation is likely to involve both cognitive and pragmatic exchanges.[9]

Recognizing the complexity of manipulative comportments, Greimas and his associates have distinguished between two complementary structures in the process of manipulation, one "modal" and one "contractual." The *modal structure* of manipulation involves "transformation of the semiotic competence of the addressee." A deed *(faire)* depends on the doer's acquisition of the competence (e.g., desire, power, know-how, obligation, etc.) to perform it. This competence is classified by *modalities*. The manipulator characteristically undertakes a persuasive tactic designed to transform the victim's "actualizing modality" *power-to-do (pouvoir-faire)* into either one of two "virtualizing modalities", *obligation-to-do (devoir-faire)* or *volition-to-do (vouloir-faire)*.[10]

We can readily see this modal transformation at work in our inventory. In the fable, the initial situation of the crow is one of freedom to eat the cheese or to sing, the former option being the more plausible given the location of the cheese. It is the fox's flattery—

> "Ha!" fist il, "tant as le corps beau,
> et ton chant plain de melodie!"
>
> (vv. 446–47)

("Ah, you have such splendid feathers and your song is so melodious")—

which initiates the stronger virtualizing modality of desire *(vouloir-faire)*. The way in which Sympathiquelin gets cloth on credit is more complex. At the outset, the clothier is indisposed to transactions on credit, especially when they occur very early in the day (vv. 296–97). Pathelin prepares the way to credit by emphasizing an identity of physical and moral qualities between the clothier and his father, thus hinting at Guillaume's obligation to carry on the upright policies of trust and credit allegedly established by his father (vv. 172–79). This implicit duty *(devoir-faire)* is later buttressed by the offer of gold and roast goose which awakens gluttonous, avaricious *volition (vouloir-faire)*, whence a combination of flattery followed by temptation, both "euphoric," or affectively positive, carriers of incentive. By contrast, Pathétiquelin creates the alarmingly "dysphoric" spectacle of sickness and imminent death, so seriously disrupting (vv. 707–31) and finally paralyzing (vv. 975–76) Guillaume's power to distinguish between reality and illusion that he finally acquires an overpowering volition to flee, while ascribing the incident in his boutique to the work of the Devil (vv. 989–90). Finally, by interfering with the process of inquest, in which the power of the court to distinguish between right and wrong conduct resides, Antipathiquelin ultimately inspires within the judge both a compelling *volition* and a sense of legal *obligation* to absolve the shepherd. In all of these examples, Manipathulin imposes upon his victim either an obligation or a desire, or both, sufficiently persuasive to overcome the addressee's awareness that there still exists a choice between accomplishing or not accomplishing the objectives toward which the manipulator is moving him.

In contrast with the modal structure of manipulation, which has to do with the manipulated individual's acquisition of the disposition to accomplish the objectives of the manipulator, the *contractual structure* contains the elements of the narrative program which the manipulator proposes to the addressee. We can consider the play's major contractual structures in the light of what the Greimassian semioticians have identified as the "canonical structure" of the proposition of a contract:[11]

$$S_1 \rightarrow [S_2 \cap O_1 ((O_2 [O_3]))]$$

Where:

S_1 = manipulator-addressor
S_2 = manipulated-addressee
O_1 = /savoir/ (knowledge)
O_2 = /vouloir/ (desire)
O_3 = Real. (NP of S_2), that is, the realization of the Narrative Program of which S_2 is the subject.
$\cap$ = conjunction

The arrow indicates that the manipulator, S_1, imposes the manipulative contract, indicated in brackets, upon his victim, S_2, by effecting a conjunction ($\cap$) with 0_1, an object of knowledge made known to the victim. Thus, the proposition of a contract is depicted in terms of the victim's exposure to knowledge—/*savior*/—manifested by the manipulator, this frequently misleading knowledge being determined by the latter's manipulative will, or /*vouloir*/. This will to manipulate is normally awakened by the object of the manipulator's desire (0_2). Especially interesting in this representation of contractual structure is the nature of the conjunction ($\cap$) achieved by the manipulated addressee. S_2 has direct access to only one of three objects, 0_1, which is the delusive persuasive knowledge made available by S_1, the manipulator. Conversely, S_2 remains *totally* unaware of other items in the contract. That which motivates the selection and manifestation of the delusive knowledge is the object of the manipulator's desire (0_2) as well as the process, or narrative program, of its attainment, or 0_3. The latter in effect designates the accomplishment of the manipulative program. As the double parentheses indicate, O_2 and O_3 are never disclosed to the addressee. According to this view, manipulation would appear to involve a "hidden agenda" conceived by the manipulator.

Such an abstract account of what is surely one of the more complex and varied of human phenomena must be tested with reference to a wide variety of specific instances. Scrutiny of our inventory according to this scheme will enable certain precisions to be disclosed. We can represent the fourfold investment of this structure in *Pathelin* as follows:

	FABLE	DS^1	DS^3	DS^5
S_1	fox	P	P/G	P
S_2	crow	C	C	J
O_1	flattery	flattery/ money & food	terminal illness	juridical persuasion
O_2	cheese	cloth	cloth	gold
O_3	crow to sing	allow mdse. on credit	clothier's departure	shepherd's acquittal

P = Pathelin; C = clothier; G = Guillemette; J = judge

Here we can see that, in the fable as in Pathelin's deceptive strategies, O_2 is a tangible object of value in every instance, while O_3 is the function, or narrative action, which, if accomplished, would make the realization of O_2 possible. O_2 and O_3 are the covert objectives of the manipulative program. In order to realize these, O_1, the *manifest process of manipulation*, must first take place. Thus the fox flatters the beauty and vocal talent of the crow; likewise, Pathelin flatters the Joceaulme family, then offers generous payment and a meal, feigns death and mounts a courtroom dramatization.

Notice that in this inventory O_1 is only once pragmatic, with the offer of food and money in DS^1, yet it is noteworthy in terms of the structure of exchange that these items are *never* transferred to the addressee but, like the proverbial carrot suspended on the stick, they are held out to make this "donkey" move. Pathelin:

> Je suis certain qu'il viendra *braire*
> pour avoir argent promptement.
> (vv. 462–63)

(I know he'll come whining [literally, "braying"] to have his money immediately.)

The much discussed food and money never materialize: words never become things. Those eighty gold crowns (vv. 198–99) and the goose crackling on the spit (vv. 300–301) are merely signifiers that produce more signifiers: "Ilz ne verront soleil ne lune,/les escus qu'i me baillera" (vv. 344–45); (Those gold pieces he gives me won't see daylight for a whole year . . .). Pathelin's manipulation, like that in the fable, is based exclusively on the exchange of words for things, as he himself acknowledges (vv. 1587–91).

Whether cheese, cloth, or gold, however, things are the catalysts of verbal manipulation. Moreover, there is an invariant order in the progression from words to things: $0_1 \rightarrow 0_3 \rightarrow 0_2$. The process of cognitive and verbal persuasion, 0_1, leads to the accomplishment of the function projected in 0_3 which then results in the attribution of 0_2, the desired object of value (except for the gold in DS^5, which is never transferred because of the shepherd's counterstrategy). This progression of three objects originates from the disequilibrium of "haves" and "have-nots":

Initial Situation:
  $(S_1 \cup 0_2 \cap S_2)^*$
Transformations:
  $S_1 \blacktriangleright [(S_1 \cup 0_1 \cap S_2)]$
  $S_2 \blacktriangleright [(S_2 \cap 0_3 \cup 0_2 \cap S_1)]$
Closing Situation:
  $(S_1 \cap 0_2 \cup S_2)$

$*(\cup)$ = Disjunction

The very simple exchange of roles, whereby the "have-nots" become the "haves" and vice versa, is mediatized by a manipulative discourse (0_1) which provokes an interpretative function (0_3) of which the transfer of the desired object is, in the case of cheese and cloth, an involuntary action resulting from a momentary distraction.

In all cases in the inventory, exchange follows a circular system in which S_1 is "operant" in the cognitive world of nonbeing and appearing, or Delusion, generated verbally, while S_2 is "responsive" in the pragmatic world of being and appearing, or material "Truth", as depicted within the discourse:

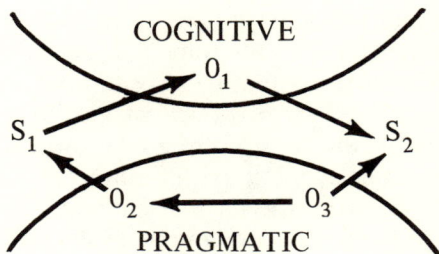

Not unlike many manipulators, particularly those of the more subtle, subliminal, less coercive variety, Pathelin creates an *illusion* of how things are by using his superior mastery of cognitive production, while the concomitant verisimilar reality effect of this illusion moves the "literalized" victim toward action in the material world. (The pattern is familiar to any Coney Island conman with sparkling nails, a pin-stripe suit, an eye for suckers, and a smooth line.)

The fact that O_2, the ultimate object of manipulative desire, is always a tangible object in this inventory—food, clothing, capital, that is, the basic elements of subsistence in a capitalistic society—raises the issue of *values* and their place in the phenomenon of manipulation.[12] As for the manipulator, we know from the outset that his dossier is contaminated. Once a prominent and successful lawyer (vv. 8–13), Pathelin has since acquired a reputation for deceptive practice that has lowered his professional standing (vv. 41–57) and resulted in public humiliation (vv. 483; 486–89). Little wonder, then, that he would resort to manipulation in order to clothe his household. Nor is it any more astonishing that, once engaged in a legal case, he would be willing to sacrifice justice in order to earn a tidy fee. The values of the operator are part of a type, the deceiver or swindler, and these basic type-related values are sufficient to account for his adoption of manipulative behavior.

The question of values becomes more complex when we consider S_2, the manipulated addressee, whether it be the crow, Guillaume, or the judge. The various elements invested in O_1—flattering discourse, food, money, phony deathbed rituals, trumped up evidence—are not sufficient in themselves to manipulate persuasively. These elements *must* interact with the manipulated subject so as to call into being attitudes based on systems of values that ultimately valorize in a decisive way one course of action as opposed to another. It is this interaction of cognitive and pragmatic manipulative devices with the values of S_2 that moves him to act according to the objectives set in O_3.

Consider the variety of values that underlie the responses of S_2 in our inventory. The fable sets up an opposition between the values of mere subsistence and those which have to do with personal esthetic and artistic qualities: the truly vain are seldom obese. Personal values combine with economic values in the clothier's allowance of credit. He reveals at least a moderate susceptibility to the emotional evocation of his honorable lineage but is even more tantalized by prospects of gratification of hunger and thirst. Yet, above all else, the prospect of gold crowns sends Guillaume out in search of his client while evoking a rich fantasy of hoarded wealth. Later, when finally convinced by the spectacle of Pathelin's imminent demise, he departs hastily, which suggests a fundamental valorization of the euphoric, or affectively positive qualities, over the dysphoric, or negative ones, of life over death. His willingness to attribute the purchase to supernatural demonic intervention (v. 989) shows a fearful recognition of moral values (evil vs. good). In the courtroom scene, manipulation and values interact in a far more straightforward way. The judge is a representative of the juridical institution, and it is this strongly institutionalized system of values which determines the manipulative strategy, whereby the discourse of inquest is eventually made to correspond to the legal criteria for a judgment of acquittal.

We can therefore see, even in these four relatively simple instances of manipulation, that the addressee is moved by varying combinations of material, emotional, moral, and economic values that represent either personal or social value-systems. In the case of the clothier, the complex interaction of these systems is a good illustration of the fact that it takes a great many signs of different colors, shapes, and significations to get the manipulated addressee to the right address at the end of the crooked, one-way, dead-end street named Cannotnot.

8
Illocupathelin, Speech Actor

The critical attention of the preceding chapter was directed primarily to the nonverbal processes and structures that enter into a *making-to-do*. Yet, having seen that manipulation has modal, contractual, and value structures, all of which are reflected in numerous ways in the figures of deceit examined, we have still to consider fully the communicative and, especially, the *verbal* aspect of Manipathulin. Although manipulative behavior is not restricted to the titular character, we can readily see that he, more than the others, repeatedly *makes to do by doing things with words*. Laced as they are with oaths and obscenities, the languages of Pathelin enable him to portray cleanly, to plead cleanly, even to perish cleanly, that is, according to the conventions in which his languages are couched. With greater fidelity to the representational dimension, we could say that Pathelin's doings are mimetic, both words and gestures being suggested by the institutions to which they implicitly refer. Yet these institutional and gestural attitudes are anchored in and conveyed by language. If Pathelin could be described as "une force qui va," that dynamic aspect has many of the essential elements of an illocutionary force.[1] His mimetic manipulative doings, in which it must appear that only clean hands are involved, are founded by the *speech acts* that mobilize doings delegated underhandedly to the gullible Guillaumes of this world.

Or, rather, of *that* world in which Pathelin and Guillaume enter into relations of communication. For the question of speech acts inevitably leads to a necessary distinction between what John Searle has called "normal real world talk"—the world with which speech act theory characteristically deals—and "parasitic forms of discourse such as fiction, play acting, etc."[2] In order to broach the matter of speech acts in drama, understood here as a specific play, we must emphasize that the focus is at one remove from "normal real world talk" since what is uttered is truncated from the intentions of a real speaker and thus only represents or dramatizes such talk. If we attempt to consider it according to "real world" criteria, its illocutionary force is immediately invalid from a theoretical perspective. On the other hand, if we consider it as *mimetic* communicative discourse and analyze its illocutionary value entirely *within* this discourse-specific context, the analytical criteria retain their pertinence to the study of communication as a manipulative force within the play.³

In addition to this distinction between theatrical and everyday discourse, it is necessary to make an allowance for nonverbal communication as part of the illocutionary act. Searle states that "often, in actual speech situations, the context will make it clear what the illocutionary force of the utterance is, without its being necessary to invoke the appropriate explicit illocutionary force indicator." Such indicators as "I promise," "I state," "I command," and so forth, need not be explicitly present in order to show what illocutionary act is being performed.⁴ In recognition of this broader context, Umberto Eco has viewed "the notion of 'speech act' . . . as concerning not merely verbal acts but every kind of expression (images, gestures, objects)," proposing the term "communicational acts" to include these nonverbal perspectives.⁵ The importance of nonverbal behavior in daily communication has been demonstrated in many studies,⁶ but one might well anticipate its even greater importance, and especially the necessity that it be exaggerated, in theatrical representation. Indeed, Anne Ubersfeld has with good reason suggested that the discourse of the theatrical text possesses an *illocutionary* force and "appears as a speech act supposing and creating its own conditions of enunciation. . . ."⁷ The role of nonverbal elements in speech acts might in fact be characterized as indicative of an illocutionary context of enunciation.

We can readily identify three basic types of illocutionary acts in our inventory, after Searle's classification.⁸ The fox attempting to get the crow to sing would be a *directive*. Devised to elicit a particular action from the addressee, directives normally include inviting, daring, and pleading, as well as commanding and requesting. Pathelin commits himself to pay in gold crowns. This is a *commissive,* an act that "commits" the addressor to do something by promise, threat, oath, and so forth. Later efforts to convince the clothier that Pathelin is dying, then to persuade the judge to absolve the shepherd, are examples of *representatives,* whereby a "state of affairs" is represented as either occurring in time or as hypothetical, whence such acts as statements, claims, hypotheses, descriptions, predictions, etcetera. Normally, an illocutionary act is considered theoretically as a discrete sentence or, in some cases, as a group of related sentences.⁹ Rather than view the fable, DS¹, DS³, and DS⁵ as complex illocutionary acts, we may consider them as segments the organizing principle of which is either a directive, a commissive, or a representative.

As far as the logic of illocutionary acts in the play is concerned, Pathelin's promise to pay in gold crowns entails two subsequent representations of a state of affairs, each of which is accessory to the invalidation of the earlier promise. It is thus the commissive which enjoys the greatest seminal prominence because of its *insincerity* which makes necessary the later representatives. We shall return to this presently.

In DS¹, the commissive, or promissory, aspect of Pathelin's purchase on credit develops from a series of utterances throughout the sequence. Well before the actual promise is expressed, Pathelin establishes an amiable rapport by preparatory, accessory speech acts, such as the representatives in his portrait of the clothier's family or even by his initial greetings: "Sa, ceste paulme!", v. 106, or "comme celluy qui est tout vostre," v. 110. (Here, shake. . . . I'm as well as ever, i.e., at your service.) Although greeting is characterized as an act of "courteous recognition of H[earer] by S[peaker]," these greetings are accessory to the later commissive in that they increase the hearer's receptivity to the addressor.[10] "Comme celluy qui est tout vostre" acquires its intimate connotations within the conventional sphere of courtesy, while "Sa, ceste paulme!" would be incomprehensible outside the cultural context that recognizes shaking hands as a gesture of recognition and greeting. These are relatively trivial examples of a fundamental concept in speech act theory, according to which a great many utterances acquire coherence only as they are understood within the context of "institutions," created by "systems of constitutive rules."[11]

This is certainly the case with regard to Pathelin's offer of an earnest, or "denier à Dieu," a gesture whose coherence depends on an understanding of the late medieval institution of promising. Even before reaching agreement as to the quantity and price of the merchandise, Pathelin makes this pious utterance:

> Avant, combien me coustera
> la premiere aulne? Dieu sera
> payé des premiers, c'est rayson:
> vecy ung denier, ne faison
> rien qui soit ou Dieu ne se nomme.
>
> (vv. 229–33)

(First, how much will a yard cost me? Wait, here's a penny. God's share should be paid first; it's only right. "Let no bargain be made before God's share is paid." *He puts the coin in a collection box.*)

Lemercier has observed that "for Pathelin as for Guillaume, the 'God's penny' conforms to a pious usage which places under divine protection the sales contract that will intervene as soon as they can agree on the object and the price."[12] Less a formal, binding agreement than a fiduciary contract between parties, the earnest is calculated to allay the clothier's suspicions about the motives of his client.

Later, Pathelin tells Guillemette that, instead of offering this traditional token, he could just as well have had recourse to a gesture with similar connotations:

> Ce fut pour le denier a Dieu,
> et encore, se j'eusse dit

> "la main sur le pot!", par ce dit
> mon denier me fust demeuré.
>
> (vv. 394–97)

(It was God's penny that sealed the bargain. If I had asked him to drink on it instead, I could have kept the penny.)

According to Lemercier, "the expression used by Pathelin alludes to a gesture whereby contracting parties place their hands on the tankard of wine they will drink to seal their agreement."[13] Retrospectively, earlier statements become clear in this context. As Pathelin enumerates what he will buy at the fair, Guillemette admonishes:

> Alez! n'ombliez pas a boire,
> se vous trouvez Martin Garant.
>
> (vv. 94–95)

(Go ahead then and don't forget to drink on the bargain if you find a gullible creditor.)

In other words, buy on credit if you find a creditor who will drink to the bargain, because we have no money. Later, when Pathelin invites the clothier around to his house for a drink, the latter replies:

> Et! par saint Jaques, je ne fais
> guares aultre chose que boire.
> J'iray, mais il fait mal d'acroire,
> ce sçavez vous bien, a l'estraine.
>
> (vv. 294–97)

(By Saint James, I hardly do anything but drink to seal the bargain with my customers. I'll go, but it's bad luck, you know, to give credit on the first sale of the day.)

The clothier is not confessing a penchant for alcohol, but rather lamenting that he all too frequently drinks to seal transactions on credit in the first sale of the day.

Thus, as a structural element of the promise Pathelin makes to the clothier, the earnest and the evocation of the gesture of clasping hands over a tankard serve as nonverbal illocutionary force indicating devices. Less explicit than the terse utterance "I promise," they nevertheless acquire the same value within the institutional context of late medieval promissory acts. Their chief role is to connote the illocutionary force of a commissive.

As for the promise itself, Pathelin expresses it in distinct phases:

> J'avois mis appart quatre vings
> escus, pour retraire une rente,
> mais vous en aurez vingt ou trente . . .
>
> (vv. 198–200)

(I've saved up 80 gold pieces to pay off a debt, but I can see you're going to get 20 or 30 of them.)

> vous les prendrez
> a mon huis, en or ou monnoye.
>
> (vv. 282–83)

(You'll have your money, in gold or in francs, as soon as you reach the door.)

> Et si mangerez de mon oye,
> par Dieu, que ma femme rotist.
>
> (vv. 300–301)

(By God, we'll even eat the goose that my wife is roasting.)

> LE DRAPPIER
> Je vous pry que vous me baillez
> mon argent dez que j'y seray.
> PATHELIN
> Feray. Et! Par Dieu! non feray
> que n'ayez prins vostre repas ...
>
> (vv. 316–19)

(THE CLOTHIER: Please give me my money as soon as I arrive. PATHELIN: Of course I will. No, I won't, by God, not until you've been well fed.)

First foreseeing merely handing the money over at the front door, Pathelin subsequently depicts an interlude of food and drink as a necessary prerequisite to the exchange. Since the latter is to be consequent upon dinner, postponement or even cancellation of the meal would in fact suffice to postpone or cancel the debt, if we follow the tortured logic of Pathelin at this point. But the offers of meal and money are both commissives and failure to provide both will eventually constitute two broken promises.

It is instructive to attempt to inscribe this promise into Searle's analysis of the illocutionary act of promising. It will be recalled that Searle stipulates nine conditions that must obtain for "sincere and nondefective" promises.[14]

1. "Normal input and output conditions obtain" (p. 57). True. Pathelin and Guillaume speak the same language and hear and understand each other.[15]

2. "[Pathelin] expresses the proposition that [promises] in the utterance of [a sentence]" (p. 57). We have seen that the promise emerges from multiple sentences which can be located and recognized as a promissory utterance.

3. In promising, Pathelin does indeed "predicate a future act" of his own doing (p. 57).

4. "[The clothier] would prefer [Pathelin's] doing [the act predicated] to his not doing [it], and [Pathelin] believes that [the clothier] would prefer his

doing [it] to his not doing [it]" (p. 58). True. Unlike a threat, a promise is "a pledge to do something for you, not to you" (p. 58).

5. "It is not obvious to both [Pathelin] and [Guillaume] that [Pathelin] will do [this act] in the normal course of events" (p. 59). True. Leaving the boutique with merchandise obviously creates anxieties for the clothier, and the whole point of the promise is to assure that such conduct will lead to due payment. So far so good.

6. "[Pathelin] intends to do [the act promised]" (p. 60). Waterloo! We know that this is *not* the case (see vv. 85–86). To allow for "insincere promises," Searle substitutes for "intends to do" simply "takes responsibility for intending to do," so that, lacking the intention, the speaker nevertheless "purports to have intentions which he does not have" when his speech act is insincere.[16] Whence the applicability of clause 6a in Searle: "[Pathelin] intends that the utterance of [the promissory sentence] will make him responsible for intending to do [the act promised]" (p. 62).

7. "[Pathelin] intends that the utterance of [the promissory sentence] will place him under an obligation to do [the act promised]" (p. 60). Again true. Although from his own point of view, as well as from our privileged position as spectators, he has never for a moment intended to *fulfill* the promise, whence the need for (6a). However, Pathelin, by promising, *must* intend that this act will place him under an obligation, especially from the perspective of the clothier. Otherwise, his promise would be meaningless, and the clothier would probably refuse to sell the cloth on credit. Only when the force of an obligation is created by the utterance does the promise become distinct from other, nonpromissory statements. We can thus see why Searle calls this the "essential condition" of the promise.

8. "[Pathelin] intends (i-I) to produce in [the clothier] the knowledge (k) that the utterances of [the promissory sentence] is to count as placing [Pathelin] under an obligation to do [the act promised]. [Pathelin] intends to produce k by means of the recognition of i-I, and he intends i-I to be recognized in virtue (by means of) [the clothier's] knowledge of the meaning of [the promissory sentence]" (p. 60). This is the *illocutionary effect* which Pathelin attempts to produce in the clothier. By using the institutionalized conventions of promising (utterance, gestures, customs, etc.), Pathelin intends to make the clothier understand his vow as a promise intentionally made so that he will consent to the transaction.

9. "The semantical rules of the dialect spoken by [Pathelin] and [the clothier] are such that [the promissory sentence] is correctly and sincerely uttered if and only if conditions 1–8 obtain" (p. 61). If, as does Searle for insincere promises, we drop "sincerely" from this proposition and substitute (6a) for (6), this final condition assures that, *albeit insincerely*, the promise is uttered as a promise according to the semantical rule for formulating such an utterance in a given dialect.

This application of the formula devised by Searle is of course made with an acute awareness that Pathelin is not a "real world" Speaker, no more than Guillaume is a "real world" Hearer. When one observes that Pathelin "intends" something, we must recognize that this is at best an inference made on the basis of represented statements and actions which replicate the effect of intentional behavior characteristic of "real world" Speakers and Hearers.

On the evidence available, Pathelin's mimetic replica of a commissive act in DS^1 produces the effect of meeting all nine conditions of the illocutionary act of nondefective *insincere* promising. Before tracing the legacy of this speech act in later segments of the play, it should be noted that condition 8, the illocutionary effect, marks an important point of tangence between the Greimassian model of the canonical structure of the proposition of a contract in manipulation and the theory of speech acts. Specifically, the Speaker's deliberate production of "knowledge" in the Hearer, according to condition 8, corresponds quite closely in this instance to the transfer of "knowledge" (O_1 = /savoir/) from S_1 to S_2. More on this later.

In contrast with the rather straightforward manner in which this knowledge is communicated in DS^1, DS^3 contains a representative in which it is much more difficult to identify the nature of communication in terms of felicitous speech act conditions. Part of the problem stems from the nature of the representative in question. This broad category is defined as including "illocutionary acts that undertake to represent a state of affairs, whether past, present, future, or hypothetical; e.g., stating, claiming, hypothesizing, describing, predicting, telling, insisting, suggesting, or swearing that something is the case."[17] Obviously the "state of affairs" that Pathelin and Guillemette are representing is false. Yet, just as we may have insincere promises that are nonetheless promises susceptible of analysis as commissives, we may have insincere representatives that are still representatives. In other words, they fulfill the conditions of representatives except that, instead of representing a state of affairs according to the *sincerity condition,* the speaker merely "takes responsibility for representing a state of affairs."

An insurmountable difficulty emerges immediately if we attempt to measure the Speaker-Hearer relationship between Pathelin and Guillaume in terms of speech act conditions. In fact, condition 1 alone, according to which "normal input and output conditions obtain" suffices to exclude this communicative relation from further serious consideration along these lines. Inasmuch as "'output' covers the conditions for intelligible speaking and 'input' covers the conditions of understanding,"[18] this condition is violated by Pathelin's dialectal utterances, which are incomprehensible to Guillaume. Moreover, from the very outset of the first of his two interviews with Pathelin, the clothier's queries about remuneration are met with complaints by Pathelin that the medical "input" from his "physician" has resulted in an abnormal "output," most likely because of the incorrect "input" of the suppositories.[19] In addition to this talking at cross purposes involving a humorous play on /merchandise/ vs. /medicine/, whence /money/ vs. /excrement/, condition 1 is further violated by the fact that Pathelin, the personage in the role of Speaker in DS[1], has now adopted another persona and, by "play acting" for the benefit of the clothier, has in effect entered the realm of a "parasitic form of communication." He is no longer on the same communicative plane as his interlocutor.

Despite the fact that speech act conditions do not obtain for the Speaker-Hearer relationship between the lawyer and the clothier at this point, they *do* obtain for Guillemette and Guillaume. It is *she* who now assumes the role of Speaker, as well as the primary responsibility for the illocutionary act of the representative. To the gullible Guillaume she is the guileful Guillemette,[20] a speech-actress who, though an accomplice to Pathelin's "play-within-a-play acting," remains her represented "real-mimetic-world" self at all times and thus on the same communicative plane as Guillaume.

Without an elaborate, meticulous reiteration of the formal conditions of the representative, we can see that with Guillaume she shares normal input and output conditions. Moreover, it is she and not Pathelin who expresses the representative utterances:

> Il est en tel parti,
> le povre homme, qu'il ne partit
> du lit y a unze sepmaines.
>
> (vv. 565–67)

(The poor suffering man is in the same place he's been without budging for eleven weeks now.)

> Il s'en va.
>
> (vv. 905; 932)

(He's sinking fast.)

> Il se meurt . . .
>
> (v. 941)

(. . . he's dying . . .)

In expressing these statements, she predicates a future act of Pathelin, specifically, that he will die at any moment, and she does so because it is not immediately obvious to Guillaume that this is about to take place. According to the modified *sincerity condition*, she "takes responsibility for representing a state of affairs." The *essential condition*, which "counts as an undertaking to the effect that [the proposition] represents an actual state of affairs"[21] is also valid, witness Guillemette's unflagging insistence that the illness has already endured eleven weeks and that it is terminal. Likewise, in her performance of this representative in the literal utterance of the above proposition, Guillemette intends to produce a certain effect—the clothier's knowledge that Pathelin is at the point of death—by getting the clothier to recognize her intention to produce that effect. Using the words *literally*, she intends this recognition to be achieved in virtue of the fact that the rules for using the expressions she utters associate the expression with the production of that effect.[22] Thus, positive marks for the illocutionary effect. Finally, the representative is uttered according to the semantical rules for representative utterances in the dialect spoken by Guillemette and Guillaume.

What, then, is the role of Pathelin in this illocutionary act? In terms of quantity of speech, it is he who produces, by far, more utterances than either Guillemette or Guillaume. Moreover, despite the fact that a major portion of his dialectal utterances are either muddled or incomprehensible, they do help to communicate and render plausible the state of affairs uttered literally by Guillemette. Pathelin's delirious ravings bring to mind an anecdote related by Searle, having to do with an American soldier captured by Italian troops during World War II. To gain release by making his captors think that he is German and therefore not an enemy, the soldier utters the only German phrase he knows: *Kennst du das Land wo die Zitronen blühen?* ("Knowest thou the land where the lemon trees bloom?").[23] Like the American soldier, Pathelin says one thing with a literal, conventional meaning which has absolutely nothing to do with the meaning he is attempting to convey to the clothier. The meaning Pathelin wishes to convey by his delirium could be formulated in terms of the representative proposition: "Je me meurs." ("I am about to die.") This sort of saying one thing while meaning another lies outside the boundaries of normal speech acts occurring within a single dialect shared mutually by Speaker and Hearer. Yet it is above all this wildly deviant verbal behavior on the margin of strictly defined illocutionary acts which is of far more interest than the latter and which compels us to look beyond constitutive rules to specify its considerable importance to communication.

The nonliteral meaning of the dialects is active and effective within a broader communicative system subsumed under the institutional category of *death* during the later Middle Ages. As we saw in the study of Pathétiquelin, the discourse of death stems from the widespread cultural context created by the popular fifteenth-century *Ars moriendi*. We can represent the communicative role of the dialects by assuming the connotations of death already present in the situation of enunciation organized around the deathbed and by tracing their relations in terms of a connotative semiotics.[24] In this light, the manifest, denotative content of the dialects, though comprehensible at times and even humorous, as when Pathelin latinizes at the expense of the clothier (vv. 962–68), is less consequential for the purposes of manipulation than are the categories of connotative content. There are at least three such categories:

1. *regression,* including utterances of the type:

> Celluy qui l'aprint a l'escole
> estoit normant: ainsi advient
> qu'en la fin il luy en souvient.
>
> (vv. 902–4)

(His schoolmaster was from Normandy. Now at the end he's remembering him.)

2. *imminent death,* e.g.,

> Par mon serment, il se mourra
> tout parlant. Comment il latime.
>
> (vv. 969–70)

(I swear, he's going to die making speeches. My, how he Latinizes!)

3. *sacraments,* e.g.,

> Helas! helas! l'heure s'apresse
> qu'il fault son dernier sacrement.
>
> (vv. 856–57)

(Alas! Alas! The hour draws near when he'll need the last sacraments.)

The resulting secondary significations conveyed by a primary signification take us out of the unambiguous, orderly, antiseptic world of Searle's constitutive rules and into the hazy, infinitely expansive nebulae of Gricean implicatures.[25] At the same time, we find ourselves in an environment that resembles the conceptualization of a connotative semiotics set forth by Umberto Eco.[26] In this scheme, expression and content relate as follows:

EXPRESSION			CONTENT		
EXPRESSION	CONTENT				
Limousin (834–39)	=	X			
Picard (848–55)	=	X			
Flemish (863–71)	=	X			
Norman (886–99)	=	X	REGRESSION (vv. 789–90; 842–45; 860–61; 902–4; 939–40)	IMMINENT DEATH (vv. 791; 829–31; 941; 969–70)	SACRAMENTS (vv. 856–57; 876–77; 941–42)
Breton (919–30)	=	X			
Lorrain (943–54)	=	X			
Latin (957–68)	=	X			

The content and expression in the primary signification become the expression of another content. This secondary, connotative content is made manifest to the dull and dim draper through the glossing by Guillemette. In one utterance, she specifies, in a didactic style reminiscent of the patristics, the causative link between all three categories:

> Ce fut la mere de son pere,
> qui fut attraicte de Bretaigne.
> Il se meurt; cecy nous enseigne
> qu'il fault ses derniers sacremens.
>
> (vv. 939–42)

(His father's mother came from Brittany. But he's dying and all this indicates that it's time for the last sacraments.)

Her relation to the dialects is metalinguistic, since she provides a commentary on the verbal symptoms which is interpretative on the classemes of /speech/, /past/, /death/, /ritual/, and so forth.[27]

The locutionary roles of husband and wife in this curious instance of a representative appear to be complementary. Strictly speaking, Guillemette nondefectively utters the representative "Il se meurt" while at the same time translating Pathelin's verbal delirium into explicative, descriptive, and prescriptive utterances having to do with regression, imminent death, and the imperative appropriateness of sacraments. Cumulatively, the ravings of Pathelin and her interpretation of them serve to make plausible the proposition contained in the representative. Thus, rather than performing a nondefective speech act in this segment, Pathelin is—and with considerably more effort and verve than it would take to utter "Je me meurs"—serving the purpose of felicitous speech acts by acting—and how!—as a connotative indicator of its illocutionary force.

The shepherd does likewise in DS[5]. Again an insincere representative is involved. Although numerous allegations, charges, and countercharges are made during the hearing, it is Pathelin's statement regarding the mental incompetence of the shepherd which is decisive:

> Or est il plus fol qui boute
> tel fol naturel en procès!
> Ha! sire, envoyés l'en a ses
> brebis! *Il est fol de nature.*
>
> (vv. 1393–96)

(It takes a real ass to bring such a poor fool to trial. Your Honor, send him back to his sheep. He's just a natural-born fool.)

The judge's decision to absolve the shepherd hinges on the represented "fact" that the accused is mentally deficient and thus not accountable before the law:

> Je l'assoulz de vostre demande,
> et vous deffendz le proceder.

> C'est ung bel honneur de plaider
> a ung fol!
>
> (vv. 1471–74)

(I absolve him of your charges and forbid you to proceed. A fine thing it is to bring suit against a fool.)

Thibault's iterative ovine utterance is thus decisive evidence, as well as the connotative illocutionary force indicator needed by Pathelin to win his case. As in the preceding segment, one of the two deceivers is "play-acting" by using incomprehensible language. (For all the judge knows, Thibault could be inquiring about the location of the land of lemon trees!) Once again, the requisite normal input and output conditions for the speech act are violated. Yet just as Guillemette glossed the dialects of Pathelin, thereby turning them into accessories to her representative, so, too, does Pathelin interpret the shepherd's sheepish bleating to the advantage of his own insincere representative argument before the bench.

Having considered ways in which speech act theory would be helpful in analyzing the manipulative strategies featuring Pathelin, we are now in a position to entertain the possibility of the useful merger of a semiotics of manipulation, as sketched along Greimassian lines in the preceding chapter, with the foregoing analysis of illocutionary acts in the play.

There is an obvious similarity between S_1 and S_2 in the Greimassian contractual structure of manipulation and Speaker and Hearer in Searle's illocutionary relation, provided that S_1 is a *verbal* manipulator. This resemblance suggests that the contractual structure

$$S_1 \rightarrow S_2 \cap O_1 ((O_2 [O_3]))$$

might be invested with the elements of speech acts in instances of verbal manipulation. Like the illocutionary effect, in which knowledge is transferred from Speaker to Hearer, or rather, deliberately induced in the latter so as to effect Hearer's recognition of the literal and intentional meaning of the utterance, the relation between S_1 and S_2 involves a transfer of an object of knowledge (O_1) to the latter in order to "transform the competence of S_2" by persuasion.

This raises the question of whether or not an equivalence exists between O_1 and the illocutionary effect. It is immediately apparent from our examples that the two are not theoretically equivalent in all cases. In DS^3, the S_1-S_2 relation could be applied to Pathelin and Guillaume, respectively. This case would satisfy the more abstract theoretical parameters of O_1, inasmuch as Pathelin may be said to "transfer" knowledge to Guillaume connotatively, by gestures and irrelevant babbling. Yet we have seen that this relation does not lie within the criteria of speech acts, as does the S_1-S_2 relation between Guillemette and Guillaume. The illocutionary effect would thus seem to be one possible subcategory of O_1, as it is in at least three cases in the play: Pathelin-Guillaume (DS^1); Guillemette-Guillaume (DS^3); Pathelin-

Judge (DS^5). The fact that in DS^3 Pathelin's verbal manipulative behavior requires for its effectiveness a second agent to explicate his delirium in an illocutionary act is a good illustration of how nonspecific O_1 really is with regard to actual cases of verbal manipulation.

If O_1 may thus in some cases involve an illocutionary act and produce an illocutionary effect, then what are O_2 and O_3 with regard to speech act criteria? O_2, the object of the manipulator's desire, is what compels S_1 to initiate the transformation of S_2's competence by persuasion. Inasmuch as S_1 does not normally disclose this object to S_2, but instead discloses O_1 as a means of realizing some other objective unrelated to O_2 but which will nevertheless make it accessible, we may expect a strongly positive correlation between *insincere* illocutionary acts in O_1 and manipulative behavior geared to the attainment of O_2. Thus, Pathelin promises insincerely (O_1) to gain the immediate release on credit of the bolt of cloth (O_2), while Guillemette represents insincerely in order to keep it. Likewise, Pathelin later represents insincerely in order to win his case and the gold crowns as fee (O_2). It follows that stratagems of verbal manipulation make extreme demands on speech act theory because it was not elaborated with the eccentric structure of the manipulative contract in mind. In order to include such a contract, in which the illocutionary act is a *means* rather than an end in itself, the insincerity clause must be invoked as a *norm* to account for the presence of O_2, which motivates and necessitates insincere utterances.

O_3, defined in the Greimassian model as the realization by S_2 of the narrative program originally conceived and covertly sought by S_1, is consequent upon what in speech act analysis is known as a *perlocutionary effect*, conceived by J. L. Austin and here summarized by Searle:

> Correlated with the notion of illocutionary acts is the notion of the consequences or *effects* such acts have on the actions, thoughts, or beliefs, etc. of hearers. For example, by arguing I may *persuade* or *convince* someone, by warning him I may *scare* or *alarm* him, by making a request I may *get him to do something,* by informing him I may *convince him (enlighten, edify, inspire him, get him to realize).* The italicized expressions above denote perlocutionary acts.[28]

Unlike the somewhat more procrustean relation between the illocutionary effect and O_1, the perlocutionary effect is analyzable into specific constituent elements of O_3 in our inventory. This is owing to the fact that the perlocutionary effect is complex and more loosely defined than the illocutionary effect. It includes the effects of both cognitive persuasion and delegation of pragmatic action. Within its limits lie S_2's response to persuasion by an *interpretative doing* [ID] *(faire interprétatif)* as well as fulfillment of the function [F] contained in the predicate of O_3: realization of the narrative program of which S_2 is the subject. Examples of the perlocutionary effect all display these two aspects:

DS¹: ID = Guillaume's assent to the terms of Pathelin's promise.
 F = release of the cloth on credit.
DS³: ID = Guillaume's assent to the proposition that Pathelin is dying.
 F = departure/relinquishment of plans to collect for the merchandise.
DS⁵: ID = The judge's assent to the proposition that the shepherd is mentally incompetent.
 F = dismissal of the shepherd from further accountability before the law/payment of gold (abortive because of the shepherd's counterstrategy).

In all three sequences, the fulfillment of manipulation as delegated action—*a making-to-do (faire-faire)*—depends upon a prior *making-to-believe (faire-croire)*. A subject induces certain beliefs in an antisubject, and these beliefs in turn prompt the antisubject to perform a certain action or series of actions.

It was asserted near the outset of this study that "delusive persuasive doing"—a deceptive *making-to-believe*—characterizes the manifestations of "deceit" around the instances of which the figures of deceit are organized. It is now apparent that delusive persuasion is a manipulative comportment anchored in speech acts. Where instances of verbal manipulation are involved, we have seen that the Greimassian formulation of the manipulative contract may be made more precise by the account of speech acts provided by Searle. Substitution of the Speaker-Hearer relation for the more general addressor-addressee (S_1-S_2) opposition, and the analysis of O_1 and O_3 in terms of illocutionary and perlocutionary effects, respectively, render the contractual structure more sensitive to the particular qualities of verbal manipulation.

On balance, this necessarily limited investigation suggests that speech act theory would be of considerable importance to the elaboration of a theory of manipulation. After all, speech act theory is centrally concerned with the situation of utterances within their institutional context, and it might be argued, as does Greimas, that manipulation is an institutional infrastructure with definable constitutive rules which are descriptive of behavior conforming to its conditions. Yet this characterization of Greimas's view is slightly reformulated to show its pertinence to speech acts, for Greimas is at this point concerned with a wide range of "comportments" rather than with utterances *tout court*. Therein lies the value of speech act theory to a semiotics of *verbal* manipulation. Although it originated in order to analyze normal, "everyday" utterances, speech act theory would seem to hold as yet unexplored possibilities for the study of eccentric types of verbal behavior that are nonetheless commonplace occurrences. Using Searle's work as a primary reference, one might develop a typology of illocutionary acts that may occur in verbal manipulation. Albeit with insincerity (for which the theory of Searle already allows), he who verbally indulges in lying, delusion, and manipulation is attempting to act and provoke action with words. Whence the importance of research toward a speech act theory of manipulation.

Despite the importance of speech acts to the organization of the manipulative contracts in this play, we note that many truly interesting aspects of manipulation are found in the suburbs of Illocution. These include all of the adjuvants of the speech act, especially the connotative illocutionary force indicators, that compel more attentive scrutiny from both the naive receptor and the literary critic. Pathelin's delirium is certainly more absorbing than assertions made about it by Guillemette. The monotonous repetition of "Bée" by the shepherd at crucial junctures in the court scene serves not only to connote illocutionary force in Pathelin's argumentation but to punctuate and emphasize in a humorous way various details that might otherwise go unnoticed, such as Pathelin's pseudopiety and charitable facade or the judge's growing frustration with the spectacle unfolding before his Incredulous Honor. More vivid and fascinating than a straightforward promise to pay is the elaborately constructed blazonry used by Logopathelin to create a propitious environment for effective illocution. If in all these segments, the speech act is an essential ingredient of delusive persuasion, it remains a relatively *hidden* persuader in comparison with the stunning array of foregrounded language that is only marginally pertinent to a speech act of literary discourse.

The latter perspective must therefore be superseded by critical recognition of the complementary and quantitatively far more extensive abundance of ludic language to which this study has so far been a small and far from exhaustive tribute. Perhaps the ultimate theory of manipulation must culminate in an awareness of the power of language by virtue of its sheer copiousness and infinite power of signification. Pathelin's use of Latin is especially pertinent here. While for a latinate audience it may be understood perfectly well as a metacommentary on the deceptive designs involving gastronomical metaphors, it acquires incantatory value when intoned as liturgical chant which to the nonerudite clothier connotes the fearful drama at death's door.[29] Language can acquire an almost hypnotic power when signifiers are liberated from their traditional function in the sign and deployed in overabundance as epideictic elements of portraiture (Sympathiquelin), incomprehensible dialects (Pathétiquelin), or barnyard bleating.[30] Even when divorced from conventional significations, signifiers can induce affective states—fear, anger, desire, etcetera—when they occur with other communicative acts (gesture, motion, intonation, etc.), as in the manipulative strategies of shamanism and psychiatric practice, or even masterful *pathelinage*.[31] It is this broader discussion which in the final analysis must furnish the criteria by which to evaluate the unsullied handiwork of the artful manipulator.

PART III

Pathelin and the Discourse of Deceit in Medieval French Drama

9
Protopathelin: the Medieval Dramatic Heritage of Deceit

The medieval French drama consists of hundreds of plays, some well known even today, others fragmentary or irretrievably lost. Although it appears to have originated late in the twelfth century, its expansion and diversification run through the fifteenth and beyond. The affective spectrum of its subject matter ranges from sublimely austere, didactically religious sobriety to grotesque, carnivalesque mockery of human enterprises and institutions, sometimes crossing the entire spectrum in a single play. Its settings may be as humble and unprepossessing as a peasant's cottage or as grandiose as the Cosmos itself. Even the terms by which its constituents were normally identified—mystery, miracle, morality, *jeu*, farce, *sottie*, etcetera—suffice to evoke the curious blend of sacred and profane, natural and supernatural depictions for which it is often either praised or passed over in favor of the drama of other periods. Given this massive, eminently heterogeneous corpus strewn across nearly four centuries of French culture, one may understandably marvel that "the medieval French drama" could be identified as a single, coherent phenomenon. Yet it has been the subject of more than one effort to trace its origins, growth, and ultimate decline, as well as to admire the splendid diversity of its elements.

Such is not to be the emphasis of this chapter, though some attempt will be made in passing to conceptualize an important aspect of French drama of the Middle Ages. Disclosure of the figures of deceit in *Maistre Pierre Pathelin* now makes its desirable and possible to see how such a play relates to this vast repertory of medieval French drama. In this effort the classeme /deceit/ will continue to serve as the analytical basis. It is not a matter of reviewing, play by play, all of the major antecedents of *Pathelin*, but rather of considering how /deceit/ signifies or tends to signify in earlier plays and of situating the figures of deceit in *Pathelin* with respect to these tendencies. In the process of locating *Pathelin* within the context of medieval French drama, it will be possible to identify a main current that unifies much of the dramatic output of earlier centuries. We may thus glimpse a new perspective on the semiotics of medieval drama while broadening the context of our analysis of *Pathelin*.

It has been shown that /deceit/ coordinates the narrative, paremiological, epideictic, juridical, and other discursive registers in *Pathelin*. Although /deceit/ is a prominent classeme of organization in other late medieval comic plays, its extensive influence on every aspect of *Pathelin* makes the play stand out as a kind of illustration of the potential latent in the late medieval farce constructed on deceptive strategies. Within the far broader context of medieval French drama, however, *Pathelin* and its congeners stand out in another way, for the classematic dominance of /deceit/ is not at all characteristic of the corpus as a whole. It is much more usual to find that /deceit/ is tributary to the organizing classeme which is its exact opposite, /veridiction/. While /deceit/ subtends a process of *concealment* of knowledge concerning the distinction between "true" and "false" within a given context, /veridiction/ entails the eventual *disclosure* of this distinction.

Normally, strategies of deceit and veridiction involve semiotic processes that occur *within* a discursive context in which the distinction between "true" and "false" is signified independently of extradiscoursive, absolutist notions of "Truth" or of "Falsehood."[1] This obtains no less with drama than with narrative. However, there may exist a mimetic illusion whereby the discourse constructs a distinction between "true" and "false" which is evocative of or analogous to some extracontextual, "real-world" situation. We find such a function in dramatic representation, in which the encoded spectacle contains various sorts of references to extradramatic reality and thus produces a "reality effect" upon the spectator.[2] Patrice Pavis has in fact characterized a "semiological attitude" with regard to dramatic representation as being the introduction, "between the sign and the object, of a certain distance, so that the theater not be reality, but a secondary system which signifies the real."[3] A play may thus in some cases signify the True as determined or believed according to some extradramatic convention or institution.

In this chapter, general identification will be made of a very prevalent type of representation in medieval drama, one in which a *veridictory function* determines the manner in which the dramatic systems signify their basic affinity with cultural institutions. It will then be possible to see how the discourse of deceit in *Pathelin* constitutes a type of drama which is transgressive and contestatory of the representational norms of this veridictory function. It will become evident that the semiological status of *Pathelin* is characterized by a mode of "signification of the real" which differs considerably from the mainstream of medieval drama and anticipates a type of drama which is liberated from the dominance of earlier medieval cultural models.

Owing to its remoteness in time from the so-called "modern stage," medieval French drama is not easily characterized with regard to the veridictory function which informs a major portion of its plays. Paradoxically, a modern French theoretician of drama provides the most illuminating insights pertinent to the veridictory function in European drama during the three centuries prior to *Pathelin*. Upon due consideration of the implications of certain views expressed by this critic, the nature of veridiction and deceit in medieval dramatic representation may be more readily expressed.

*
* *

We must believe that the essential drama, the one at the root of all the Great Mysteries, is associated with the second phase of Creation, that of difficulty and of the Double, that of matter and the materialization of the idea.

These are the words of Antonin Artaud, in *The Theater and its Double*.[4] For Artaud in 1938, such "essential drama" has long been suffocated by trivial plays catering to the shallow tastes of a middle-class elite. As remedy, Artaud prescribes a return "by present-day means to [a] superior idea . . . of poetry-through-theater capable once more of entertaining a religious idea of the theater . . . [and] of recovering within ourselves those energies which ultimately create order and increase the value of life . . ." (p. 80). We might then find freedom by sacrificing what he calls "our little human individuality" to the collective, universal, vibrant power of Myth (p. 116). The Double of the theater is abstract and metaphysical, hence ineffable, yet is accessible, not through the textual language of the play, but through the incantatory, affective power of theatrical performance. He speaks of "magic and sorcery" in the *mise en scène*, and the self-styled "alchemy" of his ideal theater is founded on a scenic "concretization of the metaphysical" through ritual invocation and even violent solicitation of the mythic Double.[5]

Artaud was inspired chiefly by Balinese theater—certainly not an Occidental model—and the "Great Mysteries" mentioned in the citation above refer not to medieval Mysteries but to those of antiquity. Yet many of his key ideas are pertinent to a major current in the drama of medieval Europe, of which the French drama is amply representative. When in his proposal of a Theater of Cruelty, Artaud calls for "mass spectacle" depicting "famous personages, atrocious crimes, superhuman devotions" and seeking "a little of that poetry of festivals and crowds when, all too rarely nowadays, the people pour out into the streets" (p. 85), one is reminded of the late medieval mystery cycles and festival plays. When he asserts that "the theater must become a sort of experimental demonstration of the concrete and the abstract" (p. 108), one might recall that the physical violence of the Passion plays is vital to disclosure of the profound mystery of divine intervention in human history. When Artaud says that performance should evoke "ideas which touch on Creation, Becoming, and Chaos . . ., [ideas] of a cosmic order" (p. 90), one thinks of how, from its twelfth-century vernacular emergence, French drama implies collective celebration of a cosmic model of order reflected in both intellectual and popular culture. His appeal for actors in "symbolic dress" and for depictions of a "battle of symbols" suggests the vestimentary iconography in the mysteries and the Psychomachia of the moralities (pp. 54; 27). His proposal to place the spectators "in the middle of the action . . ., [which] will take place all around them" (p. 96), is precisely the norm in certain medieval theaters-in-the-round such as those unearthed in France or the one used to stage *Castle of Perseverance*.[6] Given these unacknowledged affinities between medieval drama and a theory of the Double, it is not surprising that Artaud cites Saint Augustine's denunciation of the awesome power of drama (pp. 26–27) or that, in an effort to illustrate this power in exemplary paintings, he chooses such biblical and hagiographic subjects as the "Daughters of Lot" by Lucas van Leyden, El Greco's "Resurrections" and "Transfigurations," and the "Temptation of Saint Anthony" by Hieronymus Bosch (p. 120), for these participate in the same culture that is the heritage of medieval religious drama. In a word, Artaud's Double is "performed myth", and despite its anti-Occidental bias, the treatise is often evocative of the truly mythopoeic spectacle of medieval religious drama and *its* Double.

If a reading of *The Theater and Its Double* can be used to make a case for a "medieval drama of the Double," it is obvious that a late comic play like *Maistre Pierre Pathelin* must lie outside the confines of such drama. A theory of the Double adapted to the European Middle Ages would apply primarily to vernacular religious drama and certain secular plays with strong didactic overtones, as in some of the moralities. The plays circumscribed by a medieval drama of the Double would thus represent only one current, but that current is a powerful—one might say a dominant—factor in French drama from its late twelfth-century emergence through the middle of the sixteenth century. Moreover, it is precisely this massive body of individual plays and extensive cycles in which we find the workings of a *veridictory function*. Yet as with the Double conceived by Artaud, veridiction is not merely an intrinsic criterion of "truth" as a construct of a given written text. It is a question of drama which signifies connotatively an identity between "truth" as a value specific to the discourse and Truth as some form of transcendental signified, validated by the unconscious according to Artaud, but by collectively or divinely sanctioned authority in the case of medieval drama. The medieval drama of /veridiction/ realizes, in performance, a "concretization of the metaphysical" through a ritual which is at once mimetic and mythopoeic, an iteration of universal history in the signs of performance and the performance of signs. Thus a discovery of discoursive "truth" within the play of /veridiction/ is to be received connotatively by the medieval public as Truth in the register of collective belief. By virtue of such connotation, the values of the scene are conservative of mythopoeic and cultural values.

Before comparing the veridictory function and its opposite, the deceptive function, we should identify the mechanisms of veridiction apparent in a limited number of models that subtend the veridictory Double in medieval plays.

The models in question are fundamentally intertextual in the broad sense defined by Kristeva.[7] That is, the models reflected by the text written by the playwright, as well as the performance of this text, are literary in the diachronic dimension, while in the synchronic dimension they are social and cultural. In the latter dimension, performance signifies sociocultural realities or ideals, while in the former, it signifies the written text and, in some cases, the nondramatic sources on which this text is based.

The first of these models, the literary model, could be called "the model of the doubles," for veridictory drama of the Middle Ages is very often a parasitic medium whereby the dramatic text upon which performance is based "doubles" the narrative and discursive coherence of a nondramatic source, usually a written source. Under these circumstances, medieval drama in which the veridictory function is operant is usually a secondary modeling of collectively venerated texts.[8]

The "model of the doubles" is familiar to all who follow traditional scholarship devoted to medieval drama. In such scholarship, the plays are received primarily—to paraphrase Artaud—as the written projection of nondramatic narrative. For the sake of example, consider the doubling, or intermedia transposition, among some of the "firsts" in medieval French drama.

The first known French vernacular play and earliest Old Testament mystery is the late twelfth-century *Ordo representacionis Ade,* or *Mystère d'Adam.* Among its doubles are the Vulgate Book of Genesis and a pseudo-Augustinian sermon. Moreover, the dialogue is punctuated by liturgical lessons and responsories that recount the biblical message represented by the play, whence an intrinsic doubling of liturgy and *ludus,* or *mise en abyme.*[9] The contemporaneous *Seinte Resureccion*—the first surviving French play to deal with a subject related to the life of Christ—uses the apocryphal Gospel of Nicodemus and the New Testament as models. *Courtois d'Arras* is the first totally vernacular dramatization of a New Testament parable. The *Jeu de Saint Nicolas* by Jean Bodel, the earliest vernacular miracle play, is a radically amplified double of two twelfth-century Latin *iconia* plays and an earlier legend, while the first dramatized miracle of Our Lady, the *Miracle de Théophile* by Rutebeuf, combines elements from Latin and French narrative prototypes. Multiple doubling occurs in many of the collections, as in the fourteenth-century *Miracles de Nostre Dame,* which contains plays replicating hagiographic accounts, epics, romances, and folk narratives. The earliest of the Passion plays, *Palatinus* and the Autun fragments, are biblically inspired, and they also adapt long segments of the versified narrative *Passion des jongleurs*. *L'Estoire de Griseldis* (1395), first among the serious secular plays, doubles a story made famous by Boccaccio and adapted by Petrarch, Chaucer, and Philippe de Mézières.

In "the model of the doubles," the veridictory function is fulfilled by the play's signification of a preestablished *auctoritas* which effectively authorizes, sanctions, and to a considerable extent informs the structures, systems, and meanings of the play. Such doubling does not originate with medieval vernacular drama, however. The "primeval mitosis" begins to occur in earlier liturgical drama, where Christian rite has acquired representational features by the tenth century. Yet because it is bound to specific liturgical texts and music and spatially circumscribed by the enclosed sanctuary, liturgical drama is a highly conservative, pseudodoubling of Christian rite. Mythically it is ritualized reactualization of the sacred Double.[10] In contrast, the intertextual relations between vernacular French plays and their sources are to a greater degree transgressive, the play often being an amplified, elasticized, sometimes distorted reflection of its nondramatic narrative Other.

To answer the question of why, from the late twelfth century on, the "model of the doubles" prevailed, we must look to the exordia of some of the plays. Unlike the access of the written manuscript to the privileged few who read or listened to readings at communal gatherings, the plays appealed to a larger public, and their exordial devices may include solicitation of silence and the attention of the spectators.[11] Public readings were the norm for centuries, and from this to dramatization was an important move that increased the power of the story to hold an audience. The cognitive appeal of drama is superior to that of oral narration because of the visible dimension, and this power may enhance esthetic and moral values—the veridictory substance—latent in the source. In the prologue to his late fourteenth-century *L'Estoire de Griseldis*, Philippe de Mézières says that by retelling an exemplary narrative *par personnages*, he will appeal not to the ear alone, but to the eye as well.[12] Like Artaud, Mézières sought to materialize the idea on the scene by multiple sensory stimuli.

Although medieval vernacular drama became a secondary modeling medium in order to emphasize the moral and spiritual qualities of its sources, its attitude toward its sources is not uncommonly transgressive. There are several reasons for this.

First of all, as we go from source to play, beginnings and endings are preserved while middles are modified. If in the source the narrative trajectory from A to Z is an unbroken line, it is likely to follow a "zig zag" pattern in the play. In the *Grands Mystères* this may result from what Sr. Mary Faith McKean has called a "flamboyant" style of amplifying the laconic *sermo humilis* of biblical discourse, to achieve realism of detail and conversational flow.[13]

In some cases, the dramatist and public share a prior knowledge of the source, from readings of the Vulgate, preaching, iconography, or oral narration. To revitalize the interest-value of the source and "make it new," the dramatist could defy expectations and create suspense or surprises by devising elaborate middle sections for the dramatic double, while the largely unmodified *dénouement* would preserve the veridictory message. A case in point is *Courtois d'Arras*. In the Vulgate parable, the prodigal son wastes his substance in riotous living, but this is confined to one verse in thirty-two, whereas 90 percent of the play is devoted to his profligacy, including scenes of his downfall at the hands of tavern denizens and his later suffering as a swineherd. His return is precedented by the biblical source, whose value as parable is not lost in the dramatization.[14]

This need to *defamiliarize a familiar narrative* to increase its impact is paradoxically as frequent as the obverse tendency to *familiarize the remote values of the narrative double*. For example, the discourse of Abel in the *Mystère d'Adam* is a new element that explains more fully the necessity to tithe, which is not an elaborate lesson in the biblical prototype.[15] In the same play, a new, quasi-feudal contract relates God and Adam, while the figure of Satan, nowhere in the Genesis episode, speaks a courtly ideolect and dramatizes the Augustinian view of the Fall as a corruption of will.[16] Although we sense what Rainer Warning has called the "insuperable hermeneutic strangeness" or "alterity" of medieval drama in these plays, we must not forget that they in turn represent the attempts of medieval culture to transcend the alterity of *its* sources by recasting them according to contemporary social practices and institutions.[17]

Perhaps the most effective means of achieving this is by producing a profound shock of self-recognition in the Other. Adam is plausibly an obstinate Anglo-Norman farmer or Courtois one of what Georges Duby has identified as the "jeunes," the younger siblings in noble families and thus victims of primogeniture, as well as of a declining agrarian aristocracy and, eventually, of the evils of an emerging urbanism.[18] The public for which Jean Bodel wrote would surely have found as much if not more of itself in the fallen Crusaders and the Artesian tavern customs as in the miracle of the legendary icon of Saint Nicolas. There is evidence that dramatists deliberately sought to cultivate the dramatic medium as a "distant mirror". In the prologue to the third Journée of his *Mystère de la Passion,* Arnoul Gréban invites the spectator to find his own reflection in the "mirror" of the spectacle so as to become mindful of his place in the "divine immortal essence" (v. 2004).[19] This comes very close indeed to Artaud's belief that "the action of the theater . . . is beneficial, for, impelling men to see themselves as they are, it causes the mask to fall, reveals the lie, the slackness, baseness, and hypocrisy of our world; . . . in revealing to collectivities of men their dark power, their hidden force, it invites them to take, in the face of destiny, a superior and heroic attitude they would never have assumed without it" (pp. 31–32). Likewise, transgressive intertextual doubling of source in medieval drama seems less a double-dealing than an effort to remythify old narratives so as to situate the collectivity "within" the Myth where, as Artaud says, reside "powers rediscovered in the Past" (p. 116).

Such, then, was the importance of "the model of the doubles" to the creators of medieval veridictory drama. The plays are intertextual projections of their narrative sources and connotative signifiers of a transcendental signified.

The "model of the doubles" accounts for only a part of the veridictory function, that which concerns the dramatic text and its antecedents as they are signified in performance. We come closer to the notion of a veridictory function, and to the notion of the Double as conceived by Artaud, as we move from the intertextual zone between narrative source and dramatic text to the second major axis, the one which links the dramatic text with representation and performance. For Artaud, the dimension of performance is not slavishly bound to its textual model, however. He says that "the *mise en scène* must be considered, not as the reflection of a written text, the mere projection of physical doubles that is derived from the written work, but as the burning projection of all the objective consequences of a gesture, word, sound, music and their combinations" (p. 73). If, for Artaud, the inscribed dramatic text might be made to serve, though dubiously at best, as a resource of representation, it must never impose tyrannical limitations upon the scenic performance.[20] In performance, the written text must dissolve into

> the conception of a metaphysics derived from a new use of gesture and voice . . . [creating] the sense of a new physical language, based upon signs and no longer upon words . . . spiritual signs [having] a precise meaning which strikes us only intuitively. . . . These powerful signs . . . [correspond] . . . to a sort of spiritual architecture, created out of gesture and mime but also out of the evocative power of a system. . . . (pp. 54–55)

Artaud's emphasis on nonverbal signifying systems in theater would seem to make him one of the first semioticians of theater.[21] Inasmuch as the materialized idea, or Double, is the chief product of theatrical performance, study of the dramatic text must give way to semiotic analysis of nonverbal performative systems involving gesture, proxemics (the semantic aspects of space), iconicity (props, sets, actors, etc.), and the relation these bear to the signifying totality of performance.

When Artaud postulated the Double, he did not locate it in some noumenal *Au-delà* but saw it rather as idea "materialized" in performance (p. 51). Likewise, the performative aspect of the veridictory function in medieval drama is the one which addressed performative properties to the ideational competence of the community in which they signified. The resulting "spiritual signs" were the material signifiers of a collective, mythopoeic coherence. The signifying power of the performance, whose denotative and connotative systems would have appealed to the higher senses and thence to both the emotions and the intellect, could well have induced within the spectator a comprehensive sense of this coherence.

The resources of critical prose could not begin to describe adequately either the collectively intuitive appeal of Artaud's Double or the way in which the kind of medieval Double being suggested here retained its hold on the fifteenth-century spectator. Criticism generally deals more effectively with dramatic texts than with elusive dramatic performances. If there is no suitable way of recapturing the performative immediacy of the medieval Double, consideration of some of its causes is nonetheless in order, for a major objective of semiotic analysis is not only the ultimate comprehensive coherence of meaning but the system of relations vital to its production as well. We should therefore attempt to understand how the representation of medieval veridictory drama involved "matter" in "the materialization of the idea," that is, how it made the perceptible features of dramatic performance serve as "spiritual signs" to signify a reality of a higher order.

Figures 4 through 6, which represent models of the "Spatialization of Axiologies," attempt to suggest, albeit in a very primitive fashion, how in medieval French drama the performative dimension might have evoked conceptual and ideational dimensions prevalent in the cultural sphere. This analysis takes us into the domain of *proxemics,* or the study of how space signifies in dramatic representation. The models show that major spatial *loci* in the medieval dramatic scene signify, denotatively or connotatively, important systems of values in medieval culture, whence a dramatic "spatialization" of value-systems, or "axiologies," the latter term being inspired by that branch of philosophy known as "axiology," which deals with the nature and types of values.

These models do not illustrate the spatial value-structures of three distinct plays but are rather the distillation of tendencies noted within a cross section of plays. Each represents a system of cultural coherence toward which the valorization of space in many plays tends to converge. In terms of manifest discursive features, however, any given play is to a greater or lesser degree "extrasystemic" with regard to the models. Thus, a given play may explicitly signify its participation in only a few limited aspects of a model, while the rest remains implicit and understood on the basis of a cultural mentality shared by producers and public.

Each of the three models is based on the logical model of elementary signification, or "semiotic square," created by sets of contrary and contradictory relations within a given semantic universe.[22]

Figures 4–6

SPATIALIZATION OF AXIOLOGIES IN MEDIEVAL FRENCH DRAMA

Ecclesiological Model

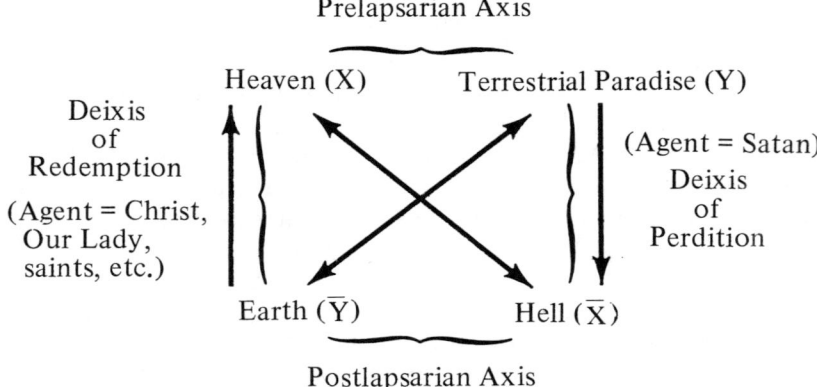

Figure 4. The *Ecclesiological Model* is reflected in contradictions and oppositions present in religious plays such as the *Mystère d'Adam,* the *Seinte Resureccion,* the Passion tradition, and aspects of the Grands Mystères. In terms of both space and values, a contradictory schema (X and X̄, or "not X") relates Heaven and Hell on a cosmic scale. The same contradiction of values is manifested on the terrestrial scale between Terrestrial Paradise and Earth (Y and Ȳ). Before the Fall, the values of Heaven and Terrestrial Paradise are positively related on the axis of contraries (X and Y), or Prelapsarian Axis, while thereafter the values of Earth and Hell are related on the axis of subcontraries (X̄ and Ȳ), or Postlapsarian Axis. The vertical relation between the contrary and subcontrary axes in the logical model of elementary signification is achieved by either (X and Ȳ) or (Y and X̄) and is known as the "deixis," because the two terms are normally related in such a manner that one implies, selects, or is demonstrative of the other. In the three models, each Deixis is created by a mediatory agent. In Figure 4, Terrestrial Paradise and Hell are negatively mediated by Satan at the Fall, whence a Deixis of Perdition; Earth and Heaven are positively mediated on the Deixis of Redemption by Christ at the Redemption and Last Judgment, as well as by Our Lady and a host of intercessory saints at other moments. The Ecclesiological Model is thus a concise representation of the major spatial elements of Judeo-Christian universal history, understood in medieval thought as a linear elaboration of cyclical divine manifestations in mundane time between an initial and final *eschaton,* Creation and Last Judgment, respectively. It is also representative of the value-relations, or axiologies, that bring these spatial elements into pertinent oppositions. Either integrally or in part, it also evokes the spatiality of many medieval mystery plays.

Military Model

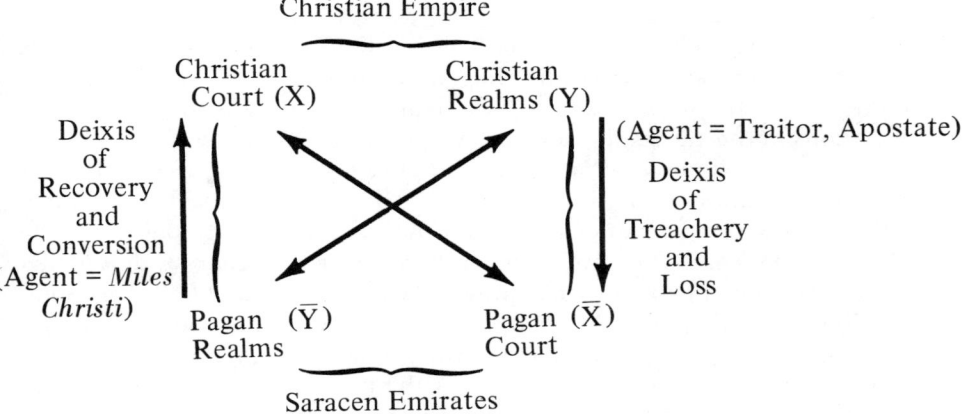

Figure 5. The *Military Model,* which happens to be descriptive of spatial axiologies in some *chansons de geste,* is evoked in large part in the *Jeu de Saint Nicolas* by Jean Bodel. The contradictory relations between Christian and Pagan Courts (X and $\bar{X}$) and their respective Realms (Y and $\bar{Y}$) obtain on the basis of space and values, while the Christian Empire (X and Y) and Saracen Emirates ($\bar{X}$ and $\bar{Y}$) each comprehend spatially proximate political entities with shared values. The Deixis of Treachery and Loss is characteristically mediated by a traitor (e.g., Ganelon in the *Chanson de Roland*) as well as by epic battles, while the Deixis of Recovery and Conversion is mediated by various figures of veridiction (e.g., the angel and the Preudom in the *Jeu de Saint Nicolas*).

Socioeconomic Model

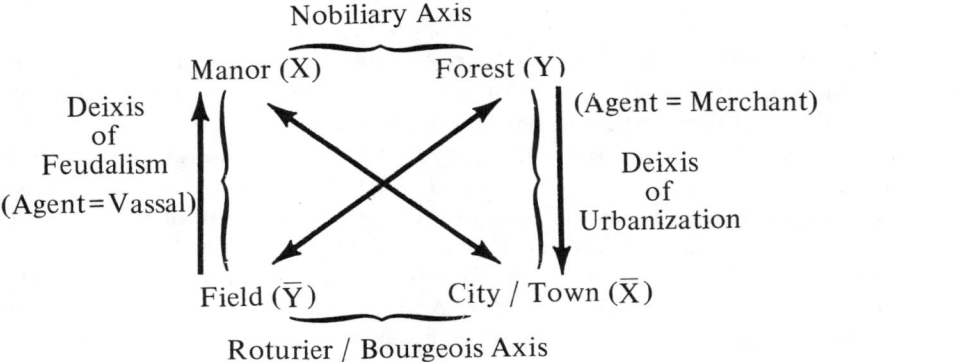

Figure 6. A wide range of secular and comic plays participate in the

Socioeconomic Model. The contradiction between Manor and City/Town articulates the axiological tensions that oppose the Nobiliary Axis of feudalism to the emergence of an exchange economy dominated by the Roturier/Bourgeois Axis. The Deixis of Feudalism is mediated by the vast network of vassals and vavassors, while the Deixis of Urbanization features the merchant as the primary agent of exchange. Mediation is subject to many variations in this model, however, as for example in *Courtois d'Arras,* where Courtois himself and later a bourgeois figure occupy these roles. In *Jeu de la feuillée,* emphasis is on the axis of subcontraries and especially the conflict between urban values and the remote heritage of courtly poetry in the Nobiliary Axis as it is degraded in the Puy, or literary contest, dominated by wealthy urban patricians and presided over by the ignoble Robert Sommeillons. (The degraded image of fairies evocative of the courtly tradition and the antiportrait of Maroie are pertinent here as well.)

These models are not constituents of the narrative code nor of surface elements of the plays but rather of relations susceptible of manifestation at *various* narrative and discursive levels. Consequently, we find elements of the models at different levels of a given play. For example, the Deixis of Perdition in the Ecclesiological Model is *narrativized* in the *Mystère d'Adam* while the Deixis of Redemption is merely prefigured in Adam's lament and the *Ordo Prophetarum.* The farce normally narrativizes the Roturier/Bourgeois Axis of the Socioeconomic Model while evoking indicially the Nobiliary Axis. If the models are set forth here as analytically discrete, their properties are reflected to varying degrees in any particular play. Moreover, we are likely to find evidence of more than one model in a single text. For example, the *Jeu de Saint Nicolas* significantly participates in all three models, as do many of the later miracle plays, while the dramatically orientated *Aucassin* reflects both the Military and socioeconomic Models.

It will be immediately evident that the categories which make up the contrary, subcontrary, and contradictory terms are drawn from the representational sphere. Medieval plays reflecting the model either designate specific *lieux* or *mansions* that represent these "places" in their staging or else allude to them without actually depicting them spatially. Of special significance for the present inquiry is the fact that, although designating spatial relations in dramatic representation, these three models are illustrative of value categories as well. For example, the opposition of Heaven and Hell in the Ecclesiological Model signifies an absolute contradiction of good and evil, while the opposition of Terrestrial Paradise and Earth concerns the involvement of mankind in this contradiction. The Prelapsarian Axis reflects an original relation of God and man on the basis of shared values, while the Postlapsarian Axis depicts the alienation of man from God and the negative values potentially shared by mankind and Hell as a result of the Fall. According to the myth, Perdition was a result of the negative mediation of Terrestrial Paradise by Satan, while Redemption is a result of the positive mediation of Earth by Christ and other agents of divinely sanctioned good.

Like the Ecclesiological Model, the Military and Socioeconomic Models also reflect an axiology implicit in spatial categories. In the Military Model, the Christian Court and the Pagan Court are valorized according to the same absolute disjunction of good and evil as in their counterparts in the Ecclesiological Model. Like Terrestrial Paradise and Earth in the latter, Christian Realms and Pagan Realms are loci, respectively, of loss through treacherous evil agents or of recovery through agents of conversion. The Axis of Christian Empire reflects the harmony of divine and mundane spheres, while the Axis of Saracen Emirates denotes alienation from transcendental Christian values. In the Socioeconomic Model, the Nobiliary Axis links Manor and Forest into the closed feudal microcosm of earthly order ostensibly in harmony with the divine. The Roturier/Bourgeois Axis comprehends a world no longer self sufficient but instead dependent upon the exchange systems evolving from cultivation and commerce. The feudal, nobiliary world is based on vertical relations with God at the summit of the pyramid, while the Roturier/Bourgeois Axis subsists on horizontal relations in which transcendental values are not directly involved. The prototype of the abundant Forest is Terrestrial Paradise, both of which provide without cultivation, while the cultivated field is the place of fallen man, among whose prototypes are Adam, Eve, and Cain, all cultivators. In contrast with the spiritually sanctioned order of the Manor, the order of the City is inherently vulnerable to corruption, as Saint Augustine maintained.[23] The City is the mimetic counterpart of Hell, inasmuch as it is frequently the site of the tavern and its tempters. The Merchant is the chief agent of transformation of feudal values, including those modeled on the spiritual hierarchy of feudal ideology, into urban exchange values. In contrast with the Merchant is the Vassal, who is the primary agent in the maintenance of the feudal order, though less in fact than in principle.

Figure 7 shows that there exists a *hierarcy of relations* among *spatial* terms in the models. Thus, the category "Earth" in the Ecclesiological Model circumscribes the spatial terms in the Military and Socioeconomic Models, while "Christian Realms" in the Military Model includes the spatial terms in the Socioeconomic Model.

However, when we consider the *axiological bias* inherent in the spatial categories in medieval veridictory plays, we find that all three models tend toward congruence, so that there results an *axiological homologation of spatial categories,* as in Table 1. Thus, for example, the Court of the King of Heaven in the Mysteries is an anagogical counterpart of the Christian Court, as at the end of *Griseldis,* or of the feudal manor, as in *Courtois d'Arras.* Earth in the *Mystère d'Adam,* the Pagan Realms in the *Jeu de Saint Nicolas,* and the Field in Cain and Abel plays, or the middle, agrarian section of *Courtois d'Arras,* represent the consequences of nonadherence to

Figure 7
HIERARCHY OF INTERMODEL SPATIAL RELATIONS

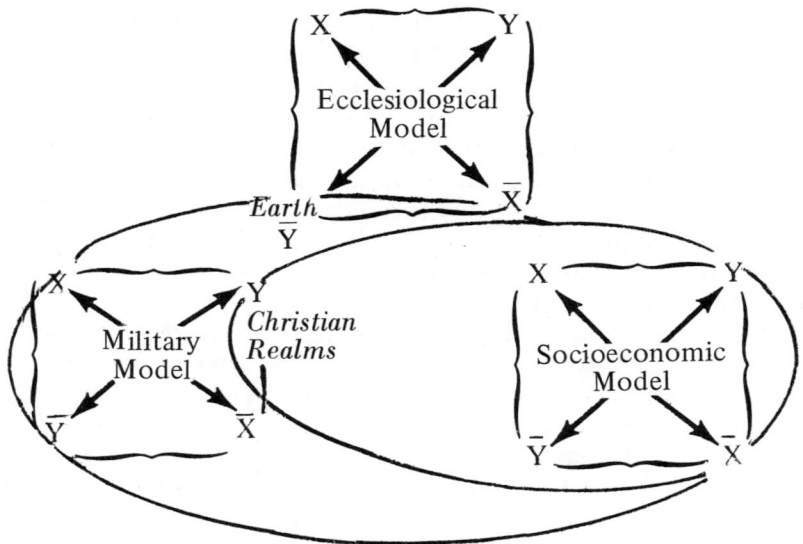

the values of either the prelapsarian idyll of Terrestrial Paradise, the collective ethos of the Christian Realm, or the nobiliary privilege represented by the Forest. As Earth and Field, so must the Pagan Realms be "cultivated" and converted to a productive life by Christian warriors. Finally, City and Town, as in the thirteenth-century Artesian tavern dramas, and the Pagan Court, as in the *Jeu de Saint Nicolas,* are normally at stage left, and thus spatially as well as ideationally associated with Hellmouth and its significations, and with the image of the city vulnerable to corruption.

The models are quite rudimentary, and they are obviously by no means exhaustive of spatial categories in medieval dramatic representation. They are nonetheless pertinent to medieval French plays as well as to other forms of contemporaneous literature. In the present context they are not proposed as objects of profound significance in their own right but rather

Table 1
AXIOLOGICAL HOMOLOGATION OF SPATIAL CATEGORIES

Ecclesiological Model		*Military Model*		*Socioeconomic Model*
Heaven (X)	$\simeq$	Christian Court (X)	$\simeq$	Manor (X)
Terrestrial Paradise (Y)	$\simeq$	Christian Realms (Y)	$\simeq$	Forest (Y)
Earth ($\bar{Y}$)	$\simeq$	Pagan Realms ($\bar{Y}$)	$\simeq$	Field ($\bar{Y}$)
Hell ($\bar{X}$)	$\simeq$	Pagan Court ($\bar{X}$)	$\simeq$	City/Town ($\bar{X}$)

$\simeq$ = Homologation

as a deliberately oversimplified means of emphasizing *the frequently positive correlation between represented spatial and value categories in medieval drama*. They also reveal in a simple way the veridictory ingredients of a truly medieval theater of the Double, for they suggest that representational "matter" is simultaneously "materialization of the idea." Theatrical space is invested with and signifies extradramatic cultural values, so that the ethos of collective belief-structures is represented by spatial categories. The veridictory function in performance thus relies on connotation of the spiritual and the ideational by means of the visual.[24] When this function is operative in medieval plays of the veridictory type, cultural values in the ecclesiological, military, or socioeconomic spheres are connotatively signified and reaffirmed. The visible décor and tangible properties of the scene are signifiers in that "physical language" of the medieval dramatic Double, a language "based upon signs" rather than upon words alone.

*
* *

In the veridictory function in medieval drama, /deceit/ often plays a subordinate but important role. There is frequently an abundance of figures of deceit, for deceit is a staple of the conflict essential to veridiction, and its incarnations are legion. One finds structures based on deceptive strategies (temptations, seductions, delusions, etc.), characters who deceive (e.g., Satan, Judas, thieves, merchants, peasants, spouses, even clergymen), deceptive situations and tactics (disguise, mistaken identity, misleading reports, vows, oaths, and contracts later abrogated willfully), ecetera. Yet in plays featuring the veridictory function, figures of deceit are invariably counterbalanced and neutralized by *figures of veridiction*. In ecclesiological drama, these include supernatural manifestations of all sorts (miracles, angelic proclamations, prophecies that come to pass, auspicious signs of divine will, etc.), and characters who utter veridictory proclamations (narrators, preachers, angels, prophets, allegorical figures of virtues, Christ, Figura, etc.). Their secular counterparts in plays that implement the Military and Socioeconomic Models vary widely among rulers, Christian warriors, venerable elders, magistrates, hermits, faithful servants, chaste maidens, devout peasants, etcetera, all of whom participate in the disclosure of an unequivocal identification of the "right," the "true," and the "just," and who affirm or connote the medieval Christian world view which sanctions their representation. By virtue of such figures of veridiction, the play maintains a rigorous disjunction between positive and negative value-systems and thus an unambiguously *monological* ethos from which the exceptional, the marginal, and the generally "gray" issues are normally excluded.[25] As an accessory of veridiction, the discourse of deceit is identified negatively and defeated in exemplary fashion, thus reassuring us about the implicit vertical relation between represented human conduct and the transcendental cultural values which it connotes.

The three models of representational veridiction are descriptive of what might be called an "analogical bias" in medieval dramatic discourse, whereby the ethical axiology of the Ecclesiological Model serves as a paradigm for medieval institutions and their representation. Systems of human institutions are vertically sanctioned according to the fundamental ethos of this cosmic model. Judson B. Allen has suggested that this type of "*assimilatio* of parallel systems" is widespread in medieval culture and that it is proliferated in a wide variety of intellectual and artistic contexts.[26] Much of the so-called "decline" or "waning" of the Middle Ages may be reflected in the gradual displacement of such analogical modes of thought.

Symptoms of this shift are apparent in the sphere of later medieval drama. Julia Kristeva has observed that until the end of the fourteenth century the life of Christ was portrayed dramatically on the inspiration of the canonical and apocryphal Gospels and the Golden Legend, as in the Mysteries from the manuscript of the Bibliothèque Sainte-Geneviève or the *Palatinus*. Early in the fifteenth century, however, she notes that ". . . the transcendental background evoked by the symbol seems to waver. A new signifying relation announces itself, between two elements both of which are placed in this world, 'real' and 'concrete'."[27] The later Mysteries become more inclusive of the resolute worldliness that will eventually lead to their proscription.[28] Rainer Warning documents the profoundly ambiguous, earthy, coarse depictions of Jesus and Mary Magdalene in the later German Mysteries and attributes this current to the deliberate exploitation of an ambiguity latent in the Gospels.[29] Throughout Europe, late medieval drama is marked by a greater fascination with the marginal, so that figures of evil, deceit, ambiguity, and equivocation, though still in some cases accessories to the veridictory function, are nevertheless accorded a far greater importance, or lingered over, so to speak, by the dramatists. Noah's shrewish wife, Cain, and Tittivillus in the Corpus Christi Cycle, or the allegorical types in the *sottie*, or the grotesque fare of the farce, may still further sacred or satirical veridictory objectives at times, but they also shock, disgust, or delight as part of a general entertainment function quite apart from any signification of transcendental values. In short, there is a decline in the importance of veridiction in European drama of the later Middle Ages.

It is not the purpose of this essay to document this decline, but rather to situate the discourse of deceit in *Pathelin* with regard to the heritage of deceit in medieval veridictory drama. Clearly, the veridictory function as we have defined it is not of great consequence in *Pathelin*. This is not to assert by any means that *Pathelin* "signifies the real" as a secondary modeling system any less than plays embodying the veridictory function. No discourse is totally innocent, that is, wholly devoid of signifying relations with its cultural context. Even the effort to achieve a culturally neutral or a culturally subversive discourse necessarily signifies some sort of cultural determinant in its production.

We may usefully contrast the semiological status of plays of the veridictory type with the semiological status of *Pathelin*. In veridictory drama we have seen that *conditions of signification connote their equivalence to conditions of truth,* both as a discourse-specific criterion and as a cultural value. The discursive identification of "truth" is an implicit reaffirmation of its ostensible cultural equivalent. By contrast, we have seen that *conditions of signification in Pathelin are equivalent to conditions of lying,* so that the extratheatrical "real" is signified subversively, if at all. No veridictory claims are connoted on its behalf. If we recall Eco's comparison of lying and signifying discussed in Chapter 1, conditions of signification in *Pathelin* are also equivalent to the minimal conditions of the sign-function, "which is to signify (and then to communicate) something to which no real state of things corresponds." We have seen how *Pathelin* again and again "signifies the real" with reference to literary and popular conventions, to the *Ars moriendi,* to juridical institutions, etcetera, but its sign-functions serve only to emphasize the contrast between signified cultural institutions and their distorted counterparts in the play. In effect, the play signifies a ludic double-cross of the cultural institutions it evokes.

Before weighing the significance of this contrast, it is perhaps useful to describe it in terms of the Greimassian cognitive model set forth in Chapter 1. Figure 8 is an adaptation of the model to the phenomenon of dramatic Representation within the context of its relations to Production and Reception as they are coordinated by Performance.[30]

In dramatic representation, the coherence of Reception (A + B̄) from the perspective of the spectator, is determined by the expression and content of Representation. The expression of Representation is the actual Performance of the play, while its content consists of the resources of Production (B + Ā), including the written text of the play and its source(s). In plays of the veridictory type, the level of expression and content constituted by Performance and Production becomes in turn the expression plane of a secondary content, consisting of the cultural objects of value as signified on the Axis of Veridiction (B + A). One may visualize this in terms of the model of a connotative semiotics conceived by Eco:[31]

EXPRESSION		CONTENT
Expression	Content	
A + B̄ = B + Ā		B + A

The secondary content (B + A) in medieval veridictory drama, consisting of culturally venerated values, often tends to be denotative of the culturally

152   Pathelin *and the Discourse of Deceit in Medieval French Drama*

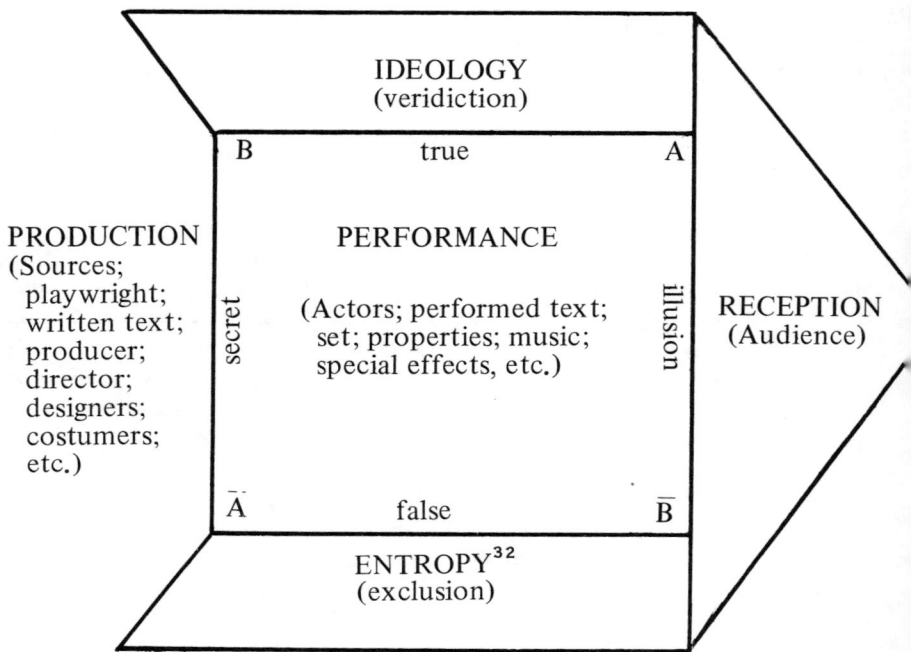

Figure 8

The Structure of Dramatic Representation in Performance

venerated narratives of the play's source(s), while it is invariably connotative of the values inherent in the axiology of these sources. Cultural models of the sort shown in Figures 4–6 above determine the axiology of the source and the axiology signified on the axis of cognitive veridiction. It is this relation of *conservative intertextuality* between the resources of Production, or the literary intertext (B + Ā), and the axis of cognitive veridiction, or the sociocultural intertext (B + A), which assures that the veridictory function is operative in Performance and Reception.

In *Pathelin*, on the other hand, the veridictory function is made inoperative by virtue of the *transgressive intertextuality* between the resources of Production (B + Ā) and the axis of cognitive veridiction (B + A).[33] As has been disclosed in the preceding chapters, the play constructs an intertext that signifies among the resources of its Production the tradition of the encomium, the *Ars moriendi,* contemporaneous juridical practices, and so forth, but these are expressed in Representation within a context which *subverts* their normal institutional usage so that in the coherence of Reception the public may recognize the discrepancy between the distorted expression of institutions in Performance and their integrity as a source of Production. The axis of cognitive veridiction (B + A) therefore becomes the locus of an affirmation of representational realities that do not correspond to their intertextual counterparts, whence a situation of appearing and not being (A + B̄). In short, that which the dramatic discourse in *Pathelin* presents as "true" is not recognized as True in any extrinsic, cultural sense. The "true" in this instance is tantamount to the Delusion or Lie.

As indicated at the end of Chapter 5, transgression of either the literary or the sociocultural intertext does not occur as a function of satire of intertextual referents. Derision, mockery, or irony is not aimed outward to any great extent at the models. Instead, sociocultural models and sources evoked by the play are tributary to the ostentation of ludic variants of delusion and lying from one end of the play to the other. In a sense, the veridictory function has been turned inward in order to affirm the authenticity of delusion and its mechanisms.

In contrast with medieval veridictory drama, then, *Pathelin* is autoreferential, evoking its sociocultural context as a means of calling greater attention to the narrative and discursive mechanisms of its figures of deceit. Such is the semiological status of *Pathelin*.

What is the significance of this status in terms of the development of dramatic discourse in medieval France? We should perhaps recall that the origin of veridictory drama in medieval Europe lies in the medieval Church and its rituals, which are veridictory of a mythopoeic, transcendental order. Robert Guiette has drawn an extremely valuable opposition between the dominance of symbolic *signification* in liturgical drama and mimetic *representation* in medieval vernacular drama.[34] Yet representation in medieval vernacular drama retained its symbolic signifying dimension for centuries after representation had begun to displace the pure symbolism of liturgical drama. Like many of its late medieval dramatic counterparts, *Pathelin* is a play whose semiological status is symptomatic of the decline of the veridictory dramatic function inherited from the ecclesiological context in which drama was reborn in the tenth century. By its insistent, repetitive, conspicuous violation of the veridictory function, achieved by setting up the context of its operation only to subvert it through idiosyncratic signfunctions, the transgressive attitude of *Pathelin* goes right to the foundations and tacit assumptions about the mainstream of medieval dramatic discourse. With regard to the heritage of medieval drama, then, it is apparent that obsessive short-circuiting of the veridictory function is the fundamental figure of deceit in the play.

Because this major advance beyond the limited monological perspective of earlier dramatic types entails dialogical play with the possibilities of "appearing and not being," which is the fundamental cognitive mode of

Representation itself, *Pathelin* is a late medieval dramatic text which connotes the liberation of European drama from its roots in powerful ecclesiological and feudal traditions.

The concluding part of this essay will weigh the significance of the foregoing assessment of the dramatic heritage of *Pathelin* within a cross section of similar tendencies evident in other areas of the contemporaneous cultural and ideational spheres.

PART IV

The Cultural Dimension of Deceit

10
Ideopathelin: The Signs of the Times

The task of characterizing the "cultural dimension" in *Pathelin* presupposes an understanding of what is meant by *culture* in the context of this essay. Above all, the term is *not* meant to designate an architectonic perspective whereby the sum of cultural building blocks viewed comprehensively at a given moment is what constitutes the edifice of Culture. If the scholar-mason were to describe the structure of late medieval European "culture" according to such a view, he would probably mortar the block labeled "*Pathelin*" into its appointed place among hundreds of other blocks bearing labels such as "*Mystère de la Passion,*" "Second Rhetoric," "Hundred Years' War," "Death," "Basoche," "Joan of Arc," "incunabula," etcetera, until the edifice was completed to the satisfaction of his scholarly blueprint. The blocks would not be placed at random, of course, but according to a certain sense of chronological succession and taxonomic arrangement. For example, the chapter on the blocks in the historical facade would probably come first, that on literary and artistic embellishments somewhere near the conclusion. If the study were of a literary or dramatic work only, a sketch of the entire edifice would have to precede or follow the chapters devoted to the work itself, so that we might feel that we have a "correct" sense of the place the work occupies in Culture and History.

In this essay, the approach to cultural perspectives is of a different sort. Having examined the play intrinsically, it is not now at last a matter of performing an established critical ritual by inserting a "sensible" discussion of *Pathelin and* late fifteenth-century "culture," as if the latter had some kind of existence outside the play but contiguous with it. On the contrary, the assumption throughout the essay has been that literary and dramatic works are not merely formal entities with no relation whatsoever to a broader cultural context. Proverbs, mercantile gestures, the *Ars moriendi,* juridical procedures, etcetera, all are extrasystemic, that is, they emanate from cultural systems lying outside the play. If on the one hand the artistic work has an immanent structure, its coherence cannot be perceived in isolation, without implementing the codes that relate it to these extrasystemic dimensions.[1] Codes of all sorts, and not just the linguistic, make possible the patterned sharing of information without which culture would disaggregate into chaos and entropy.² For a work of art is the complex message in a channel of communication whose codes link the addressor who produces the work with a real or imaginary, virtual or actual public to whom it is addressed. The representational models in the preceding chapter rest on precisely this assumption of the communicative dimension in performance and its tributaries. Moreover, the coherence of a work of art reflects the cultural grounding of its producer and thus benefits from cultural input of all sorts, while its output represents the recombination and modification of this generative influx.³ Thus, in the present context, the play exists with respect to "culture" not as a discrete entity among others, but rather as a coherent sign system whose polysemic hierarchies correlate with the sign systems that feed the mechanisms of its production and interact with the sign systems that make up the competence of its public. Potentially, then, the play both subsists on and modifies culture.⁴ In a certain sense, the play itself *is* culture, to the extent that from within itself, by virtue of its systemic organization of discourse, it projects a coherent synthesis of culture to which are tributary a wide variety of other syntheses that constitute its input. Thus, an objective in this essay has been to examine how the play, as an integrated system, *signifies culture* as its levels of discourse are fed by tributaries from other cultural systems.⁵ Such is the approach inspired by a semiotics of culture, a fundamental object of which is "the study of the functional correlation of different sign systems."⁶

In this approach, an adequate notion of "text" is essential, so as to avoid an unduly limited conceptualization of the textual dimension with regard to its tributaries. As for the verbal literary text, Julia Kristeva characterizes it as being a "translinguistic mechanism which redistributes the order of *langue* by relating a communicative *parole* bearing information with different types of anterior and synchronic utterances." The text is the locus of a "*productivité*," as well as of a "permutation" of texts and thus of an "intertextuality": "In the space of a text several utterances, absorbed from other texts, intersect and neutralize each other."⁷ In contrast with the formalistic notion of the literary text as a hypothetical *verbal* structure, the "culture text" may be either verbal or nonverbal, the latter type being operative as a message in a signifying and communicative channel, as is its verbal counterpart.⁸ Accordingly, culture may be viewed as "an assemblage of texts," as Clifford Geertz puts it.⁹ Likewise, Cesare Segre characterizes "the texts which combine into culture" as not merely literary or verbal texts but as "all utterances which are public and conspicuous."¹⁰ Intertextuality in the broad cultural sense thus concerns not only interliterary relations but correlative relations with extraliterary, indeed, extraverbal, "texts" as well.

The preceding chapters have evoked relations between *Pathelin* and antecedent or synchronic "texts" of both the verbal and the nonverbal type. Yet the mere identification and labeling of these relations, a task under way long ago, must not be the chief objective of criticism of the literary or dramatic text. Again Segre:

> A literary text constructs a model of the world. Semiotics—which here coincides with literary criticism—must take upon itself the difficult task of finding out what in the text represents reality in terms of the stereotypes of the given culture, and what proposes different realities as deformation or prefiguring, as utopia or satire, as expectation or desecration: realities embedded in our own, still to be realized, etc.[11]

In our analysis of the dramatic text, then, it is a question of receiving it as more than the pure product of other dramatic texts, but as a complex redistributive product of the input of other culture texts *including* those of the dramatic type. Moreover, it is of capital importance to determine how input from other culture texts is recombined in a new synthesis of culture. From the evidence of the preceding chapters, we must now consider how, using "the stereotypes of the given culture," *Pathelin* "proposes different realities as deformation or prefiguring" and in so doing constructs a new view of the world.

This essay began with one fundamental stereotype of popular culture—the narrative structure of the "deceiver deceived"—disclosing that the "bonne disposition" amounts to a kind of clockwork whose mechanism functions so that it might produce a potentially endless cycle of duperies. In keeping with the metaphor of time, one could say that the pendulum swings in rhythm with the duper and victim, who emerge at regular intervals from their rustic little cottages and exchange roles. Because the mechanism is common to many cultures, schematic analysis of its particular adaptation in *Pathelin* is hardly tantamount to showing what particular cultural determinants make it tick. What kind of spring tension, hands, and calibrated face—the values and indicators of input from culture texts—concur to make the play a complex of signs of the times?

Although the public striking clock was an invention of the fourteenth century, there are no clocks in *Pathelin,* and it is not until much later that they play any major role in literary and dramatic works.[12] Among postmedieval dramatic clocks there is one which would seem to meet our needs rather well. It chimes at the opening of *La Cantatrice chauve* [*The Bald Soprano*] by Eugène Ionesco. It will furnish one example of how a dramatic work creates an intertext with a nonverbal "culture text," and by analogy it will provide an image of how *Pathelin* uses cultural stereotypes to propose different realities as "deformation and prefiguration."

We recall that this lovely old grandfather clock sits alone in a corner of the Smith household. It figures in a lengthy passage describing in detail the appurtenances of the set.[13] Ionesco depicts a scene in which everything is *on ne peut plus anglais,* including the attire, furniture, attitudes, right down to the impeccably trimmed, untweakably correct English moustache of Mr. Smith. Even the English clock chimes—seventeen (!)—English times, whereupon Mrs. Smith remarks drily that it is 9:00 P.M.

Prior to this last incongruous moment, one has the impression of a modest, tidy, content English family in its finest hour. The properties become descriptive indices that concur in the realization of a powerful icon which evokes the "middle-class household" as an extradramatic, stereotyped culture text. The visual icon is rich in connotations.[14] There is an atmosphere of complacence, self-satisfaction, and domestic tranquility, a feeling that all is indeed what it seems to be. The scene is animated only by the regular ticking of the clock and the reassuringly productive darning needle of Mrs. Smith. Absolutely nothing would appear capable of marring the clockwork order and harmony that reign in this home. One look at the set and already it appears that this is a household where the clothier, had he arrived in time to dine, might have been offered a genuine slice of roast goose, one like those elegantly served up at Christmas in Victorian novels. One also imagines that, instead of the promised gold, he might have been paid promptly in pounds sterling. The exaggerated identification of this scene with things allegedly English makes it function as a heavy-handed, comic symbol of Englishness, a rival of tourist brochures displaying the marvel of Stonehenge, or the Tower of London, or Big Ben, that most striking of all public striking clocks.

But wait! What of the bizarre striking of this private striking clock? Has time gone haywire from High Holborn to Haymarket and Hampstead Heath? On the contrary, the disconcerting discrepancy between seventeen and nine in no way signifies to Mrs. Smith that the world is at sixes and sevens. Seventeen chimes will do as nicely, thank you, as nine, to indicate nine o'clock in her eccentric orbit. Yet for the spectator, the contradiction between the chimes and the time holds a different meaning. The symbolism of a perdurable, quasi-Platonic Englishness conjured by this scene is suddenly dispelled by the incongruity of the chimes. The clock makes us aware that between the chiming signifier and the abstract signified there is no necessary resemblance. Moreover, like time, Englishness is a transcendental signified, yet one suddenly realizes that the manner in which both are signified derives not from some absolute, invariant, privileged model but rather from cultural conventions which are, as Mrs. Smith reveals, both arbitrary and mutable. As the clock is cut loose from its conventional mooring, it acquires the "drift" of a dynamic signifier and in so doing summons us away from the stasis of the symbol and back into the realm of time, a realm where signs constantly modify and renew the world in the free play of their signifiers.[15]

Whence the appropriateness of Ionesco's clock as an indicator of the types of values that in *Pathelin* drive the intricate narrative mechanism and shape every cog of its verbal and semantic components. For Pathelin is a kind of dramatic timepiece, but one which always chimes incongruously as its hands point to medieval culture texts indicated around its face. What Ionesco's clock is to its stereotyped English household, *Pathelin* is to the medieval cultural heritage which it signifies, and study of the play as a cultural object is like locating that clock in a vaulted recess of some vast Gothic chamber.

Despite all its many affinities with the cultural heritage of the late Middle Ages, the world of *Pathelin* consistently reminds us of its own play with institutions and their conventions. As we have seen, the "medieval scene" acquires a bizarre kind of elasticity before our eyes, and the polymorphous distortions create a carnivalesque counterworld that parodies its social and historical precursors and models. Illusion reigns: it is no less feasible that bladders be lanterns or that shepherds speak like sheep than that seventeen equal nine. Just as the clock introduces transgression into the banal sanctity of the middle-class drawing room, *Pathelin* subverts the conventions of portraiture, of the dignified demise, of jurisprudence, and of a host of other anterior texts. It does this by constantly creating a discrepancy between signifying systems, weighted and buckled by the cumulative inertia of the medieval centuries, and the traditional spheres of European culture which they had come to signify.

These circumstances serve to identify *Pathelin* as a timepiece in yet another sense, for one cannot fail to see the pertinence of what others have said concerning literary contemporaries of the play with regard to the movement away from an earlier world view. Paul Zumthor has shown how "the poetry of the *rhétoriqueurs* belongs to an epoch balance between an older *épistémè*, dominated by an analogical view of nature, and another that will shortly emerge triumphant, crystallized around a desire for representation."[16] Likewise, asserting that between the thirteenth and the fifteenth centuries, European culture underwent a major transition from a "semiotics of the symbol" to a "semiotics of the sign," Julia Kristeva has identified as exemplary of the latter Antoine de la Sale's *Jehan de Saintré* (1456).[17] The literature of the fifteenth century, and especially of the second third of the century if *Saintré* and *Pathelin* are indicative of trends, is the fulcrum of this epistemic seesaw as well as the most vivid indication of the extent to which the symbolic *hortus conclusus* of the twelfth-century renaissance had begun to open onto a vast playground of signs.

The chief characteristic of these fifteenth-century "pivotal" texts would seem to be that, like a snowbank which in springtime melts from underneath while preserving its outer surface, the traditional forms were maintained while their content was emptied from within. Always from within, the *rhétoriqueurs* exploited tendencies already latent within the heritage of poetic language, "evacuating, by hyperbole, traditional types of their metaphorical references, and accumulating to the point of absurdity . . . all of the verbal games that earlier generations had played."[18] Likewise, the clear-cut early epic disjunctions of good and evil, heroism and cowardice, virtue and vice, and the like, underlie the proto-novelistic *Saintré*, but largely as they crystallize in nondisjunctive figures of ambiguity, duplicity, illusion. "The novel is possible," says Kristeva, "only when the disjunction of the two terms can be denied while at the same time being present, confirmed and approved. Rather than as *two irreducible* terms, it appears as a *double*. The figure of the traitor, of the ridiculed sovereign, of the defeated warrior, of the unfaithful wife, all stem from this non-disjunctive function found at the origins of the novel."[19]

All of which constantly recalls the figures of deceit examined in preceding chapters of this study. Yet if the values which inform these figures stem in large part from a highly complex, massive shift away from a declining cosmogonic model passed down from the high Middle Ages, they cannot be synthesized in any terse, formulaic manner. Just as the "non-disjunctive function is concretized at all levels (thematic, syntagmatic, actantial, etc.) of the global novelistic utterance,"[20] evidence of an ideological shift in *Pathelin*'s figures of deceit is apparent at several levels of narrative and discoursive coherence. It is worthwhile to recall earlier phases of this essay in order to obtain a more comprehensive view of the cultural significance of the shift as it is expressed within the play.

To begin with, consider its narrative structure. In Chapter 2 we saw that, unlike the type of mythic story or folktale frequently analyzed by Propp, Bremond, Greimas and others, *Pathelin* has all of the characteristics identified in narratives that embody the "deceiver deceived" structure. In the former type of narrative, there normally obtains a disjunctive axiology that unequivocally distinguishes "good" from "evil," "hero" from "villain," "right" from "wrong"; the progression, no matter how circuitous or convoluted it may become, inevitably culminates in a closing situation in which the "good" are rewarded and the "wicked" punished. The nonproblematic closing situation is one from which ambiguity and contradiction have been forever eliminated. The good-bad, villainous hero or heroic villain will finally acquire an unambiguous status, whether by being sent packing back to the Paynim stronghold, or won over to the host clad in the shimmering armor of virtue. Pierre Van Nuffel and Larry S. Crist have shown how this type of narrative is pertinent to epic masterpieces like the *Chanson de Roland*, and I have elsewhere explored its heritage in medieval romance.[21] In terms of Kristeva's symbol-sign dichotomy, we are here in the realm of literature of the symbol, where contradictions are resolved into "exclusive disjunction." Conversely, *Pathelin* features a nondisjunctive axiology whereby the actors are normally devious and the deceived struggle to exchange roles with the deceiver. Consequently, the closure of *Pathelin*, like that of the "deceiver deceived" story, contains a latent disequilibrium: for every deceiver there is necessarily a deceived party, whence the potential for a renewed struggle between the actors who occupy these two roles. The nondefinitive closure of the swindler tale and exploitation of the interchangeability of its two basic roles account for the cyclical tendencies of this type of narrative, as in certain of the trickster "cycles" or in the "branches" of the *Roman de Renart*.[22] Likewise in *Pathelin,* the clothier who is last seen on his way to verify the identity of the shepherd's lawyer as Pathelin, or the latter who vows to imprison the shepherd, are potential overtures to new conflicts. Characteristically, *Pathelin*'s "open" closure behaves as do works classifiable under the rubric of "literature of the sign," where we find an "illusion of an *open* structure, impossible to terminate, and having an *arbitrary* ending."[23] The play was in fact followed by two others featuring Pathelin, though a true cyclical dimension, despite potential, never occurred.[24]

Our ability to distinguish between texts of the "symbol" and those of the "sign" depends upon recognition of discourse-specific values that inhere in the two types of literature. Here, the distinction between "monological" and "dialogical" discourse is crucial. The former is characteristic of epic texts in which a narrator and/or characters establish and maintain the axiological bias and monological equilibrium which orientates reception of denoted and connoted values. An elementary example from the *Chanson de Roland:* "Paien ont tort e chrestïen ont dreit" (v. 1015; The Pagan cause is wrong, the Christian right). In terms of the Greimassian cognitive model set forth in the Introduction, such utterances serve to organize the axes of contraries and subcontraries: (being + appearing) = True; (not being + not appearing) = False. The axis of contraries valorized in the univocal utterances of narrator and speaker never enters into dialogical coordination with the axis of subcontraries, which is confined to the infrastructure of narration. "At the level of manifest textual organization (historical enunciation/discursive enunciation), dialogue does not occur; the two aspects of enunciation remain limited by the absolute point of view of the narrator which coincides with the unity [*tout*] of a god or of a community. We find in epic monologism this 'transcendental signified' and this 'self-presence' described by J. Derrida."[25] By contrast, "dialogical" discourse consists of the simultaneous manifestation of the monological by means of traditional figurations as well as of their transgression, creating what Kristeva calls, after Bakhtine, a "carnivalesque" structure: "The laughter of the carnival is not simply parodic; it is no more comic than tragic; it is both at once, *serious* if you wish, but only thus is its scene neither that of the law, nor that of its parody, but its *other*."[26] The epic and the carnivalesque would be the two opposing currents that make up European narrative, and one dominates the other "depending upon epochs and authors."[27]

We might thus see the *Pèlerinage de Charlemagne* and the *Cligés* of Chrétien de Troyes as examples of works in which elements of the dialogical are numerous, and which are somewhat eccentric with regard to the majority of twelfth-century epic and romance narratives that pay tribute, albeit often precariously, to monological values. The function of signs in semiosis is always potentially dialogical. Inherent in any system of sign production is a virtually infinite process of semiosis involving dialogical fluctuations.[28] This propensity of the sign is foreclosed upon in texts that reflect an imposition of the powerful monological values of a dominant ideology. The type of relatively isolated dialogical fluctuation in twelfth-century texts, when an analogical world view is dominant, is to be distinguished from a pivotal epoch like the fifteenth century when the dialogical permeates cultural models to such an extent as to distort the monological and challenge its authority at every turn.

Such is the springtime of *Pierre Pathelin*, in which the thaw has progressed so far that the flecked and sooty covering of snow readily gives way underneath with every advancing step that Pierre takes on his way to the clothier's stall. . . . Consider the soft, slushy underside of deceit. Figures of the dialogical are everywhere apparent.

Take, for example, the intertextual relation between the *Ars moriendi* and the scene of feigned death. Emile Mâle has characterized the Art of Dying as a devotional aid which particularizes the long-standing medieval theme of Psychomachia—the struggle between good and evil, allegorized by Prudentius and adapted in all sorts of contexts for centuries thereafter.[29] Whence its adherence to the symbolic mode, whereby "symbols refer to unrepresentable and unknowable universal transcendence(s)," according to a "cosmogonic semiotic practice" by which the noumenal is represented in restrictive categories,[30] e.g., angels and demons. This figural disjunction characterizes the "vertical" dimension of the symbol, while its "horizontal" elaboration moves to the elimination of paradox, as in the clash between the Seven Deadly Sins and the Seven Cardinal Virtues, or between the heavenly hosts and the dark forces of Satan's armies. In the aftermath of the skirmish, there are no ambiguous actors with respect to the original cosmic opposition. Even very casual comparison of the bedside "psychomachia" in the *Ars moriendi* with the animated scene in Pathelin's chamber suffices to show how far we have strayed from a semiotics of the symbol. The fact that they both share the same actantial configuration of subject, adjuvant, and adversary belies significant contrasts. In the *Ars moriendi*, of course, these are respectively invested by the moribund, a guardian angel, and Satan, the latter two categories being variously augmented by the cohorts who help to produce either dysphoric or euphoric visions. It would be tempting to draw an absolute equivalence between dying man, angel, and demon in the woodcuts of the treatise, and Pathelin, Guillemette, and Guillaume in this scene were it not for the fact that Pathelin's agony is feigned while Guillemette and the clothier both fall far short of representing a satisfactory opposition of good and evil. By no stretch of the imagination could their struggle at the bedside of the deceiver be characterized as a variant of Psychomachia.

Unless it be so characterized in terms of transgressive intertextuality arising from a semiotics of the sign. Although oppositions of the type life-death, love-hate, virtue-vice, good-evil, etcetera, are still irreducibly disjunctive in literature of the sign, they are constantly minimized or dissimulated by nondisjunctive figures based on ambiguity, disguise, pretense, duplicity, etcetera.

Whence a cast of characters to which these terms apply with particular aptitude. There is the lawyer whose practice combines *avocacïon* with *trompacion*, his wife whose name onomastically signifies deceit and whose presentation takes on muted overtones of the Parisian prostitute.[31] Of course the clothier is dishonest, but even the judge, who has often been depicted as an unambiguous, rather wan emblem of justice, seems to place pecuniary values above those of charity, witness his reaction when Pathelin offers to defend the shepherd without fee: "c'est Peu d'Aquest!" (v. 1375; i.e., not lucrative). Thus we find that the play is deprived of its only potential monological enunciator, its only unequivocal figure of veridiction, without whom there is no imposition of disjunctive values, thus no manifestation of an axiological equilibrium. Of all the characters in the play, however, it is the shepherd who is least deceived and who triumphs at deception against even the master of deceit himself. It is he alone who enjoys ill-acquired alimentation and, what is more, with total impunity. By virtue of its ecclesiological associations, his lamblike animality takes on strong overtones of innocence. So it is, then, that the figure of the shepherd as *pastor bonus* or even *imago christi* is evacuated of its traditionally positive axiological status and made ambiguous.[32] A disjunctive symbol in medieval iconography, the lamblike shepherd is now "on the lam," leaving an empty scene with a fleeting, bleating, cheating image—a nondisjunctive sign, retrospectively revealing that in no way does the play distinguish clearly the "bons" from the "méchants" but rather confronts us with ambiguous figures of deceit whose fleecy white coats are lined on the underside with the dark fur of sleek brown foxes.

Nevertheless, the name most frequently invoked is no less than *the* transcendental source of immutable Truth. Although named in ritualized vows to sanctify exchanges—

> vecy ung denier, ne faison
> rien qui soit ou Dieu ne se nomme.
>
> (vv. 232–33)

(Wait, here's a penny. God's share should be paid first; it's only right. "Let no bargain be made before God's share is paid.")

or in an attitude of pious generosity, as when Pathelin declines his fee:

> Moy je vous jure
> qu'aussi n'en vueil je riens avoir.
> Pour Dieu soit!
>
> (vv. 1375–77)

(I swear I have no thought of gain. Let it be for love of God.)

—these utterances no longer govern the beliefs, sincerity, or conduct of their speakers. The name of the Deity joins a host of saints who figure in the ubiquitous expletives and oaths that punctuate nearly every utterance of the characters. Count them as a special category in the stockpile of surplus signifiers emptied of their traditional signified like so many empty shells after an all-night clambake. The univocal gives way to duplicity. God, that sweet Bernardian Totality toward which all earthly effort must evolve, is now evoked as a means of achieving a dubious end. Judgment having been put off until "le jour du jugement," professed spiritual values may become accessory to exchange values, and even these are mostly transgressed, for exchanges seldom take place, unless it be language for loot.[33] He who dupes last dupes best—until the next time.

Above all, communication is deceptive—there are few unambiguous messages. Saintré, poor chap, "loses sight of the pretense and becomes ensnared in the game of univocal (thus erroneous) interpretation of a rigorously double message."[34] Likewise with goose-eaters and ganders led by goslings. Praise is blame. Death is life. The end of the play is a replay of the beginning. Like the pseudolaudatory lambasting of the Joceaulme family, epideictic utterances such as the *blason* "lose their univocity and become ambiguous, praise and blame at one and the same time. In the fifteenth century, the *blason* is already a non-disjunctive figure *par excellence.*"[35] So, also, is the book.[36] While an object of veneration and prestige—the *maire* has read his "grimaire" and Pathelin declares

> et si n'aprins oncques a lettre
> qu'ung peu; mais je m'ose vanter
> que je say aussi bien chanter
> ou livre avecques nostre prestre
> que se j'eusses esté a maistre
> autant que Charles en Espaigne.
>
> (vv. 22–27)

(It's true I don't know much Latin, but when I chant with our priest from the mass-book, it sounds like I've studied for as long as Charlemagne stayed in Spain.)

—the book, whether it be ecclesiastical or juridical, is of little use in a way of life that involves studious deviance from the authoritative systems that it represents. The Bible, the liturgical missal, the pious conduct book, the legal document, by virtue of their cultural prominence in the fifteenth century, all are just so many signifying systems ripe for transgression in *Pathelin.*

The shards and debris of antecedent oral culture attest to the degree of vitality still remaining at the level of preliterate enterprises. Allusion to Charles in Spain of Roland fame (v. 27), to the swarthy hero of later epic, Renouart au Tiné (v. 886), to countless local saints, and to figures drawn from dramatic types (e.g., Peu d'Aquest) all suggest the enduring popularity of oral epic and hagiographic traditions surviving in toponymy and allusion as well as of the importance of drama in the popular culture of markets, fairs, and festivals.[37] Add to this the mercantile gestures of "God's penny," ritual quaffing to seal a transaction, the proverbs, and the setting of the play within the "(bourgeois) space of the fair, the market, the street" and we have ample evidence of how the sign, in its "vertical," hierarchical dimension, assimilates the metaphysical tendencies of the symbol to the concrete and the immediately perceptible.[38]

Conversely, concretization of language may lead to a new, paradoxical "metabolization" of the real in which metaphysical tendencies mingle with the quotidian to produce grotesque or bizarre effects akin to those experienced by a child on his first visit to a fun-house. Having witnessed the (eleven-week) illness of the person whose identity he nonetheless identified with that of a client earlier in the day, our man of minimal conclusions—Pathelin's epithet: "Dieux! qu'il a dessoubz son hëaume / de menus conclusions!" (vv. 997–98; Now he's really got some confused ideas under that bonnet of his)—waxes eloquently inconclusive on the nature of the madness he has just sampled:

> Dea! or je vois savoir:
> Je sçay bien que j'en doy avoir
> six aulnes, tout en une piece,
> mais ceste femme me depiece
> de tous poins mon entendement . . .
> Il les a eues vrayëment . . .
> Non a. Dea! il ne se peult joindre:
> j'ay veu la Mort qui le vient poindre;
> au mains ou il le contrefait.
> Et! si a! il les print de fait
> et les mist dessoubz son esselle . . .
> Par saincte Marie la belle! . . .
> Non a! . . . je ne sçay se je songe:
> je n'ay point aprins que je donge
> mes draps en dormant ne veillant
> a nul, tant soit mon bienveillant;
> je ne les eusse point acreues . . .
> Par le sanc bieu, il les a eues!
> Par la mort bieu, non a! Ce tiens je!
> Non a. Mais a quoy donc en vien ge? . . .
> Si a! Par le sanc Nostre Dame,
> meschoir puist il de corps et d'ame
> se je soy qui sauroit a dire
> qui a le meilleur ou le pire
> d'eulx ou de moy: . . .
>
> (vv. 707–31)

(Now I've got to figure this out. I know I should have six yards of cloth in one piece. But that woman addles my brain so much I can't think. He really did take the cloth. . . . No, he couldn't have, damn it! It just doesn't fit. I saw Death coming to strike him down—at least he so pretended. . . . Yes he did! He did take the cloth and he put it under his arm, by Saint Mary! . . . No, he didn't. Maybe I'm dreaming. But even in my sleep I'd never give my cloth away to anybody, no matter how much I liked him. I just wouldn't have given credit. . . . God's blood! He did take the cloth! . . . No, damn it all, he didn't. I know he didn't. But where does that leave me? . . . Yes he did, by our Lady's blood! . . . Misfortune take me, body and soul, if I know who could decide who got the best of this deal, them or me: . . .)

In the rapidly shimmering, clear-obscure twilight zone between reality and illusion, that zone in which no apparent cleavage exists between yes-no, life-death, true-false, waking-dreaming, being-seeming, a muttering merchant, looking in silhouette for all the world like Molloy, trudges lamely down the slushy sidewalks of Cannotnot. He is swallowed into the gloom rising to obscure, totally, the crepuscular evanescence—gilded momentarily before vanishing—of faint epic effulgences. From afar, a dejected murmur:

> . . . je n'y voy goute. [*fade*]

(. . . I just can't figure it out.)

Thus the enunciator of veridiction—be he Figura, Christ, prophet, preacher, venerable *senex,* monarch, or some other authoritative character who in earlier religious and secular plays imposes upon the represented spectacle its monological values, including an unmistakable sense of the transcendental signified—is displaced in *Pathelin* by this myopic merchant who dramatizes only a profound anxiety generated by the equivocal effects of the dialogical. Yet he alone is lost in the fun-house, while the other three delusive persuaders in the play share with the audience considerable joy and delight with this topsy-turvy world.

As this evocation of the highlights of earlier chapters would suggest, the deformed world in question is a mosaic of reminiscences of culture texts past and contemporaneous. *Pathelin* is a kind of cultural palimpsest overlaid with successive traces of textual coherence. There is the faint, fragmented textual image of the medieval cosmos, whose order, reflected in the eschatological text presided by God, inscribed by the saints, and closed on Judgment Day, is prismatically dispersed in countless allusions and oaths. There are the more discernible contours of the agrarian, mercantile, monetary, thanatopic, juridical, paremiological, biblical, and ecclesiastical texts. There are also evocations of specific secular literary texts, some of which, like the fable, are more explicit than others. Throughout this essay, it has been of far less interest to determine the fidelity of the play to such culture texts than to trace the striations and convolutions of its ludic distancing from these precursors. For the play is not a complex, derisive statement about mercantile practices, exchange values of currency, legal institutions, or contemporaneous ecclesiastical and political figures. The parody is in service to semiosis, not satire. Nor is the play's primary objective to present a faithful toponymic, geographical, and sociological account of the milieu in which it was created, nor to involve the critic in a guessing game as to the identity of its anonymous creator. It is rather a dramatized manifesto of the power and the independence of the signifier. To receive the play otherwise, by reinstitutionalizing the "realia" signified in its figures of deceit, though perhaps commendable as an academic exercise, has sometimes led to a serious diminution of its vitality, as if a "hard, gemlike flame" had been smothered under a wet blanket of erudition.

To what extent, then, does *Pathelin* use the stereotypes of its input, its cultural background? What different realities does it propose in its output, as deformation and prefiguration? In the preceding chapter we saw that the semiological status of European drama at its inception involves a situation in which conditions of signification connote an equivalence to conditions of truth in the dimension of collectively held values, whence a mode of signifying culture which is fundamentally conservative of the values of its cultural input. In *Pathelin*, on the other hand, we disclosed a situation in which conditions of signification subvert this truth-connotation and call attention auto-referentially to conditions of lying, hence of semiosis, hence of the phenomenon of representation itself. This was taken as an instance of late medieval theatrical discourse liberated from its referential "vassalage" to values inherited from the high Middle Ages. By its obsessive-repetitive play with the mechanisms of deceit, *Pathelin* constantly subverts the principle of resemblance, whereby appearances signify a reality of a higher order, upon which medieval European modes of expression had so extensively relied.

It is precisely these figures of deceit created as variants of the structure of Delusion—appearing and not being—which constitute the essential output of *Pathelin* as a signifier of culture. Through the discourse of deceit, the play repeatedly "gives the lie" to its cultural input by setting up, through parody, an intertext constructed upon resemblances between the text of the source and its dramatic counterpart, only to announce gleefully its independence of the latter. Like Ionesco's clock, the mechanisms of lying and deceit repeatedly assert the freedom of the signifier with regard to its ostensible signified and of the dominance of appearance over being, illusion over reality. It is almost as if we could perceive the repressed, mischievous, instinctive spirit of the Middle Ages take leave of the solemn cadaver that was once its host and prance merrily on its way.

In less anthropomorphic terms, the difference between input and output emerges from a distinction between analogy, a dominant form in the aesthetics of the high Middle Ages, and representation, the principles of which will become well established in seventeenth-century theories of discourse. It becomes apparent in the preceding chapter that the drama of veridiction is a drama of analogy, conceived as a faithful replica of ecclesiologically grounded collective values and endowed with the transcendental signified of the symbol.[39] It was shown that these plays are linked with the notion of *assimilatio* of parallel systems based on an understanding of homology and isomorphism between language and things in nature. At the opposing extremity lies the classical theory of language as a representational mode which no longer assumes an identity between words and things. Michel Foucault has sketched the broad outlines of this displacement of resemblance by representation, as it entails a shift from the medieval notion of language as "the material writing of things" to the view of discourse as an expression of "that which is, but [as being] nothing more than what it says."[40]

Although Foucault locates the center of this displacement of one *épistémè* by another in the sixteenth century, it is evident that *Pathelin* is among fifteenth-century precursors of this moment. Thus, like the contemporaneous *rhétoriqueurs,* in whose works Zumthor finds a consistent preference for transgressive as opposed to integrative types of intertextuality,[41] *Pathelin,* while resembling its intertextual precursors at times, emphasizes its profound dissimilarity to them through parody and equivocation. By dialogically transgressing the norms of cultural texts while maintaining their manifest forms, *Pathelin* realizes the very spirit of Carnival, stirring up the sediment accumulated over the centuries and applauding as it drifts downward, like so much confetti, creating new and delightful distortions of order.[42] If we think of the play as a cultural repository, then it is a repository of the languages of late medieval cultural play.

Conclusion

This essay was conceived and written as a semiotic approach to medieval drama and its cultural context. It would have been impossible in a single study to deal exhaustively with such a vast subject. In keeping with the rigorous economy and scientific aspirations of modern theories of discourse analysis, it was thought best to adhere to the notion of "minimal units" as a point of departure, and thus the classeme /deceit/ served as the focal point for a multi-leveled study of its narrative and discoursive ramifications in a single play. To date, the analytical methodologies of textual semiotics have lent themselves more readily to examination of a single text, frequently with copious results, witness Barthes's *S/Z* or Greimas's *Maupassant,* both of which are lengthy books devoted to relatively brief short stories. Obviously, such an approach to the full corpus of medieval drama, even that in a single vernacular language, would be neither writable nor readable. Nonetheless, the liminal analysis of a single text is of great value to a study of the broader context, due to the intertextual dimension which, as we have seen, relates the work to its literary, dramatic, and cultural contexts.

The *classematic approach* taken here "anchors" the whole enterprise and lends itself readily to an expanding focus involving thematic, narrative, dramatic, and cultural perspectives. It thus became possible to locate the play, always on the basis of /decit/ and its textual configurations, with respect to medieval dramatic traditions from the twelfth century forward, and in so doing, to identify and describe a "drama of veridiction" fundamental to the dramatic production of medieval Europe. Concurrently, the same elementary structural configuration of the Delusion or Lie proved to be a valid basis for the elaboration of a theoretical model of representation in performance which bears further scrutiny for its pertinence to other types of drama. Finally, the figures of deceit in the play were replaced within their synchronic cultural dimension.

This progressive expansion from classeme to culture could perhaps more properly have been designated as a series of related "approaches" rather than as a unitary Approach. For semiotic research in both the East and the West has contributed an array of complementary perspectives and methodologies that have come into play in this essay. These pages reflect a plurality of disciplinary approaches, stemming from narrative and discoursive semiotics, semiotics of manipulation, theatrical semiotics, and semiotics of culture. All have been brought to bear in various ways on problems of signification and communication. Apart from the particular demonstrations of it arguments, this essay has attempted to show in a particular case that these various semiotic approaches are indeed interrelated, and possess a unity just as do the sign systems they purport to study. One thinks here of the complementarity among semiotic perspectives acknowledged by the Tartu-Moscow group in their "Theses on the Semiotic Study of Cultures": "Together with an approach which permits us to construct a series of relatively autonomous sciences of the semiotic cycle, we shall also admit another approach, according to which all of them examine particular aspects of the *semiotics of culture,* of the study of the functional correlation of different sign systems" (1.0.0.). It is hoped that this essay has made a modest case for just such a view of the relatedness of diverse semiotic perspectives, all of which are directly related to the developing approach known as semiotics of culture.

The foregoing chapters are offered not as the culmination of developments either in semiotic theory or literary analysis but rather, it is hoped, as an appeal for further study of the hypotheses and the arguments set forth along the way, in terms not only of medieval semiotic practices, but as concerns those of other ages as well. It may be that the semiological status of *Pathelin* with regard to its medieval dramatic background conceals a cyclical model of the origin, rise, and eventual decay of successive Western dramatic currents. As we have seen, the semiological status of vernacular European drama at its origins involves a situation whereby conditions of signification connote an equivalence to conditions of truth. Three centuries later, its decline is marked by a situation, detectable in texts like *Pathelin,* in which conditions of signification undermine referential allusions to conditions of extratheatrical truth. As conditions of signification become autoreferential and begin to denote conditions of lying, hence of semiosis and of representation itself, European drama, considerably evacuated of its traditional content, embarks on a new quest for conditions of veridiction that will eventually be based on Classical, Romantic, and post-Romantic models. And now in the plays of Ionesco, Beckett, and Pirandello, as in the experimentation of the Living Theater, do we not find the earmarks of a new theater of infinite semiosis whose ludic heritage includes the devious doings of a late medieval semiopath?

Master Pierre Pathelin
Translated by Alan E. Knight

[Scene I]

PATHELIN: Holy Mary, Guillemette, for all the trouble I take to scrimp and save we just can't get ahead. I've seen the day, though, when I was a real attorney.

GUILLEMETTE: By Our Lady of the Law Trade! I was just thinking about that. But now people don't think you're nearly as clever as they used to. I remember when everybody wanted you to take his case. Now they all call you a prattling pettifogger.

PATHELIN: And I don't mean to brag, of course, but there's not a sharper fellow in the whole circuit, except maybe the mayor.

GUILLEMETTE: Yes, but he's studied his Latin grammar and he knows how to conjure his verbs.

PATHELIN: Whose case don't I expedite if I decide to take it on? It's true I don't know much Latin, but when I chant with our priest from the mass-book, it sounds like I've studied for as long as Charlemagne stayed in Spain.

GUILLEMETTE: But what's it worth to us? Not a thing! We're starving to death, our clothes have as many holes as a sieve, and we have no idea how we can get new ones. So, what's all your knowledge worth to us?

PATHELIN: Hold your tongue! I swear, if I really put my mind to it, I'll find out where to get some clothes—and some headgear too. God willing, we'll pull out of this and be back on our feet in no time. "God does a deed with all due speed," they say. If I really have to apply myself to further my practice, you won't be able to find my equal.

GUILLEMETTE: By Saint James, certainly not in swindling. At that you're a past master.

PATHELIN: By God, you mean a master of proper lawyering.

GUILLEMETTE: By my faith, you're a master deceiver. I know, because, despite your little learning and less common sense, you're taken for one of the slyest wits in the parish.

PATHELIN: Nobody knows the finer points of the law the way I do.

GUILLEMETTE: Or the finer points of cheating, by God. At least that's the reputation you have.

PATHELIN: And so have those who wear fine clothes of silk and velvet, who claim to be lawyers, but aren't. Enough of this chatter, I'm off to the fair.

GUILLEMETTE: To the fair?

PATHELIN: Yes, by Saint John! *(He sings.)* "To the fair, my pretty maid . . ." Would it displease you if I bought some cloth or some other little thing that we need? Our clothes are nothing but rags.

GUILLEMETTE: But you don't have a penny to bless yourself with. What'll you do there?

PATHELIN: Don't ask too many questions, my lady. But if I don't bring back enough cloth to outfit us both, then call me a liar to my face. What color would you like? A gray-green, a Brussels black, or what? I need to know.

GUILLEMETTE: Whatever you can get. Beggars can't be choosers.

PATHELIN, *counting on his fingers:* Two and a half yards for you and three for me, or maybe four. That makes . . .

GUILLEMETTE: You count off the yards very generously, but who the Devil will give you that much cloth on credit?

PATHELIN: What do you care who? Somebody will give it to me and with payment due on Judgment Day, because it won't be paid for any sooner.

GUILLEMETTE: Very well then. In that case, no matter what happens, we'll be covered.

PATHELIN: I'll buy some gray or green, Guillemette, and for a waistcoat I'll need three quarters of a yard of fine black cloth . . . or maybe a yard.

GUILLEMETTE: Indeed! God help me! Go ahead then and don't forget to drink on the bargain if you find a gullible creditor.

PATHELIN: Take care of things here. *(He leaves.)*

GUILLEMETTE: Oh God! But what merchant . . .? Whoever it is, I just pray he's blind as a bat.

[Scene II]

PATHELIN *(approaching the Clothier's shop):* Isn't that the one there? No, I don't think so. Yes it is, by Saint Mary. He deals in cloth goods. *(To the Clothier)* God be with you.

GUILLAUME JOCEAULME, CLOTHIER: And God give you joy.

PATHELIN: So help me, you're just the person I wanted to see. How's your health, Guillaume? Are you hale and hearty?

THE CLOTHIER: Yes, thank God.

PATHELIN: Here, shake. How are things going?

THE CLOTHIER: Pretty well. *(They shake.)* At your service. And how are you?

PATHELIN: By Saint Peter, I'm as well as ever. So, you're enjoying life?

THE CLOTHIER: Yes, but believe me, merchants can't always do as they please.

PATHELIN: And how's business? Are you able to keep the wolf from the door?

THE CLOTHIER: So help me God, Master Pierre, it's hard to say. It's always work, work, work.

PATHELIN: Ah, what a wise man your father was! God rest his soul. By Our Lady, it seems to me that you're like him in every way. What a good and clever merchant he was. *(He stares at the Clothier.)* Your face resembles his, by God, like a perfect picture. If God ever had mercy on one of his creatures, may he grant true pardon to his soul.

THE CLOTHIER: Amen! And to us too if it please him.

PATHELIN: By my faith, he often predicted in great detail the times we live in now; and I often think of what he said, for he was considered one of the best.

THE CLOTHIER: Please sit down, sir. It's high time I remembered my manners.

PATHELIN: I'm fine like this. By heaven, your father had . . .

THE CLOTHIER: Truly, you must sit down.

PATHELIN: Very well. *(he sits down.)* "Ah," he used to say to me, "you will see great marvels." *(He stares at the Clothier again.)* Look at those eyes, those ears, that nose, that mouth! So help me God, never did a son more closely resemble his father! And look at that dimpled chin; you're really a chip off the old block. If anyone should say to your mother that you're not your father's son, he'd just be itching for a quarrel. Truly I can't imagine how nature in all her works formed two faces so much alike that one is blemished exactly like the other. Why, it's as if somebody had spit you both out in the same way, like two gobs against a wall. You're the very spit and image of your father. By the way, what about the good Laurence, your lovely aunt? Did she pass away?

THE CLOTHIER: No, certainly not.

PATHELIN: How beautiful she was when I saw her, tall and straight and graceful. By the precious Mother of God, you resemble her in shape as if someone had made you both of snow. I think there's not a family in the whole region whose members look so much alike. *(He gets up and stares more intently at the Clothier.)* By God, the more I look at you, the more I see your father. You're more alike than two drops of water, without a doubt. What a gentleman he was, what an honest man, who would sell his goods on credit to anyone who asked. May God have mercy on him. He always used to give me a hearty laugh. Would to Christ the worst in the world were like him; then people wouldn't rob and steal from one another the way they do. *(He feels a piece of cloth.)* What a fine piece of cloth this is, so soft and smooth, and so attractive.

THE CLOTHIER: I had it specially made from the wool of my own sheep.

PATHELIN: Ah, what a good business man you are! But you wouldn't be your father's son, if you weren't. You just never stop working.

THE CLOTHIER: So what do you expect? If a man wants to make a living, he's got to toil and sweat.

PATHELIN *(feeling another piece of cloth):* And this cloth, is it dyed in the wool? It's as strong as leather.

THE CLOTHIER: It's a very good fabric from Rouen, and well made I assure you.

PATHELIN: Well, I'm really tempted. By the Lord's passion, I had no intention of buying cloth when I came. I've saved up 80 gold pieces to pay off a debt, but I can see you're going to get 20 or 30 of them. I like that color so much it hurts.

THE CLOTHIER: Gold pieces? Indeed! Is it possible that the people you're indebted to would take some other coinage instead?

PATHELIN: Oh yes, if I wanted them to. It doesn't matter to me how it's paid. *(He feels another piece of cloth.)* And what cloth is this? The more I look at it, the crazier I am about it. I'll have to have a coat made of it, and another for my wife.

THE CLOTHIER: As you know, cloth is very expensive these days. I'll sell you some if you wish, but 10 or 20 francs won't buy very much.

PATHELIN: That doesn't matter; it's worth the price. Besides, I have a few sous put away that have never seen the light of day.

THE CLOTHIER: God be praised! By Saint Peter, that doesn't displease me a bit.

PATHELIN: To be brief, I'm so taken with this cloth that I just have to have some of it.

THE CLOTHIER: All right. First you must decide how much you need. Take as much as you want. In fact, I could let *you* take the entire bolt even if you didn't have a sou.

PATHELIN: That's kind of you. Thanks very much.

THE CLOTHIER: Do you want some of this light blue?

PATHELIN: First, how much will a yard cost me? Wait, here's a penny. God's share should be paid first; it's only right. "Let no bargain be made before God's share is paid." *(He puts the coin in a collection box.)*

THE CLOTHIER: By God, that's the talk of an honest man; you've really cheered me up. Do you want my last word on the price?

PATHELIN: Yes.

THE CLOTHIER: It will cost *you* only 24 sous per yard.

PATHELIN: Never! 24 sous? Holy Mother!

THE CLOTHIER: That's just what it cost me, by my soul! I'll have to charge at least that, if you take it.

PATHELIN: The Devil take it! It's too much.

THE CLOTHIER: But you don't realize how much cloth has gone up. All the sheep died last winter in the great freeze.

PATHELIN: Twenty sous! Twenty sous!

THE CLOTHIER: I swear to you I have to charge 24. Just wait till market day on Saturday and you'll see what it costs. A fleece that used to cost 20 pence when they were plentiful, cost me 40 pence last July.

PATHELIN: By God, if that's the way it is, then without more haggling I'll buy. Com on, measure it.

THE CLOTHIER: How much do you need?

PATHELIN: That's easy to figure out. What's the width?

THE CLOTHIER: The standard Brussels width.

PATHELIN: Three yards for me and two and a half yards for my wife—she's tall. That makes six yards, doesn't it? . . . No it doesn't. How stupid of me!

THE CLOTHIER: It only lacks half a yard of being six exactly.

PATHELIN: Then I'll round it off at six. Anyway, I need a hat.

THE CLOTHIER: Take that end and we'll measure it. I'm sure we've got a good six yards here. One . . . two . . . three . . . four . . . five . . . and six.

PATHELIN: Saint Peter's gut! It's six on the nose.

THE CLOTHIER: Shall I measure it again?

PATHELIN: No, for Pete's sake! There's always a little gain or loss in business deals. How much is that altogether?

THE CLOTHIER: Let's see. At 24 sous a yard and six yards, it comes to nine francs.

PATHELIN: That makes six gold pieces, right?

THE CLOTHIER: That's right, by God.

PATHELIN: Then, Sir, will you give me that much credit for the short time it takes to come to my house? It's not really credit. You'll have your money, in gold or in francs, as soon as you reach the door.

THE CLOTHIER: By our Lady! I'd have to go far out of my way to get there.

PATHELIN: I swear to God, not a word has passed your lips since you failed to speak the gospel truth. You say it's far out of your way. The thing is, you've never wanted to find an occasion to come drink at my house. But this time you will have a drink there.

THE CLOTHIER: By Saint James, I hardly do anything but drink to seal the bargain with my customers. I'll go, but it's bad luck, you know, to give credit on the first sale of the day.

PATHELIN: Isn't it worth it if I pay you in gold coins instead of the common currency? By God, we'll even eat the goose that my wife is roasting.

THE CLOTHIER *(aside):* This man is driving me crazy! *(To Pathelin)* Go ahead then. I'll come later and bring the cloth.

PATHELIN: There's no need for that. Will it burden me if I just tuck it under my arm? Not in the least.

THE CLOTHIER: No, don't bother. It would be more fitting and proper if I carried it.

PATHELIN: May Mary Magdalene send me misfortune if I put you to that trouble. As I said, under the arm. It'll give me a nice hump. *(He puts the cloth under his arm inside his robe.)* There, that's perfect. You'll have plenty of drink and good cheer before you leave my house.

THE CLOTHIER: Please give me my money as soon as I arrive.

PATHELIN: Of course I will. No, I won't, by God, not until you've been well fed. And I'm glad I didn't have any money on me. At least you'll come sample my wine. Your late father, when he passed my house, used to call out: "Hi there, friend," or "What do you say?" or "What's new?" But now you rich people don't care a straw about us poor people.

THE CLOTHIER: God in heaven, I'm a lot poorer than you are.

PATHELIN: Well, so long; goodbye. Come to my house as soon as you can and we'll drink well, I promise you.

THE CLOTHIER: I'll do that. Go on ahead, but see that I get the gold.

PATHELIN: Gold? I give you my word. And the Devil take me if I ever broke my word. *(He leaves the shop.)* Gold, indeed! Well, hang him! He wouldn't sell to me at my price, only at his. But he'll be paid at mine. He needs gold, does he? Fool's gold he'll get. By God, if he had to run from now till he's paid, he'd get to the end of the world first.

THE CLOTHIER: Those gold pieces he gives me won't see daylight for a whole year, I swear, unless somebody steals them. Well, there's no buyer so clever that he won't find a seller who can outwit him. That would-be trickster was stupid enough to pay 24 sous a yard for cloth that's not even worth 20!

[Scene III]

PATHELIN: Well, did I get it?
GUILLEMETTE: What?
PATHELIN: What happened to your old worn-out dress?
GUILLEMETTE: That's just what it was. What do you want with it?
PATHELIN: Nothing. Nothing. So, did I get it? I told you I would. *(He takes the cloth from beneath his robe.)* How's that for a piece of cloth?

GUILLEMETTE: Holy Mother! I'll stake my salvation there's been a swindle. Oh, God! What have you gotten us into now? Alas! Alas! Who'll pay for it.

PATHELIN: Who'll pay for it, you ask. By Saint John, it's paid for. The draper that sold it to me wasn't as crazy as all that, my love. May I be hanged if I didn't bleed him white as a sack of plaster. The thieving ragpicker got what he deserved.

GUILLEMETTE: How much did it cost?

PATHELIN: I owe nothing. He's been paid, so don't worry.

GUILLEMETTE: He's been paid? But you didn't have a penny. What did you use for money?

PATHELIN: I swear to you, woman, I did have money. I had one Paris penny.

GUILLEMETTE: You either signed a note or used a magic formula; that's how you got it. And when the note comes due, they'll come and seize all our goods. Everything we have will be taken away.

PATHELIN: I swear to God, the whole thing cost only a penny.

GUILLEMETTE: *Benedicite Maria!* Only a penny? That can't be.

PATHELIN: You can pluck out this eye if he got more than that or ever does get more, no matter what tune he sings.

GUILLEMETTE: Who's the merchant?

PATHELIN: It's a certain Guillaume whose last name is Joceaulme, if you must know.

GUILLEMETTE: But how did you get it for one penny? What was the trick?

PATHELIN: It was God's penny that sealed the bargain. If I had asked him to drink on it instead, I could have kept the penny. Still, it was a pretty good deal. He and God can divide that penny if they want to, because it's all they'll get from me, no matter how much they rant and rave.

GUILLEMETTE: How did he decide to let you have the cloth on credit? He's so bullheaded.

PATHELIN: By Saint Mary, I flattered him and his whole family tree so much that he almost gave it to me. I told him that his late father was such a worthy man. "Oh, my friend," says I, "what good stock you come from! Your lineage," says I, "is the purest in the whole district." But I swear to God that guy comes from the scurviest lot of scoundrels and the vilest riffraff in the country. "Guillaume, my friend," says I, "how much you resemble your good father in looks and in every other way!" God knows I piled on the flattery, and all the while I was throwing in remarks about his cloth. "Holy Mary," says I, "how easily he gave his merchandise on credit, and without pretense! I can see," says I, "that you're his spit and image." But you could pull all the teeth of that sea-hog of a father and that baboon of a son before they'd give you anything on credit or even give you the time of day. Anyway, I talked so fast that he finally gave me six yards on credit.

GUILLEMETTE: Really? And you never have to return it?

PATHELIN: That's right. If I return anything to him, it'll be the Devil.

GUILLEMETTE: That reminds me of the fable of the crow, who was sitting up on a high cross with a piece of cheese in his beak. A fox came by and, seeing the cheese, thought to himself, "How can I get that?" Then he sat directly beneath the crow and said, "Ah, you have such splendid feathers and your song is so melodious." The vain and foolish crow, hearing his song praised like that, opened his beak to sing. His cheese fell to the ground and Master Fox grabbed it in his teeth and ran. That's just the way it was, I'm sure, with this cloth. You got it by flattery and sweet-talk, the same way the fox got the cheese. You really put one over on him.

PATHELIN: He's supposed to come eat goose with us, so here's what we have to do. I know he'll come whining to have his money immediately and I've planned a good reception for him. I'll go get into bed and pretend to be sick and when he comes you'll say, "Shh! Speak softly," and you'll moan and put on a long face. "Alas," you'll say, "he's been sick for the past six or eight weeks." And if he says to you, "That's a lot of nonsense! He just left my shop a few minutes ago," you'll say, "Alas! This is a poor time to be making jokes." Then I'll make him think he's on a wild goose chase, because that's the only kind of goose or anything else he'll ever get here.

GUILLEMETTE: I swear I'll play the role to perfection. But if you get caught again and brought to justice, I'm afraid it'll be twice as bad as it was before.

PATHELIN: Quiet. I know what I'm doing; we have to do exactly what I said.

GUILLEMETTE: But, for God's sake, think of that Saturday they put you in the pillory. You know how everybody jeered at you for your shady dealings.

PATHELIN: Enough of such talk. He'll be here any minute now and we've got to keep this cloth. I'm going to get into bed.

GUILLEMETTE: Go ahead.

PATHELIN: Now don't laugh.

GUILLEMETTE: Of course I won't. I'll be crying hot tears.

PATHELIN: We both have to be serious so he won't suspect anything.

[Scene IV]

THE CLOTHIER *(in his shop):* I think it's time for me to have a little drink before I leave. Oh, no I won't. I'll soon be drinking and eating goose at Master Pierre Pathelin's house. By the patron saint of fools, I'll get my money there and the special treat they're preparing, and it won't cost me a sou. I can't sell anything more here, so I'll be going.

[Scene V]

THE CLOTHIER *(Shouts in front of Pathelin's house):* Hey There! Master Pierre!

GUILLEMETTE *(opening the door):* Please sir, for the love of God, if you have something to say, speak softly.

THE CLOTHIER: God be with you, Madame.

GUILLEMETTE: Shh! Softer.

THE CLOTHIER: What's the matter?

GUILLEMETTE: Bless my soul . . .

THE CLOTHIER: Where is he?

GUILLEMETTE: Alas! Where should he be?

THE CLOTHIER: Who . . . ?

GUILLEMETTE: Ah, that was ill-spoken, my good sir. "Where is he," indeed! May God in his mercy have pity on him. The poor suffering man is in the same place he's been without budging for eleven weeks now.

THE CLOTHIER: But who . . . ?

GUILLEMETTE: Pardon me, but I don't dare speak louder. I think he's resting now; he was a little drowsy. Alas, he's so sick, the poor man.

THE CLOTHIER: Who?

GUILLEMETTE: Master Pierre.

THE CLOTHIER: What? Didn't he come to my shop to get six yards of cloth just now?

GUILLEMETTE: Who? Him?

THE CLOTHIER: He just left there, not ten minutes ago. Hurry up! Devil take me, I've stayed too long already. Quick, give me my money and no more foolishness.

GUILLEMETTE: Hey! No more of *your* foolishness! This is no time to joke around.

THE CLOTHIER: Are you crazy? My money! Now! You owe me nine francs.

GUILLEMETTE: Ah, Guillaume, are you making fun of me? This is no asylum for lunatics. Go tell your nonsense to fools like yourself and play your tricks on them.

THE CLOTHIER: May I renounce God, if I don't get my nine francs!

GUILLEMETTE: Alas, Sir, not everyone is as eager to laugh and gossip as you are.

THE CLOTHIER: Please, I beg you, no more joking. Just have Master Pierre come here, for the love of . . .

GUILLEMETTE: Misfortune strike you down! Will this go on all day?

THE CLOTHIER: But isn't this the house of Master Pierre Pathelin?

GUILLEMETTE: Of course! May the patron saint of lunatics *(crosses herself)* addle your brain! Speak low!

THE CLOTHIER: The Devil take your "speak low"! Shouldn't I ask for what's mine?

GUILLEMETTE: God help me! Speak low, if you don't want him to wake up.

THE CLOTHIER: How "low" do you want? In the ear? In the cellar? Or in the bottom of the well?

GUILLEMETTE: My God, how you drivel on! But that's always been your way.

THE CLOTHIER: The Devil it has! *(Calming down.)* Now that I think about it, if you want me to speak low, just say so. I'm really not used to arguments like this. The truth is that Master Pierre took six yards of cloth today.

GUILLEMETTE: What is this? Will this go on all day? The Devil take it! Now, just what do you mean by "took"? Oh, may the one who's lying be hanged! That poor man is in such a pitiful state that he hasn't left his bed in eleven weeks. Then you come along with your wild ideas. Now is that right? By God's passion, you'll leave my house at once. Oh, what misery!

THE CLOTHIER: You asked *me* to speak so low. Now, by the Holy Virgin, you're screaming.

GUILLEMETTE: So help me, you're the one who can't speak without quarreling.

THE CLOTHIER: Look, so I can go, just give me . . .

GUILLEMETTE *(shouting):* Are you going to speak low?

THE CLOTHIER: But you're going to wake him yourself. Damn it all, you're yelling four times louder than I am. I insist that you pay me.

GUILLEMETTE: What is this? Are you drunk or just out of your mind? God in heaven!

THE CLOTHIER: Drunk! Saint Peter curse you! What a question!

GUILLEMETTE: Please! Speak lower!

THE CLOTHIER: By Saint George, I demand payment for six yards of cloth!

GUILLEMETTE: You must have been dreaming. And just who did you give it to?

THE CLOTHIER: To him.

GUILLEMETTE: He's in fine shape to be buying cloth. Alas, he can't even move. He has no need for new clothes. He'll never get dressed again, except in graveclothes; and he'll never leave his room again, except feet first.

THE CLOTHIER: Then this happened since early this morning, because I spoke to him for sure.

GUILLEMETTE *(in a loud voice):* Your voice is so loud. For the love of God, speak lower!

THE CLOTHIER: You're the one shouting, damn it all, you and nobody else. God help me, this is agony. Will somebody pay me so I can go! By God, every time I've given credit, I've had nothing but trouble.

PATHELIN *(from his bed):* Guillemette, a little rose water. Prop me up. Tuck me in behind. Damn! Who was I talking to? The water jar! Give me a drink! Rub my feet!

THE CLOTHIER: I hear him in there.

GUILLEMETTE: Yes.

PATHELIN *(delirious):* Ah, wicked woman! Come here! Did I tell you to open these windows? Come cover me up. Get rid of these people in black! *Marmara carimari carimara!* Take them away from me, away!

GUILLEMETTE: What's the matter? You're tossing about so. Have you lost your senses?

PATHELIN: You don't see what I see. There's a monk in black flying around the room. Catch him. Get a stole to exorcise him! The cat! Get the cat! Look how he rises up!

GUILLEMETTE: What is all this? Aren't you ashamed? This is too much stirring about, for heaven's sake.

PATHELIN: Those doctors are killing me with all the vile potions they make me drink. And yet we have to believe them; we're like putty in their hands.

GUILLEMETTE *(to the Clothier):* Alas! Come and see him, good sir. He's suffering terribly.

THE CLOTHIER: Was he taken so ill on returning from the fair?

GUILLEMETTE: The fair?

THE CLOTHIER: Yes, by Saint John! I'm sure he was there. Master Pierre! I need the money for the cloth I gave you on credit.

PATHELIN *(pretending to take the Clothier for a doctor):* Ah, Doctor John! I shat two tiny black turds, round as balls and hard as rocks. Should I take another enema?

THE CLOTHIER: How should I know? What've I got to do with enemas? I want my nine francs or six gold pieces.

PATHELIN: Those three black sharp things—you call those pills? They nearly busted my jaws. For God's sake don't make me take any more of them, Doctor John. There's nothing in the world more bitter, and they made everything come up again.

THE CLOTHIER: No they didn't, by God. My nine francs haven't appeared yet.

GUILLEMETTE: Hang such tiresome people. *(To the Clothier.)* Go away, by all the devils, since it can't be on God's part.

THE CLOTHIER: I swear to God, I'll get my cloth before I leave, or my nine francs.

PATHELIN *(pretending the Clothier is a doctor):* And my urine specimen, doesn't it show that I'm dying? For God's sake, whatever happens, don't let me die.

GUILLEMETTE *(to the Clothier):* Be off with you! It's terrible to torment him like this.

THE CLOTHIER: Lord God in heaven! Six yards of cloth! Tell me, do you think it's right that I should lose it?

PATHELIN: Oh, Doctor John! Do you think you could loosen my bowels? I'm so constipated I don't know how I stand to sit on the throne.

THE CLOTHIER: I want my nine francs now or by Saint Peter of Rome . . .

GUILLEMETTE: Alas! You're tormenting this man so. How can you be so cruel? You can see plain as day that he thinks you're his doctor. Alas! The poor soul has had such misfortune. He's been in that bed for eleven straight weeks, the poor man!

THE CLOTHIER: By God, I don't know how this sickness came about, because today he was in my shop and we did business together—at least it seems we did. Otherwise I don't know what could have happened.

GUILLEMETTE: By Our Lady, I think your memory is slipping, my friend. If you take my advice, you'll go get some rest. Besides there are a lot of gossips around who'll think you came in here to see me. Go on now; his doctors will be here soon.

THE CLOTHIER: I don't care if others do think evil of it, because I have no such thoughts. Damn it all, how'd I get into this mess? I swear to God, I thought . . .

GUILLEMETTE: Again?

THE CLOTHIER: And don't you have a goose cooking?

GUILLEMETTE: What a question! Sir, that's not a dish for sick people. Go chase your own goose and don't come here making fun of us. You've got some nerve to do that.

THE CLOTHIER: Please excuse me, but I really thought . . .

GUILLEMETTE: Still?

THE CLOTHIER: By the sacrament! Goodbye! *(He leaves the house.)* Now I've got to figure this out. I know I should have six yards of cloth in one piece. But that woman addles my brain so much I can't think. He really did take the cloth. . . . No, he couldn't have, damn it! It just doesn't fit. I saw Death coming to strike him down—at least he so pretended. . . . Yes he did! He did take the cloth and he put it under his arm, by Saint Mary! . . . No, he didn't. Maybe I'm dreaming. But even in my sleep I'd never give my cloth away to anybody, no matter how much I liked him. I just wouldn't have given credit. . . . By God, he did take the cloth! . . . No, damn it all, he didn't. I know he didn't. But where does that leave me! . . . Yes he did, by Our Lady's passion! . . . Misfortune take me, body and soul, if I know who could decide who got the best of this deal, them or me. I just can't figure it out.

PATHELIN: Is he gone?

GUILLEMETTE: Quiet, I'm listening. I don't know what he was muttering, but he left grumbling so much that he was almost hysterical.

PATHELIN: Isn't it time for me to get up? We sure pulled that one off.

GUILLEMETTE: I don't know if he's coming back or not. *(Pathelin starts to get up.)* No, don't get up yet! Everything would be ruined if he found you out of bed.

PATHELIN: He's always so suspicious of others, but by God he met his match this time. The joke was on him and it fit like a cross on a steeple.

GUILLEMETTE: No greedy shark ever took the bait quicker than he did. It serves him right. He never gives a thing in church on Sundays. *(She laughs.)*

PATHELIN: For God's sake, don't laugh. If he came back and heard you, it would spoil everything. I'm sure he'll be back.

GUILLEMETTE: Hold in your laughter if you can, but I swear I can't help myself.

THE CLOTHIER *(at his shop):* By the sacred sun that shines, I'm going back to that backwoods barrister, I don't care what anybody says. Oh, God! That phoney financial fraud would fleece his own family. Now, by St. Peter, I know he has my cloth, the sneaky swindler. I gave it to him right on this spot.

GUILLEMETTE: When I think of the face he made looking at you, I can't help laughing. He was so greedy in asking you for . . .

PATHELIN: Peace, you cackler! I swear to God, if he came back and heard you, we might as well start running. He's such a sour old bastard.

THE CLOTHIER *(returning to Pathelin's house):* That addlepated advocate, that bibulous barrister, does he take us all for fools? By damn, the only doctor he needs is a good hangman. I'll renounce God if he doesn't have my cloth. And he played this trick on me, too. *(At the door.)* Hey, in there! Where are you hiding?

GUILLEMETTE: On my oath, he heard me and he seems to be raving mad.

PATHELIN: I'll pretend to be delirious. Go to the door.

GUILLEMETTE *(to the Clothier):* My, how you're shouting.

THE CLOTHIER: By God, you were laughing! My money, now!

GUILLEMETTE: Holy Mary! What do you think I have to laugh about? There's no sadder person in town. He's fading fast. Never did you hear such an uproar or such raving. He's still delirious. His mind wanders, he sings, he jabbers in so many languages and jumbles them all together. He won't live half an hour longer. I swear, I laugh and cry at the same time.

THE CLOTHIER: I don't know what you mean about laughing and crying. But to put it bluntly, I must be paid now!

GUILLEMETTE: For what? Are you insane? Are you going to start that again?

THE CLOTHIER: I'm not used to being paid with words when I sell my cloth. Would you have me believe the moon is made of green cheese?

PATHELIN *(delirious):* Arise! Make way for the Queen of Guitars. Let her approach without delay. I know she gave birth to four and twenty guitarlings, sired by the Abbot of Iverneaux. I'll have to be the godfather.

GUILLEMETTE: Alas! Think about God the father, my dear, not about guitars.

THE CLOTHIER: What a pair of con artists you are! Quick, now, give me my money in gold or silver for the cloth you took.

GUILLEMETTE: Good God! You were mistaken once, isn't that enough?

THE CLOTHIER: Do you know what's going on, woman? So help me, I don't know what you mean by "mistaken." But never mind, you'll either pay up or be strung up. How do I wrong you by coming here to ask for what's mine? By Saint Peter of Rome . . .

GUILLEMETTE: Alas! How you torment this poor man! Truly, I can see in your face that you're losing your wits. If only I had help, sinner that I am, I'd have you tied up. You're a raving lunatic.

THE CLOTHIER: I'm raving because I don't have my money.

GUILLEMETTE: Oh, what madness! Cross yourself. *Benedicite!* Make the sign of the cross.

THE CLOTHIER: May I renounce God if I ever again sell cloth on credit. *(Pathelin stirs.)* What an invalid!

PATHELIN: Mere de Dieu, la coronade,
Par ma fye, y m'en vuol anar,
Or regni biou, oultre la mar!
Ventre de Diou! z'en dis gigone!
(He points to the Clothier.)
Çastuy ça rible et res ne done.
Ne carrilaine! fuy ta none!
Que de l'argent il ne me sone!¹

(To the Clothier.) Did you understand, cousin?

GUILLEMETTE: He had an uncle from Limousin, the brother of his aunt by marriage. I'll bet that's what makes him babble in the Limousin dialect.

THE CLOTHIER: Damn it, he stole out of my shop with the cloth under his arm.

PATHELIN: Venez ens, doulce damiselle.
Et que veult ceste crapaudaille?
Alez en arriere, merdaille!
(He wraps himself in his blanket.)
Sa! tost! je vueil devenir prestre.
Or sa! que le dyable y puist estre,
En chelle vielle prestrerie!
Et faut il que le prestre rie
Quant il dëust chanter sa messe?²

GUILLEMETTE: Alas! Alas! The hour draws near when he'll need the last sacraments.

THE CLOTHIER: But how does he speak the Picard dialect so well? And why all this silliness?

---

1. (Limousin dialect.) Mother of God, crowned [queen of Heaven], by my faith, I want to go, or I'll renounce God, to the other side of the sea. God's belly, I say *gigone!* (He points to the Clothier.) That one there steals and gives nothing. Toll not the bell. Take your nap. Let him not speak to me of money!

2. (Picard dialect.) Come in, sweet damsel. What does that pack of scoundrels want? Get back, you shitten knaves! (He wraps himself in his blanket.) Quick, I want to become a priest. Now, may the Devil be part of that ancient priesthood! And must the priest laugh when he should be chanting his mass?

GUILLEMETTE: His mother was from Picardy. That's why he speaks it now.

PATHELIN *(to the Clothier):* Where did you come from, you carnival clown?

>   Vuacarme, liefe gode man!
>   Etlbelic beq igluhe golan.
>   Henrien! Henrien! conselapen.
>   Ych salgneb nede que maignen.
>   Grile, grile, scohehonden!
>   Zilop, zilop, en mon que bouden!
>   Disticlien unen desen versen.
>   Mat groet festal ou truit denhersen;
>   En vuacte vuile! Comme trie!
>   Cha! a dringuer, I beg of you.
>   Quoy act semigot yaue.
>   And put some water in it for me.
>   Vuste vuille, because of the frost.[3]

Quick, call Father Thomas so I can be shriven.

THE CLOTHIER: What's going on? Will he never stop jabbering in different languages? If he'd just give me my money, or even a deposit, I'd be on my way.

GUILLEMETTE: By God's passion, I'm tired of this. You're the weirdest man I ever met. Just what do you want? I don't know how you can be so obstinate.

PATHELIN: Or cha! Renouart au Tiné!
>   *(He looks into his gown.)*
>   Bé dea, que ma couille est pelouse!
>   El semble une cate pelouse,
>   Ou a une mousque a mïel.
>   Bé! Parlez a moy, Gabriel.
>   Les play's Dieu! Qu'esse qui s'ataque
>   A men cul? Esse ou une vaque,
>   Une mousque, ou ung escarbot?
>   *(He puts his hand into his gown.)*
>   Bé dea! J'é le mau saint Garbot!
>   Suis je des foureux de Baieux?
>   Jehan du Quemin sera joyeulz,
>   Mais qu'i' sache que je le see.

---

3. (The meaning of this garbled Flemish is not entirely clear.) Awake, to arms, dear good man! Fortunately I know several books. Henry! Henry! Come to sleep. I shall be well armed. Foolishness, foolishness, crazy inventions! A run, a run, a nun is bound! There are distichs in these verses. But great feasting disturbs the brain. Wait a while! Come quick! Something to drink, I beg of you! Come, look; a gift of God. And put some water in it for me. But wait a while because of the frost.

     Bee! Par saint Miquiel, je beree
     Voulentiers a luy une fes![4]

THE CLOTHIER: How can he stand to talk so much? He's going stark raving mad.

GUILLEMETTE: His schoolmaster was from Normandy. Now at the end he's remembering him. He's sinking fast.

THE CLOTHIER: Holy Mary! This is the craziest mess I've ever gotten myself into. Never would I have doubted that he was at the fair today.

GUILLEMETTE: You really believed it?

THE CLOTHIER: I did, by Saint James. But now I see it wasn't so.

PATHELIN: Is that an ass I hear braying? *(To the Clothier.)* Alas and alack, good cousin, they all shall bray in great sorrow the day that I see thee no more. And yet I must needs detest thee, for thou hast played false with me. Thy work is naught but deceit.

     Ha oul danda oul en ravezeie
     Corfha en euf!

GUILLEMETTE (to Pathelin): May God have mercy on you.
PATHELIN: Huis oz bez ou dronc nos badou
     Digaut an tan en hol madou
     Empedif dich guicebnuan
     Quez queuient ob dre douch aman
     Men ez cahet hoz bouzelou
     Eny obet grande canou
     Maz rehet crux dan hol con
     So ol oz merueil grant nacon
     Aluzen archet epysy
     Har cals amour ha courteisy.[5]

THE CLOTHIER: Alas! For God's sake, listen to him. He's going fast. How he rattles on! But what the Devil is he jabbering about? Holy Mary, how he mutters! God's bodkin, he babbles and quacks his words so you can't understand a thing. It's no Christian tongue he's speaking, nor any that makes sense.

---

 4. (Norman dialect.) Come here! Renouart au Tiné! (He looks into his gown.) What the Devil! How hairy my balls are! They're furry as a caterpillar or a honeybee. Hey! Speak to me, Gabriel. God's wounds! What's biting my ass? Is it a fly, a dungbeetle, or a cockchafer? (He puts his hand into his gown.) What the Devil! I've got dysentery! Am I one of the loose-boweled of Bayeux? Jean du Quemin would be glad to know that I am. Well, by St. Michael, I'll glady drink to his health.

 5. (The translation of the Breton passage is based on the conjectural reconstruction of J. Loth.) P: May he go to the Devil, body and soul! G: May God have mercy on you. P: May you have dizzy spells all night with much lamenting and with all your relatives praying for you, for fear that you'll vomit your guts out. There will be such weeping and wailing that even the starving dogs will take pity on you. May you receive a coffin as alms out of much love and courtesy.

GUILLEMETTE: His father's mother came from Brittany. But he's dying, and all this indicates that it's time for the last sacraments.

PATHELIN: Hé, par saint Gigon, tu te mens.
Voit a Deu! Couille de Lorraine!
Dieu te mette en bote sepmaine!
Tu ne vaulx mie une vielz nate.
Va, sanglante bote savate;
Va foutre! Va, sanglant paillart!
Tu me refais trop le gaillart.
Par la mort bieu! Sa! Vien t'en boire,
Et baille moy stan grain de poire,
Car vrayment je le mangera
Et, par saint George, je bura
A ty. Que veulx tu que je die?
Dy, viens tu nient de Picardie?
Jaques nient se sont ebobis.[6]
Et bona dies sit vobis,
Magister amantissime,
Pater reverendissime.
Quomodo brulis? Que nova?
Parisius non sunt ova.
Quid petit ille mercator?
Dicat sibi quod trufator,
Ille qui in lecto jacet,
Vult ei dare, si placet,
De oca ad comedendum.
Si sit bona ad edendum,
Pete tibi sine mora.[7]

GUILLEMETTE: I swear, he's going to die making speeches. My, how he Latinizes! Don't you see how highly he esteems the divinity? His humanity is ebbing away. Now I'll remain poor and miserable.

THE CLOTHIER: It would be better for me to go before he breathes his last. If he has some secret things to confide in you before he dies, I doubt that he would want to say them in front of me. Please forgive me, but I swear to you that I truly believed he had taken my cloth. Farewell, good woman. I beg you in God's name to forgive me.

GUILLEMETTE: May this day be blessed for you and also for me in my sorrow.

---

6. (Lorraine dialect.) Hey, by St. Gengoux, you're lying! I swear to God! Great balls, may God send you misfortune! You're not worth an old doormat. Get out of here, you bloody old boot; fuck off! Leave, you low-life lecher! You're too malicious, by God! You there! Come have a drink and give me a peppercorn; I'll really eat it and, by St. George, I'll drink to you. What do you expect me to say? Say, are you by chance from Picardy? The peasants there are dumbfounded.

7. (Latin.) Good day to you, beloved master, most reverend father. How are you burning? What's new? There are no eggs in Paris. What does that merchant want? Let him say to himself that the swindler, the one lying in bed, wants to give him, if he will, some goose to eat. If it's good, ask for some without delay.

THE CLOTHIER *(leaving the house):* By the gracious Virgin, I'm more confused now than ever. The Devil, in his shape, took my cloth to tempt me. *(Crosses himself.) Benedicite.* May he leave me in peace. But since that's the way it is, I give the cloth, in God's name, to whoever took it.

PATHELIN *(getting up):* Now then, didn't I instruct you well? There he goes, the gullible simpleton. Now he's really got some confused ideas under that bonnet of his. I bet he'll have nightmares when he goes to bed tonight.

GUILLEMETTE: We really put him in his place. Didn't I play my part well?

PATHELIN: By God, you played it to perfection. Now at least we have enough cloth to make some clothes.

[Scene VI]

THE CLOTHIER *(in his shop):* Damn it all! Everybody feeds me lies; everybody steals from me and takes all he can get. I feel like I'm the king of the wretched. Even the shepherds of the field defraud me. And my own shepherd, to whom I've always been generous, will not get away with cheating me. He'll be begging for mercy, by the Blessed Virgin!

THIBAULT AIGNELET, THE SHEPHERD *(entering the shop):* God grant you a blessed day and a good evening, gentle Master.

THE CLOTHIER: Aha! There you are, you dung-covered scoundrel! What a good fellow you are! Good for nothing!

THE SHEPHERD: Begging your pardon, Sir, but some guy, I don't know who, with stripes on his sleeve, and all kind of excited, and carrying a whip handle without a cord, came up and said to me . . . But I don't rightly recollect what it was he said. He talked about you, Master, and some kind of summons, but, Holy Mary, I couldn't make heads or tails out of it. He mixed me up so with his talk about "sheep" and "afternoon session," and he made a great fuss about things you had said against me, Sir.

THE CLOTHIER: If I don't haul you before the judge in two shakes, I pray God to strike me with storm and flood. Never again will you get away with killing my sheep, I swear. And no matter what happens, you'll pay me for those six yards . . . I mean, for killing my sheep and for all the losses you've caused me in the last ten years.

THE SHEPHERD: You shouldn't believe those poison tongues, good Master, for by my soul . . .

THE CLOTHIER: And by Our Lady you'll pay me on Saturday for my six yards of cloth . . . I mean, for what you stole of my sheep.

THE SHEPHERD: What cloth? Ah, Sir, I believe you're upset about something else. By Saint Lupus, Master, I'm afraid to say anything when I see you like this.

THE CLOTHIER: Go and leave me in peace. And answer your summons, if you know what's good for you.

THE SHEPHERD. But Sir, let's settle this now. For God's sake, don't take me to court.

THE CLOTHIER: Go! The matter is in good hands. Go on, now! I won't make a settlement, by God, and I won't agree to anything but what the judge decides. Damn it all, everybody will cheat me from now on if I don't put a stop to it.

THE SHEPHERD: Goodbye, Sir. May God give you joy. *(He leaves.)* So now I have to defend myself.

[Scene VII]

THE SHEPHERD *(knocking at Pathelin's door):* Is anybody here?

PATHELIN *(to Guillemette):* I'll be hanged if he hasn't come back.

GUILLEMETTE: No it can't be! Saint George preserve us. That would be the end.

THE SHEPHERD: God be with you and keep you.

PATHELIN: God save you, my good fellow. What is it you want?

THE SHEPHERD: They're going to fine me for not showing up, if I don't answer my summons, Sir, this afternoon, and if you please, would you, good Master, plead my case for me, 'cause I don't know nothing about it, and I can pay you good, even though I'm dressed so poor.

PATHELIN: Come here and speak up. Which are you, plaintiff or defendant?

THE SHEPHERD: Well, Sir, I work for a certain merchant, you know, and for a long time I've taken his sheep out to graze and I guard 'em, and I swear when I think about him paying me next to nothing . . . Do I have to tell everything?

PATHELIN: Certainly. A client should hide nothing from his counsel.

THE SHEPHERD: It's true, Sir, it's the truth, I struck 'em down, so that many of 'em were knocked out and fell down dead, even though they were strong and healthy, and then I made him think, so's he wouldn't punish me, that they died of the scab. "Oh," he'd say, "don't leave a diseased one with the others, get rid of it." "I'll be glad to," I'd say; and I'd get rid of it all right, but not the way he thought, for, by Saint John, I ate every one of 'em, 'cause I knew what they really died of. What else can I tell you? I kept doin' this so long and struck down and killed so many that he noticed it, and when he found out he had been deceived, so help me God, he sent somebody to spy on me 'cause you could hear 'em cry out, you know, when you hit 'em. So I was caught red-handed, I can never deny it, and now I come to ask if there ain't some way we can put the old hound off the scent, and don't worry about money, I got enough to pay you good. I know he's got a good case, but you can find some loophole, if you will, to make it worthless.

PATHELIN: I promise you'll be satisfied with the results. What will you give me if I overturn the claim of your accuser and get you a full pardon?

THE SHEPHERD: Instead of payin' in sous, I'll pay you in solid gold crowns.

PATHELIN: Then you'll have an unbeatable case even if it's twice as weak as you say. The stronger the case I argue against, the quicker I can render it null, when I put my mind to it. You'll hear how well I can spiel it off after he's presented his argument. Come over here. By God, you're wily enough to understand the trick. Now tell me, what's your name?

THE SHEPHERD: By Saint Maurus, it's Thibault Aignelet.

PATHELIN: Aignelet, did you appropriate many lambs from your master?

THE SHEPHERD: On my oath, I may have eaten thirty or more in three years.

PATHELIN: That makes an income of ten a year—the equivalent of a few games at the tavern. *(He thinks for a moment.)* I believe I have a good ruse here. Do you think he can readily find a witness to prove his allegation? That's the most important part of the trial.

THE SHEPHERD: Prove, Sir? Holy Mary! By all the saints in paradise, instead of one, he'll find ten to testify against me.

PATHELIN: That's almost enough to ruin your case. Here's what I had in mind. I'll pretend that I'm not on your side and that I've never seen you before.

THE SHEPHERD: For God's sake, don't do that!

PATHELIN: No, that's no good. But here's what we have to do. If you speak, they'll trap you one by one on all counts of the indictment, and in such cases confessions are as prejudicial and harmful as the Devil himself. So here's what will make our case: as soon as they call you to appear before the court, you'll answer only with "baa," no matter what they say to you. And if they should curse you, saying, "Hey, you stinking yokel! May God plunge you into misery! Are you making fun of the court?" just answer "baa." "Ha!" I'll say, "he's a poor simpleton who thinks he's talking to his sheep." But even if they knock themselves out yelling at you, make sure no other word comes out of your mouth.

THE SHEPHERD: Seein' as how this touches me close, I'll make sure I don't say nothin' else and I'll do it right, I promise.

PATHELIN: Now make sure you stick to your promise. And even to me, no matter what I say or ask, don't answer any other way.

THE SHEPHERD: Me? Never, by the sacrament! You can cry out that I'm crazy, if I say another word today, to you or anybody else, no matter what they say to me, except "Baa," just like you told me.

PATHELIN: If you do that, by Saint John, your accuser will be caught in our trap. But also make sure when it's over that I get a payment I'll be proud of.

THE SHEPHERD: Sir, if I don't pay you at your word, then never believe me again. But please work hard on my case.

PATHELIN: By Our Lady, I'll bet the judge is already on the bench; he always holds court around six o'clock. Now you come along after me; we won't both go together.

THE SHEPHERD: That's a good idea, so nobody sees you're my lawyer.

PATHELIN: And God help you if you don't pay generously.

THE SHEPHERD: I swear I'll pay at your word; really, Sir, have no fear.

PATHELIN *(alone):* Well now, it may not be raining money, but it's sprinkling. At least I'll get a little something out of this. If everything falls into place, I'll have a gold piece or two for my trouble.

[Scene VIII]

PATHELIN *(removing his hat to salute the Judge):* Your Honor, God grant you success and whatever your heart desires.

THE JUDGE: Welcome, Sir. Please don your hat and take your place over there.

PATHELIN *(seeing the Clothier):* Damn! *(To the Judge.)* I'm fine here, Your Honor; I'll have more room to maneuver.

THE JUDGE: If there is business before the court, let it be done quickly so I can adjourn.

THE CLOTHIER: My lawyer is coming, Your Honor. He's finishing up some other business. If the court please, we had better wait for him.

THE JUDGE: Wait? I have cases to hear elsewhere. If the offending party is present, then state the case yourself without delay. Are you not the plaintiff?

THE CLOTHIER: I am.

THE JUDGE: Where is the defendant? Is he here in person?

THE CLOTHIER: Yes, there he is, not saying a word. God only knows what he's thinking.

THE JUDGE: Since you're both here, state your case.

THE CLOTHIER: Then here's my complaint against him, Your Honor. The truth is that for the love of God and in charity I fed and clothed him in his childhood; and, to be brief, when I saw that he was strong enough to go to the fields, I made him my shepherd and set him to watching my flock. But as sure as you're sitting there, Your Honor, he wrought such carnage among my wethers and ewes that without a doubt . . .

THE JUDGE: Just a minute! Wasn't he hired by you?

PATHELIN: That's a good point! Because if he had finagled to employ him without a contract . . .

THE CLOTHIER *(recognizing Pathelin):* May I disavow God if it isn't you! You, without a doubt!

THE JUDGE: Why are you holding your hand to your face, Master Pierre? Do you have a toothache?

PATHELIN: Yes, the pain is so excruciating that never before have I been in such agony. I can't even look up. For God's sake, make him get on with it.

THE JUDGE: Proceed! Finish your deposition. Come on, be brief about it.

THE CLOTHIER: It's him and nobody else! By God's cross, it really is! Master Pierre, it was you that I sold six yards of cloth to.

THE JUDGE: What's he saying about cloth?

PATHELIN: He's rambling. He thinks he's getting to his opening statement, but he doesn't know how because he isn't used to this.

THE CLOTHIER: May I be hanged by the bloody neck if anybody else took my cloth.

PATHELIN: Look how this unworthy man goes to extremes to build his case. He means, and he's very stubborn about it, that his shepherd had sold the wool—that's what I understood—from which the cloth of my robe was made. He seems to be saying that the shepherd's a thief and has been stealing the wool of his sheep.

THE CLOTHIER: God send me misfortune if you haven't got it!

THE JUDGE: Silence! The Devil take you for running off at the mouth! Can't you get back to your deposition without delaying the court with such drivel?

PATHELIN *(laughing):* Oh, my tooth aches, but I can't help laughing. He's already so rushed he doesn't know where he left off. We'll have to lead him back to the subject.

THE JUDGE: Come now, let's get back to those sheep. What happened next?

THE CLOTHIER: He took six yards of it, worth nine francs.

THE JUDGE: Do you take us for fools or simpletons? Where do you think you are?

PATHELIN: I swear to God, he's trying to make an ass of you! And he looks like such a decent man. But I suggest you examine his adversary.

THE JUDGE: That's a good idea. He sees him often, so he must know him. *(To the Shepherd.)* Step forward! Speak!

THE SHEPHERD: Baa!

THE JUDGE: Another vexation! What do you mean, "baa"? Am I a goat! Speak to me!

THE SHEPHERD: Baa!

THE JUDGE: The bloody pox take you! Are you trying to make a fool of me!

PATHELIN: He must be either crazy or pigheaded; or maybe he thinks he's among his sheep.

THE CLOTHIER: I'll renounce God if you aren't the one that got my cloth—you and nobody else! *(To the Judge.)* Oh, you don't know, Your Honor, by what malice . . .

THE JUDGE: What! Hold your tongue! Are you dense? Set aside this accessory matter and let's get back to the principal.

THE CLOTHIER: Very well, Your Honor, but the case concerns me. Nevertheless, I promise I won't say another word about it for the rest of the day. Some other time it may be different; right now I'll just have to swallow it. Now, I was saying in my complaint that I had given six yards . . . I should say, my sheep. . . . Please forgive me, Your Honor. . . . This good Master . . . I mean, my shepherd, when he was supposed to be in the fields . . . He told me I would get six gold pieces when I came . . . I mean to say, three years ago my shepherd made an agreement that he would faithfully guard my sheep and would cause me no loss nor do me any wrong, and then . . . Now he brazenly refuses to give me either cloth or money. *(To Pathelin.)* Ah, Master Pierre, I swear . . . *(To the Judge.)* This scoundrel here was stealing the wool from my sheep, and he was killing healthy ones by clubbing them on the head. . . . When he put my cloth under his arm, he took off in a great hurry, saying that I should go collect my six gold pieces at his house.

THE JUDGE: There's neither rime nor reason in any of your railing and ranting. What is this? You mix in one thing and then another. In short, by God, I can't make heads or tails of it. *(To Pathelin.)* He prattles about cloth, then he jabbers about sheep and jumbles it all up. Nothing he says makes sense.

PATHELIN: I'll bet anything he's keeping this poor shepherd's wages for himself.

THE CLOTHIER: You can shut your mouth, by God. It's the gospel truth that my cloth . . . I know better than you or anybody else where my shoe pinches, and by God in heaven, I know you have it!

THE JUDGE: What does he have?

THE CLOTHIER: Nothing, Your Honor. But I swear he's the biggest swindler . . . OK, I'll try to control my tongue and I won't say another word about it today, no matter what happens.

THE JUDGE: Very well, but remember your promise. Now conclude quickly.

PATHELIN: This shepherd cannot answer the charges against him without counsel, and he's afraid or doesn't know how to ask for it. I would be willing to counsel him, Your Honor, if you so ordered.

THE JUDGE: Him? I should think that would be wasted effort. He's as poor as a church mouse.

PATHELIN: I swear I have no thought of gain. Let it be for love of God. Now I'll try to find out from the poor lad what he has to say, and I'll see if he can instruct me as to how to reply to the charges against him. He'd have a hard time getting out of this, if nobody helped him. *(To the Shepherd.)* Come over here, my friend. Now if we could find . . . Do you understand?

THE SHEPHERD: Baa!

PATHELIN: What is this "baa"? By the Holy Blood, are you crazy? Tell me about your case.

THE SHEPHERD: Baa!

PATHELIN: What is this "baa"? Do you hear the ewes bleating? Try to understand, this is for your own good.

THE SHEPHERD: Baa!

PATHELIN: Come on! Answer yes or no. *(Softly.)* That's good. Keep it up. *(Aloud.)* Will you do that?

THE SHEPHERD: Baa!

PATHELIN: Speak up, or you'll find yourself in real trouble, I'm afraid.

THE SHEPHERD: Baa!

PATHELIN: It takes a real ass to bring such a poor fool to trial. Your Honor, send him back to his sheep. He's just a natural-born fool.

THE CLOTHEIR: You call him a fool? By Saint Savior of Asturias, he's smarter than you are.

PATHELIN *(to the Judge):* Send him back to watch his sheep, *sine die*, never to return. A plague on him who brings charges against such natural-born fools.

THE CLOTHIER: Will he be sent back before I can be heard?

THE JUDGE: So help me, since he's a born fool, yes. Why shouldn't he be?

THE CLOTHIER: But Your Honor, at least allow me to sum up my case first. This isn't something I dreamed up or just idle discourse.

THE JUDGE: Nothing but vexation comes of bringing suit against fools and simpletons. Now hear this: to stop this senseless babble, the court will be adjourned.

THE CLOTHIER: Will they go without obligation to return?

THE JUDGE: And why not?

PATHELIN: Return! You never saw a greater fool in word or in deed. *(Pointing to the Clothier.)* And this other one isn't an ounce better. They're both brainless boneheads. By the Blessed Virgin, their brains together wouldn't weigh a carat.

THE CLOTHIER: You took my cloth by deceit, Master Pierre, without paying. As I'm a poor sinner, that wasn't the deed of an honest man.

PATHELIN: May I renounce Saint Peter of Rome if he isn't an insidious fool, or well on his way to being one.

THE CLOTHIER: I recognize you by your speech, by your clothes, and by your face. And I'm not crazy! I'm sane enough to know what's good for me. *(To the Judge.)* I'll tell you the whole story, Your Honor, upon my conscience. *(The Judge grimaces. Laughter in the audience.)*

PATHELIN *(pointing to the audience):* Please, Your Honor, bring them to order. *(To the Clothier.)* Aren't you ashamed to haul this poor shepherd into court for three or four grubby old sheep that aren't worth two buttons. *(To the Judge.)* His litany gets longer and more tedious.

THE CLOTHIER: What sheep? It's always the same old song! It's you I'm talking to and, by God, you'll give me back my cloth.

THE JUDGE *(to the audience):* You see that? I really get the cases, don't I? He won't stop braying for the rest of the day.

THE CLOTHIER: I'll bring suit . . .

PATHELIN: Make him shut up! *(To the Clothier.)* You prattle too much, by God. Let's say he did knock off six or seven sheep, or even a dozen, and ate them—Holy Christmas, you weren't crippled by it. You still earned a lot more than that in the time he's been watching your flock.

THE CLOTHIER: Look at that, Your Honor, just look! I talk to him about cloth and he answers me in sheep. *(To Pathelin.)* Those six yards of cloth that you stuck under your arm, where are they? Don't you intend to give them back to me?

PATHELIN: Oh, Sir, would you have him hanged for six or seven sheep? At least think it over. Don't be so harsh on this poor, unfortunate shepherd, who hasn't a thing to his name.

THE CLOTHIER: You're an expert in changing the subject. The Devil himself made me sell cloth to such a customer. Please, Your Honor, I charge him . . .

THE JUDGE *(thinking the Clothier is charging the Shepherd):* I absolve him of your charges and forbid you to proceed. A fine thing it is to bring suit against a fool. *(To the Shepherd.)* Go back to your sheep.

THE SHEPHERD: Baa!

THE JUDGE *(to the Clothier):* By our Lady, you've certainly shown what kind of person you are, Sir.

THE CLOTHIER: But Your Honor, I swear I want him to . . .

PATHELIN: Can't he shut up?

THE CLOTHIER: But it's you I have a case against. You tricked me with your eloquent speeches and carried my cloth away like a thief.

PATHELIN: Your Honor, I solemnly appeal! Are you going to listen to this?

THE CLOTHIER: So help me God, you're the biggest swindler . . . Your Honor, let me say . . .

THE JUDGE: It's a three-ring circus with you two—nothing but wrangling and squabbles. So help me, I've got to be going. *(To the Shepherd.)* Go, my son, and don't ever come back, even if an officer serves you with a warrant. The court grants you full pardon.

PATHELIN: Say "thank you."

THE SHEPHERD: Baa!

THE JUDGE: Is that clear? Go now and don't worry about a thing. It's all right.

THE CLOTHIER: But is it right for him to go like that?

THE JUDGE: Bah! I have business elsewhere. You're both outrageous mockers and you won't detain me a moment longer. I'm leaving. Will you come to supper with me, Master Pierre?

PATHELIN *(raising his hand to his cheek):* I can't. *(The Judge leaves.)*

[Scene IX]

THE CLOTHIER: You're an outright thief! Tell me, will I ever be paid?

PATHELIN: For what? Are you crazy? Who do you think I am anyway? By God, I've been trying to figure out who it is you take me for.

THE CLOTHIER: Indeed!

PATHELIN: No just a minute, my good man. I'll tell you right now who it is you take me for. It's the town fool, isn't it? But look! *(He lifts his hat.)* That can't be because he's not bald on top of his head like me.

THE CLOTHIER: Do you think I'm an imbecile? It was you in person; you, yourself, and nobody but you. Your voice proves it and don't think it doesn't.

PATHELIN: Me myself, and I? No it wasn't, I swear. Get that out of your head. It was probably John from Noyon; he's about my size.

THE CLOTHIER: The Devil it was! He doesn't have that besotted, witless face of yours. Didn't I leave you sick a while ago at your house?

PATHELIN: Now there's a fine bit of evidence! Me, sick? And what was I sick with? Come on, admit your stupidity; it's quite clear now.

THE CLOTHIER: I'll renounce Saint Peter if it wasn't you—you and nobody else. I know that to be absolutely true.

PATHELIN: Well don't you believe it, because it positively wasn't me. I never took a yard or even half a yard of cloth from you. I don't have that kind of reputation.

THE CLOTHIER: Damn it all, I'm going to go back to your house to see if you're there. We won't have to squabble here any more if I find you there.

PATHELIN: By Our Lady, that's a good idea! That way you'll know for sure. *(The Clothier leaves.)*

[Scene X]

PATHELIN: Hey, Aignelet!

THE SHEPHERD: Baa!

PATHELIN: Come here. Was your case well disposed of?

THE SHEPHERD: Baa!

PATHELIN: Your accuser has gone, so you don't have to say "baa" anymore. I really cooked his goose, didn't I? And didn't I counsel you just right?

THE SHEPHERD: Baa!

PATHELIN: Hey, don't worry. Nobody'll hear you. Speak up.

THE SHEPHERD: Baa!

PATHELIN: It's time for me to go now, so pay me.

THE SHEPHERD: Baa!

PATHELIN: To tell the truth, you played your part very well; you looked good. But what really fooled him was that you kept from laughing.

THE SHEPHERD: Baa!

PATHELIN: Why "baa"? You mustn't say it any more. Just pay me generously.

THE SHEPHERD: Baa!

PATHELIN: Why do you keep saying "baa"? Speak normally and pay me so I can go.

THE SHEPHERD: Baa!

PATHELIN: You know what? I'll tell you. I'm asking you, please, without any more bleating around the bush to think about paying me. I've had enough of you baa's. Pay up quickly.

THE SHEPHERD: Baa!

PATHELIN: Is this some kind of joke? Is this all you're going to do? I swear to God, if you don't escape, you're going to pay me, understand? The money! Now!

THE SHEPHERD: Baa!

PATHELIN: You've got to be kidding. Is this all I'm going to get from you?

THE SHEPHERD: Baa!

PATHELIN: You're running this into the ground. And just who are you trying to fool? Do you know who you're dealing with? Don't babble your baa's to me anymore today; just pay me.

THE SHEPHERD: Baa!

PATHELIN: Is this the only pay I'll get? Who do you think you're playing games with? I was taking such pride in your performance; now really make me proud of you.

THE SHEPHERD: Baa!

PATHELIN: Are you trying to pull the wool over my eyes? God's curse! Have I lived so long that a shepherd, a sheep in human clothing, a churlish knave can make a fool of me?

THE SHEPHERD: Baa!

PATHELIN: Will I get no other word? If you're doing this for a joke, say so and don't make me argue any more. Come and have supper at my house.

THE SHEPHERD: Baa!

PATHELIN: By Saint John, you're right: the goslings lead the geese to pasture. *(To himself.)* I thought I was the master in these parts of all the cheaters and swindlers and those who give their word in payment, collectible on Judgment Day; and now a shepherd of the fields outwits me. *(To the Shepherd.)* By Saint James, if I could find an officer, I'd have you arrested.

THE SHEPHERD: Baa!

PATHELIN: Baa, yourself! May I be hanged if I don't go find me a good policeman! and misfortune seize him if he doesn't throw you in jail.

THE SHEPHERD *(running away):* If he finds me, I'll give him a full pardon.

Appendix
Narrative and Discoursive Semiotics

The foregoing essay reflects my considerable indebtedness to certain theoretical works in semiotics, most of which have appeared within the past fifteen years. Given the rather circumscribed focus of my investigation, it would have been disruptive to include within the course of the study lengthy excurses on the theoretical background of these relatively recent concepts. Throughout I have attempted to provide a modicum of theoretical and technical background, so as not to lose my reader in some massive conceptual undertow, while at the same time avoiding undue ripples and eddies in the flow of the discussion. In the interest of further assisting readers yet unfamiliar with the developments in semiotics evoked in the preceding pages, I am including here a few brief indications regarding terminology and bibliography, with the hope that they may be of use either in providing further clarification of my analyses or, better still, in pointing out some of the important contributions to semiotic theory. An exhaustive bibliographical apparatus is impossible here, and listing is restricted to a handful of writings by semioticians whose works have been the most useful to me as a literary specialist in developing my approach to the problematics of deceit.

In the latter effort, I have occasionally attempted to adapt or to refine theoretical perspectives in the light of insights that occurred to me along the way. Semiotics lends itself to this sort of specialized use of its resources as an accessory to research in other disciplines, though not always without the possibility that impurities with regard to antecedent theory might find their way into the analysis. The theoretical background evoked here is thus an approximation only of my point of departure, and I take full responsibility for any subsequent detours from the theoretical trails blazed by others.

All studies referred to below are keyed by initials and page numbers in brackets to a bibliographical listing at the end of this Appendix. Many other contributions to semiotics are included throughout the footnotes to this essay.

The introductory chapter earmarks for analysis the "figures of deceit" in

Maistre Pierre Pathelin. Figure is understood not merely as an anthropomorphic "character" in the literary sense but as a unique and complex semantic organization of content which may characterize virtually any element of discourse, whether it be situated in characters, actions, milieu, speech, thought, commentary, or the like [*SS*, 25–27; *SNT*, 169–71; *SB*, VI, 2–3]. In later chapters figures are identified and described in proverbs, speech, and types of discourse based on institutions (rhetoric, law, religion, etc.). The study of figures involves analyses of the *form of content* [*SS*, 25–27; *SD*, 22–27].

It is hypothesized that these discoursive figures of deceit, despite the vast array of particular forms their manifestation takes in the play, are all related by some invariant property or properties which make them identifiable as constituents of "deceit." Deceit in this basic sense is not a *comportment*, or behavioral pattern, but a minimally signifying property. This property is hypothetically identified as fundamental to the *classeme* /deceit/. Minimal signifying unities, or *semes*, may combine in the definition of a term *(nuclear semes)*. For example, the word *class* combines, among many others, the semes /plural/, /human/, /instruction/, etcetera, in a pedagogical sense, and /plural/, /human/, /status/, etcetera, in a social sense. On the other hand, a single seme may serve as a classeme to identify generically several discoursive figures as constituents of the same category. Thus, "the wind and the rain in your hair" and "that old devil moon in your eyes" are figures generically related under the classeme /love/. The recurrence of the same classeme or classemes within a given set of figures is known as a semantic level of coherence, or *semantic isotopy*. This classematic redundancy contributes to the coherence of figurative networks running throughout the discourse. In the study, for example, the semantic isotopy created by the redundance of /deceit/ directly relates proverbial figures with those found in the narrative dimension of the play, and these in turn are related to the embedded discourse of the fable narrated by Guillemette [*SS*, 42–116; *ND*, 45–54; *SB*, VII].

At the end of Chapter 1, the elementary structure of /deceit/ is characterized with regard to a *model of veridiction*. This model is established on an opposition of the categories of "Manifestation," concerning that which is "appearing," and of "Immanence," concerning that which is "being," as signified within a given discoursive context. In such a context, a "True" state is one in which Manifestation and Immanence relate positively ("appearing + being"); a "False" state is the negative counterpart of this ("not being + not appearing"); a "Secret" state involves ("being + not appearing"), while the state of the "Delusion or Lie" projects ("appearing + not being"). The latter state is said to obtain in the elementary signification of /deceit/. Our classeme is thus defined differentially with regard to its articulation within this model of veridiction. *Veridiction* concerns the manner in which the discourse-intrinsic category "True" signifies differentially from the other categories in the model. The significance of veridiction with regard to medieval French drama is taken up in Chapter 9 [*SB*, IV, 4–5; *ND*, 131–36; *CD*].

The model of veridiction in Chapter 1, as well as the three medieval dramatic spatial models in Chapter 9, are specialized investments of the *model of the elementary structure of signification*, also known as the "semiotic square" *(carré sémiotique)*. This model represents the relations among minimal unities of signification and is founded on the premise that no term signifies independently since signification in its most elementary form operates on the basis of oppositions and differences. The primordial opposition in the model is created by two semes having a common denominator. Such semes are said to be in a *pertinent* opposition. (If apples and oranges were semes, they would be in a pertinent relationship on the common denominator "fruit," though not on that of "citrus.") The opposition of two pertinent terms (s1, s2) and the projection of the negation of each term (s̄1, s̄2) produces the articulations of the model:

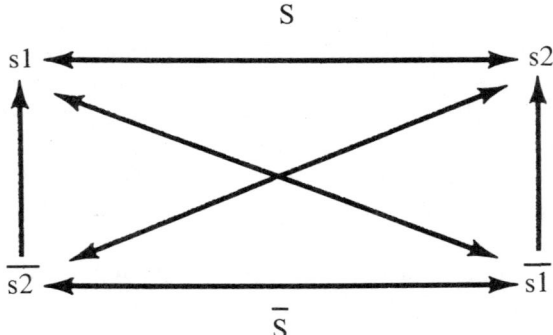

Two *schemas* are created by s1 and s̄1 (or "not s1") and s2 and s̄2, that is, by negating the two terms in pertinent opposition (s1 and s2). The *axis of contraries*, S, describes this initial opposition, while S̄, the *axis of subcontraries*, describes the opposition of the negated terms s̄1 and s̄2. A *deixis* is formed by s1 and s̄2, another by s2 and· s̄1. A relation of implication links the negative term in the deixis (s1 or s̄2) with the term to which its positive counterpart is opposed (s2 or s1). The negation of s1 by s̄1 thus "implies" s2.

As a rudimentary example of the adaptability of the square to a wide variety of logical representations, consider the opposition /A.M./ versus /P.M./, two terms which share the common denominator "temporality." The following articulations obtain:

Appendix: Narrative and Discoursive Semiotics

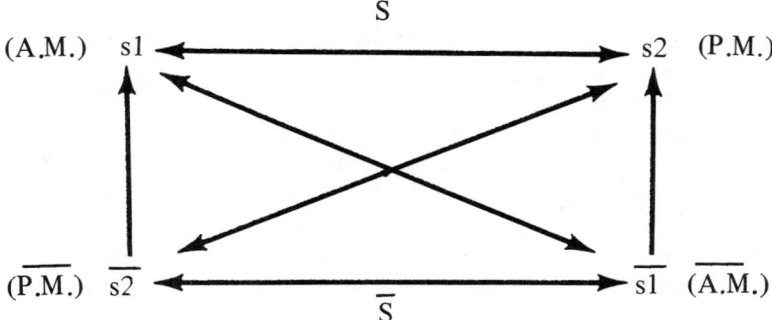

The *semantic axis* S comprehends either A.M. or P.M., or the diurnal temporality of 24 hours. The semantic axis S̄, created by the negated terms s̄2 and s̄1, logically comprehends that which is neither A.M. nor P.M., or Noon and Midnight. Deixis s1s̄2, "A.M. not P.M.," denotes the temporal segment from Midnight to Noon, while deixis s2s̄1 denotes Noon to Midnight. As invested, the model brings out the relations between durative (S) and punctual (S̄) components of diurnal temporality.

Much has been written about how this model functions in the formal representation of signification [*SS*, 18–41; *DS*, 39–48 and esp., 135–55;*L du R*, 81–102; *ND*, 53–60; *SB*, VIII]. Its primary value resides in its usefulness as a means of establishing for a text the pertinent opposition(s) which generate(s) signification. Such is the case with the Greimassian model of veridiction which permits classification of the pertinent categories of /deceit/ and of their relations while anticipating *operations* that occur at various levels of discourse on the basis of this classification. The later spatial models illustrate the *modified* use of the model as a means of describing relations that inhere in types of dramatic discourse.

One of the most prominent types of operation anticipated by the model of veridiction is the *narrativization* of /deceit/ in the elaborate linkage, or *concatenation*, of deceits analyzed in Chapter 2. The narrative dimension of a text, whether it be dramatic, cinematic, balletic, in prose, etc., signifies itself as a series of *states* and the *transformations* linking them [*DS*, 157–83; *L du R*, 11–128; *SD*, 15–145]. Semiotic analysis details the relations between these static and dynamic aspects of narrative by studying the characters and the roles that they play in the succession of transformations between states. Underlying the network of narrative actions, or *functions*, chief among the latter being *deceit* in our corpus, we find a fundamental narrative configuration in which a *subject*, S_1, and an *antisubject*, S_2, vie for an *object of value*, O, which may be either tangible (cloth, food, money, etc.) or abstract (assent, renunciation, submission, etc.). At a given moment in the narrative, S_2 may possess the object desired by S_1 and thus may be said to be in a state of *conjunction* (∩) with it, whereas S_1 is in a state of *disjunction* (∪) from the object. S_1 is thus a potential performer, or *agent*, of the function(s) that will bring him into a state of possession, or conjunction. To the extent that S_2 is a recipient of the performative actions of S_1, S_2 may be termed a *patient* [*L du R*, 131–331]. The transformation effected is in this instance an *exchange* by transfer of the object from patient to agent. The process whereby S_1 realizes this objective is called a *Narrative Program* [*SB, I–V; ND*, 62–100]. In the course of this process, a variety of performative accessories, or *actants*, assume prominence [*SNT*, 161–76]. In addition to the *subject* who, as primary agent, performs a narrative action, there may also be an *addressor* who designates the *addressee* of the *object* of value. The subject may be assisted by an *adjuvant* or hindered by an *adversary*. The *actantial model* represents these roles [*SS*, 172–91; *ND*, 62–69]:

$$\text{ADDRESSOR} \longrightarrow \text{OBJECT} \longrightarrow \text{ADDRESSEE}$$
$$\text{ADJUVANT} \longrightarrow \text{SUBJECT} \longleftarrow \text{ADVERSARY}$$

Because the actantial model defines relations of *narrative syntax* while characters are defined at nonnarrative levels of discourse, the same *actor* may assume more than one actantial role, as when Pathelin, a performative subject in the tribunal scene, is also the addressor of the verdict handed down to the shepherd, its addressee. In this instance, however, Pathelin is the *subject operator* of the narrative program because he manipulatively delegates the performance of the verdict to the judge, whence the following representation of this narrative program:

$$F(S_1) \longrightarrow [S_3 \cup O_1 \longrightarrow S_4 \cap O_1]$$

where F = a performative sequence *(faire)*
 S_1 = Pathelin, the subject operator
 S_3 = the judge
 O_1 = the verdict
 S_4 = the shepherd

As addressor, Pathelin is a subject operator in the *cognitive dimension* of delusive persuasion, while as subject of the principal performance, the judge renders a verdict in the *pragmatic dimension* of "real-world" events. Earlier, in the clothier's stall, Pathelin is the addressee of the cloth as well as the subject operator of the narrative program which entails the deceptive purchase.

To effect the *performance (faire)* of narrative functions, the actant must possess or acquire a performative *competence* made up of *modal values:* will-, obligation-, power-, knowledge-to do *(vouloir-, devoir-, pouvoir-, savoir-faire)*. The *virtualizing modalities* (will-to do, obligation-to do) establish the subject of a given action without as yet determining his capacity to accomplish it.

Virtualizing modalities are often found in the instigative attitudes of the addressor. The *actualizing modalities* (power-to do, know-how-to do) qualify the subject with regard to specific modes of action, such as reliance on ruse (know-how) or brute strength (power). The ultimate *realization modality* (to do) brings the virtualizing and actualizing modalities to bear on the principal performance of the subject operator [*TM; SB*,III]. In the processes of *manipulation* [*D*, 221–22; *SB*, XII] examined in Chapter 7, Pathelin typically occupies the role of addressor whose virtualizing modalities are used to institute the actualizing modalities of an independent subject operator.

This necessarily brief and deliberately simplified digest of important aspects of narrative and discursive semiotics reflected in the foregoing chapters will specify certain of the conceptual bases upon which the analyses were initiated. It will by no means take the place of systematic readings in the selections listed below, notably those by A. J. Greimas. Many of his theoretical principles are applied in his *Maupassant*. The best synthesis of the work of Greimas is that by Joseph Courtés; also especially helpful are illuminating segments entitled "Rudiments d'analyse" in *Sémiotique et Bible.**

Bremond, Claude. *Logique du récit* (Paris: Seuil, 1973). [*L du R*]
Chatman, Seymour. *Story and Discourse: Narrative Structure in Fiction and Film* (Ithaca, N.Y., and London: Cornell University Press, 1978). [*SD*]
Courtés, Joseph. *Introduction à la sémiotique narrative et discursive, méthodologie et application* (Paris: Hachette, 1976). [*ND*]
Greimas, A. J. *Sémantique structurale, recherche de méthode* (Paris: Larousse, 1966). [*SS*]
———. *Du Sens: Essais sémiotiques* (Paris: Seuil, 1970). [*DS*]
———. "Les Actants, les acteurs et les figures," in *Sémiotique narrative et textuelle* (Paris: Larousse, 1973), pp. 161–76. [*SNT*]
———. *Maupassant: La sémiotique du texte: Exercices pratiques* (Paris: Seuil, 1976).
———. "Pour une théorie des modalités," *Langages* 43 (1976): 90–107. [*TM*]
Greimas, A. J., and Courtés, J. "The Cognitive Dimension of Narrative Discourse," *New Literary History* 7 (1976): 433–47. [*CD*]
———. *Sémiotique, dictionnaire raisonné de la théorie du langage* (Paris: Hachette, 1979). [*D*]
Sémiotique et Bible, 1–12 (1976–78). [*SB*] *These segments were later published separately; see Groupe d'Entrevernes. *Analyse sémiotique des textes: Introduction, théorie, pratique* (Lyon: Presses Universitaires de Lyon, 1979).

Notes

List of Abbreviations

In addition to the many journals whose titles are given in full in the notes, the following abbreviations have been used:

CL	Comparative Literature
ECr	L'Esprit Créateur
LR	Langues Romanes
MP	Modern Philology
Neophil	Neophilologus
NLH	New Literary History
PMLA	Publications of the Modern Language Association of America
RN	Romance Notes
RPh	Romance Philology
RR	Romanic Review
RSH	Revue des Sciences Humaines
SMC	Studies in Medieval Culture
SP	Studies in Philology
YFS	Yale French Studies

Preface

1. See Michel Rousse, "'Pathelin' est notre première comédie," *Mélanges de langue et de littérature médiévales offerts à Pierre Le Gentil, professeur à la Sorbonne, par ses collègues, ses élèves et ses amis.* Ed. J. Dufournet and D. Poirion (Paris: S.E.D.E.S. and C.D.U., 1974), pp. 753–58.
2. At least one scholar has attempted to attribute *Pathelin* to Villon. See Jean Deroy, *François Villon, coquillard et auteur dramatique* (Paris: Nizet, 1977).
3. See the useful bibliographic section on *Pathelin* in Halina Lewicka, *Bibliographie du Théâtre profane français des XVe et XVIe siècles* (Paris: Editions du CNRS, 1970), pp. 63–73.
4. A quarrel over the identity of the author pitted L. Cons, R. T. Holbrook, and G. Bonno against M. Roques. See Cons, *L'Auteur de la farce de Pathelin*, Elliott Monographs in the Romance Languages and Literatures, 17 (Princeton, N.J.: Princeton University Press, 1926); R. T. Holbrook, *Guillaume Alecis et Pathelin* (Berkeley: University of California Press, 1928); M. Roques, "D'une application du calcul des probabilités à un problème d'histoire littéraire," *Romania* 58 (1932): 88–89; R. T. Holbrook, "La paternité de Pathelin: critiques et réponses. La première réfutation logique du calcul des probabilités appliqué à la solution du problème," *Romania* 58 (1932): 544–99; G. Bonno, "Réponse critique," *RR* 24 (1933): 30–36. M. Roques replies to Bonno in *Romania* 61 (1935): 308.
5. Daniel Poirion, "Ecriture et ré-écriture au Moyen Age," *Littérature* 41 (1981): 118.
6. For an early study of Pathelin's "tongues", see L.-E. Chevaldin, *Les Jargons de la farce de Pathelin* (Paris: Fontemoing, 1903).

Chapter One. Semiopathelin

1. Augustine identifies Cain, the eldest son of Adam and Eve, as the founder of the first city (15.1) and as a prototype of Romulus, who slew his brother, Remus, to enjoy alone the glory of founding Rome (15.5).

2. Vv. 86; 1591. The edition in use throughout this study is that of Richard T. Holbrook, *Maistre Pierre Pathelin*, CFMA, 35 (Paris: Champion, 1963).

3. See D. W. Robertson, Jr., "The Doctrine of Charity in Mediaeval Literary Gardens: A Topical Approach through Symbolism and Allegory," *Speculum* 26 (1951): p. 24–49. Robertson asserts that a fundamental precept of the medieval exegetical tradition established notably by St. Augustine in *De doctrina Christiana* is the "aim of Scripture to promote Charity and to condemn cupidity. . . ." (p. 24). If not explicit in Scripture, this aim may be disclosed through allegorical interpretation. Robertson maintains "that mediaeval literary authors frequently share the primary aim of Scripture, to promote Charity and to condemn its opposite, cupidity" (p. 25). This view has prompted Robertson and others to examine medieval secular and vernacular works using exegetical methodology. For reservations concerning this approach, see Morton W. Bloomfield, "Symbolism in Medieval Literature," *MP* 56 (1958): 73–81; and Francis Lee Utley, "Robertsonianism Redivivus," *RPh* 19 (1965): 250–60.

4. Umberto Eco, *A Theory of Semiotics* (Bloomington, London: Indiana University Press, 1976), pp. 58–59.

5. Ibid., p. 7.

6. In the context of this study, the term "Figure" is not confined to the designation of anthropomorphic figures, such as "characters" or *personnages*. Rather, it refers to any property or combination of properties, be they narrative, verbal, semantic, etc., that signifies the minimal semantic category /deceit/ as a coherent configuration.

7. See "La Farce de 'Maistre Pierre Pathelin' et son originalité," in *Mélanges de littérature comparée et de philologie offerts à Miczyslaw Brahmer*, ed. R. Brandwajn et al. (Warsaw: PWN–Editions Scientifiques de Pologne, 1967), pp. 207–17.

8. Cited by Michel Rousse, in "'Pathelin' est notre première comédie," p. 754, from Estienne, *Deux dialogues du nouveau langage françois italianizé*. Ed. P. Ristelhuber (Paris, 1883), 1:195.

9. This view of the play's contrast with contemporaneous farce is widespread. For example, in *Le Théâtre médiéval, profane et comique* (Paris: Larousse, 1975), pp. 151–56, Jean-Claude Aubailly argues that *Pathelin*, alone among its contemporaries, prefigures later psychological comedy and says that "son intrigue repose entièrement sur la psychologie des personnages." For a similar usage of "gentile" in a late medieval text, see Paul Zumthor, *La Masque et la lumière, la poétique des Grands Rhétoriqueurs* (Paris: Seuil, 1978), p. 19.

10. See the discussion of pertinent basic concepts in E. R. Curtius, *European Literature and the Latin Middle Ages*, trans. W. R. Trask (New York: Harper, 1963), pp. 68–71. For an illustration of *invention* in the *Prison amoureuse* of Froissart, see Douglas Kelly, *Medieval Imagination: Rhetoric and the Poetry of Courtly Love* (Madison: University of Wisconsin Press, 1978), pp. 156–60.

11. In "The Author in the Text: The Prologues of Chrétien de Troyes," *YFS* 51 (1974): 26–41, esp. pp. 32–33, Marie-Louise Ollier summarizes scholarship on Chrétien's use of the term and proposes the definition (cited in my own translation).

12. See D. W. Robertson, Jr., "Some Medieval Literary Terminology, with Special Reference to Chrétien de Troyes," *SP* 48 (1951): 669–92. More useful are: Douglas Kelly, "The Source and Meaning of 'Conjointure' in Chrétien's *Erec* 14," *Viator* 1 (1970): 179–200; and Ollier, p. 30.

13. See the useful synthesis by Joseph Courtés, *Introduction à la sémiotique narrative et discursive: Méthodologie et application* (Paris: Hachette, 1976). See also the appendix at the end of this study.

14. Vladimir Propp, *Morphologie du conte*, trans. M. Derrida et al. (Paris: Seuil, 1970), pp. 7-8; Alan Dundes, in *The Morphology of North American Indian Folktales*, Folklore Fellows Communications, no. 195 (Helsinki: Academia Scientiarum Fennica, 1964), adheres to this view of "morphology." For a critique of Proppian "morphology," see A. J. Greimas, "Les Acquis et les projets," in Courtés, *Introduction*, pp. 5–25.

15. A. J. Greimas and J. Courtés, "The Cognitive Dimension of Narrative Discourse," *NLH* 7 (1976): 433–47.

16. Ibid., pp. 438–39; 441–42.

17. Ibid., p. 440.

Chapter Two. Infrapathelin, the Deceived Deceiver

1. Substantial portions of this chapter were previously published in an article entitled "The Morphology of Mischief in *Maistre Pierre Pathelin*," *ECr* 18 (1978): 55–68, in a special issue on *Medieval Poetics and Semiotic Theory*, ed. D. Maddox and S. Sturm-Maddox. I wish to thank the editor of *L'Esprit Créateur* for permission to use material from that article in this chapter.

2. This tripartite conceptualization of literary discourse is discussed at length by Tzvetan Todorov in *Quest-ce que le structuralisme? 2. Poétique* (Paris: Seuil, 1973), pp. 29–91.

3. See Claude Bremond, "Le Message narratif," *Communications* 4 (1964): 4 and, by the same author, *Logique du récit* (Paris: Seuil, 1973). Bremond focuses primarily on narrative form, while in *Narrative Discourse: An Essay in Method*, trans. E. Lewin (Ithaca, N.Y., and London: Cornell University Press, 1978), Gérard Genette scrutinizes many aspects of the form and substance of content in narrative.

4. Seymour Chatman, *Story and Discourse: Narrative Structure in Fiction and Film* (Ithaca, N.Y., and London: Cornell University Press, 1978), esp. pp. 22–26: "Is Narrative a Semiotic Structure?"

5. Chatman represents the four-term conceptualization schematically, p. 26. See also Courtés, *Introduction*, pp. 38–43.

6. Vladimir Propp, *Morphologie du conte suivi de Les Transformations des contes merveilleux*, trans. M. Derrida et al. (Paris: Seuil, 1970). See the critical reappraisal of Proppian "morphology" by A. J. Greimas in Joseph Courtés, *Introduction à la sémiotique narrative et discursive: Méthodologie et application* (Paris: Hachette, 1976), Préface [by A.J.G.], pp. 5–25.

7. Cf. Roland Barthes, *S/Z* (Paris; Seuil, 1970), p. 9: Development of a grammar of narrative is a "tâche épuisante . . . et finalement indésirable, car le texte y perd sa différence."

8. *Structure and Sacring: The Systematic Kingdom in Chrétien's "Erec et Enide"* (Lexington, Ky.: French Forum, 1978), pp. 75–177. Cf. Chatman, *Story and Discourse*, pp. 10–11.

9. Patrice Pavis, *Problèmes de sémiologie théâtrale* (Montreal: Les Presses de l'Université du Québec, 1976), p. 72. In her approach to the analysis of drama, Danielle Kaisergruber details a "semiotic procedure" involving initial study of the syntagmatic concatenation of statements, followed by consideration of "the levels of semantic coherence" or *isotopies,* and of how syntagmatic and semantic elements interact. "Reading and Producing Theater," *Sub-Stance* 18/19 (1977): 163–71.

10. Greimas and Courtés, "The Cognitive Dimension of Narrative Discourse," pp. 441–42.

11. Michel Rousse, "Le Rythme d'un spectacle médiéval: *Maître Pierre Pathelin* et la farce," in *Misions et démarches de la critique: Mélanges offerts au Professeur J. A. Vier* (Paris: Klincksieck, 1973), pp. 575–81.

12. Bremond, *Logique du récit*, p. 32.

13. See T. Pavel, *La Syntaxe narrative des tragédies de Corneille: Recherches et propositions* (Paris: Klincksieck, 1976), p. 17.

14. Cf. Philippe Hamon, "Pour un statut sémiologique du personnage," in *Poétique du récit* (Paris: Seuil, 1977), pp. 115–80.

15. Stith Thompson, *The Folktale* (New York: Dryden Press, 1946), Ch. 3, "The Trickster Cycle," pp. 319–28.

16. Greimas and Courtés, "The Cognitive Dimension," p. 442.

17. Cf. A. J. Greimas, "Pour une théorie de l'interprétation du récit mythique," in *Du Sens: Essais sémiotiques* (Paris: Seuil, 1970), pp. 185–230.

18. Exemplary discussions are found in Todorov, *Qu'est-ce que le structuralisme? 2.*, pp. 67–85; and Gerald Prince, *A Grammar of Stories: An Introduction* (The Hague and Paris: Mouton, 1973).

19. Greimas, "Pour une theorie," p. 198.

Chapter Three. Paremiopathelin the Sententious

1. Indeed, the proverb is structurally akin to phrases that occur in the topos of "the world upside down." See E. R. Curtius, *European Literature and the Latin Middle Ages*, trans. W. R. Trask (New York: Harper, 1963), pp. 94–98.

2. Cf. Paul Zumthor, "L'Epiphonème proverbial," *RSH* 41 (1976): 324: "Un proverbe

constitue un micro-discours narratif, comportant actants, fonctions et transformations, dénommés et dé-temporalisés, offerts à tout investissement de valeur qui n'en modifierait pas la structure profonde."

3. Hans Robert Jauss identifies the proverb as the shortest form of the series of nine "little genres" that "form a specifically medieval system of literary communication." See "The Alterity and Modernity of Medieval Literature," *NLH* 10 (1979): 217–18. For a useful bibliography of paremiological studies, with emphasis on medieval literature, see Claude Buridant, "Sélection bibliographique: Etudes sur les proverbes," *RSH* 41 (1976): 432–36. For proverbs in French literature and a selected bibliography, see Grace Frank and Dorothy Miner, *Proverbes en rimes* (Baltimore, Md.: Johns Hopkins University Press, 1937), Introduction and pp. 85–86.

4. Cited by Grace Frank in "Proverbs in Medieval Literature," *MLN* 58 (1943): 508.

5. Ibid., pp. 514–15.

6. See David Heft, *Proverbs and Sentences in Fifteenth-Century French Poetry* (New York: New York University Press, 1942). For proverbial elements in the poetry of the Grands Rhétoriqueurs, see Paul Zumthor, *Le Masque et la lumière: La Poétique des Grands Rhétoriqueurs* (Paris: Seuil, 1978), pp. 152–60.

7. M. Le Roux de Lincy, *Le Livre des proverbes français précédé de recherches historiques sur les proverbes français et leur emploi dans la littérature du Moyen Age et de la Renaissance* (Paris: Delahaye, 1859), "Proverbes cités dans *Maistre Pierre Pathelin*," pp. 499–500. On the problems of identifying proverbs in medieval texts, see Marie-Louis Ollier, "Proverbe et sentence: Le Discours d'autorité chez Chrétien de Troyes," *RSH* 41 (1976): 329–57; Jacqueline and Bernard Cerquiglini, "L'Ecriture proverbiale," *RSH* 41 (1976): 359–75; Claude Buridant, "Nature et fonction des proverbes dans les *Jeux-Partis*," *RSH* 41 (1976): pp. 377–418; Henri Meschonnic, "Les Proverbes, actes de discours," *RSH* 41 (1976): 419–29; as well as the article by Zumthor cited in note 2 this chapter.

8. Thus Jean Paulhan provides examples of "armatures common to an entire family of proverbs," in "L'Expérience du proverbe," *Commerce* 5 (1925): 25–77. A. J. Greimas cites archaic features and binary rythmic and semantic structures as elements commonly found in proverbs. See *Du Sens* (Paris: Seuil, 1970), "Proverbes et dictons," pp. 309–14. Drawing on the work of earlier studies, Buridant proposes useful internal criteria for determining proverbial types, traits of specification and classification, and the mode of insertion in the discourse. See "Nature et fonction," pp. 391–402.

9. Grace Frank, "Pathelin," *MLN* 56 (1941): 42–47. In fact, Henri Estienne attributes *pathelin* and *patheliner* to the farce. See *Deux dialogues du nouveau langage françois italianizé*, ed. P. Ristelhuber (Paris, 1883), 1: 195–96.

10. According to Zumthor, the proverb either "confirms" or "derides" the text in which it is cited (*Masque*, p. 153). As reflexive micro-narrative, it prefigures some of the more recent types of *mise en abyme* discussed by Lucien Dällenbach in *Le Récit spéculaire: Essai sur la mise en abyme* (Paris: Seuil, 1977).

11. A. K. Zolkovskij discusses the "paremiological model" developed by G. L. Permjakov as it applies to the analysis of poetic and cultural content in proverbs, in "At the Intersection of Linguistics, Paremiology and Poetics: On the Literary Structure of Proverbs," *Poetics* 7 (1978): 309–32; bibliography, pp. 331–32.

12. "Le proverbe fonctionne comme un embrayeur référant expressément le texte à l'intertexte, intégrant de façon manifeste l'un à l'autre" (Zumthor, *Masque*, p. 160).

13. Le Roux de Lincy, *Livre des proverbes français* 1: 190. In his edition of the *Pathelin*, p. 126, Holbrook misquotes the proverb and thus erroneously assumes that the version in the play is an "inversion" of its prototype.

14. As in the proverb, "Faire voir à quelqu'un son béjaune. . . . C'est lui montrer qu'il manque d'expérience ou de savoir. Un *bec-jaune*, et, par ellipse, *béjaune*, est un oiseau qui n'est pas encore en âge de nicher; ce que l'on reconnaît à la partie membraneuse du bec, qui est restée jaune." M. de la Mésangère, *Dictionnaire des proverbes français* (Paris: Crepelet, 1823), p. 85.

15. See the examples from the *Yvain* of Chrétien de Troyes in Ollier, "Proverbe et sentence," p. 345.

16. Buridant, "Nature et fonction," p. 378 and *passim*.

17. Mario Roques, "Notes sur *Maistre Pierre Pathelin:* I. Manger de l'oie," *Romania* 57 (1931): 548–60.

18. Larry S. Crist, "Pathelinian Semiotics: Elements for an Analysis of *Maistre Pierre Pathelin*," *ECr* 18 (1978): pp. 69–81.
19. See Archer Taylor, *The Proverb and an Index to the Proverb* (Hatboro, Pa.: Folklore Associates, 1962), p. 27, who cites Greek, Aramaic-Syriac, Hebrew, and Old English terms. See also Harlan Sturm, ed., *The Libro de los Buenos Proverbios* (Lexington, Ky.: University of Kentucky Press, 1970), p. 23, for multiple Spanish terms that designate "proverb" (e.g., *palabra, proverbio, fablilla, fabliella*, etc.). Jauss, "Alterity," p. 215, includes both fable and proverb among little genres of the exemplary.
20. Taylor, *The Proverb*, pp. 27–32.
21. See Grace Frank, *The Medieval French Drama* (Oxford: Clarendon, 1954), p. 246n2; Aubailly, *Théatre médiéval*, "Les proverbes en action," pp. 118–19.
22. Cf. Cerquiglini, "L'Ecriture proverbiale," p. 366; Zumthor, *Masque*, p. 154.
23. Jauss, "Alterity," p. 218.
24. Cerquiglini, "L'Ecriture," pp. 367–69; Buridant, "Nature et fonction," pp. 401–7.
25. See Cerquiglini, "L'Ecriture," p. 367.
26. Zumthor, *Masque*, p. 154, and "L'Epiphonème proverbial," pp. 321–28.

Excursus: The Three Faces of Logopathelin

1. Robert Louis Stevenson, *Memories and Portraits* (London: Chatto & Windus, 1906), "Talk and Talkers," p. 144.
2. Richard T. Holbrook, "Pour le commentaire de *Maistre Pierre Pathelin*, premier article," *Romania* 54 (1928): 66–98; idem, "Commentaires lexicologiques sur certaines locutions françaises médiévales," *Mélanges de linguistique et de littérature offerts à M. Alfred Jeanroy par ses élèves et ses amis* (Paris: Droz, 1928), pp. 181–89; Emmanuel Philipot, "Remarques et conjectures sur le texte de Maistre Pierre Pathelin," *Romania* 56 (1930): 558–84; Omer Jodogne, "Notes sur *Pathelin*," *Festschrift Walter von Wartburg zum 80. Geburtstag. 18 mai 1968* (Tübingen: Niemeyer, 1968), pp. 431–41.

Chapter Four. Pathegyrics, or the Subversive Encomium

1. *Jeux et sapience du Moyen Age*, ed. A Pauphilet (Paris: Gallimard, 1951), p. 471, *Ysopet*, 15: "Du Renard et du corbel."
2. Further on the background of the fable as told by Guillemette in Emmanuel Philipot, "Remarques et conjectures sur let texte de *Maistre Pierre Pathelin*," *Romania* 56 (1930): 568–69.
3. Cited in Frédéric Godefroy, *Dictionnaire de l'ancienne langue française et de tous ses dialectes du IXe au XVe siècle* (Paris, 1880) vol. 1, s.v. "blason," from P. Gringore, *Foll. Entrepr.*, p. 26 (Bibl. Elz.).
4. See Alice Colby, *The Portrait in Twelfth-Century French Literature: An Example of the Stylistic Originality of Chrétien de Troyes* (Geneva: Droz, 1965), pp. 23–88, for a thorough analysis of "the stereotyped content of the twelfth-century portrait."
5. See ibid., pp. 122–69, for examples from the romances of Chrétien de Troyes. See my "Nature and Narrative in Chrétien's *Erec et Enide*," *Mediaevalia* 3 (1977): 59–82, for a study of how the Nature topos is related to the full context of this romance.
6. This pun was first singled out by Jean Frappier, "La Farce de *Maistre Pierre Pathelin* et son originalité," *Mélanges de littérature comparée et de philologie offerts à Miczyslaw Brahmer* (Warsaw: PWN-Editions Scientifiques de Pologne, 1967), p. 211.
7. Edmond Faral, *Recherches sur les sources latines des contes et romans courtois du Moyen Age* (Paris: Champion, 1913), pp. 103–5; and *Les Arts poétiques du XIIe et du XIIIe siècle* (Paris: Champion, 1924), pp. 80–81. But see Colby, *Portrait* p. 6ff., who finds scant evidence that this order is observed in vernacular narrative portraits.
8. In this respect, Pathelin is closer to the type of portraiture discussed in treatises on Latin oratory, where it is a question not only of physical description but of either praise of the virtues or defamation of the vices of an individual. See Colby, *Portrait*, p. 91.
9. See Erich Köhler, *L'Aventure chevaleresque: Idéal et réalité dans le roman courtois* (Paris: Gallimard, 1974), pp. 7–76.

10. Edmund Leach, "Anthropological Aspects of Language: Animal Categories and Verbal Abuse," in Pierre Maranda, ed., *Mythology* (Middlesex, England: Penguin, 1972), pp. 39–67.

11. Colby, *Portrait*, p. 91.

12. Ibid., p. 88.

13. Ibid., p. 90.

14. Ibid., pp. 89–103.

15. In his *Dialogues of the Orators*. See also Tzvetan Todorov, *Théories du symbole* (Paris: Seuil, 1977), pp. 59ff., for a discussion of the decline of oratorical rhetoric.

16. Provided, of course, that we subscribe to the hypothesis of Rita Lejeune concerning the localization of the play. "Pour quel public la farce de *Maistre Pierre Pathelin* a-t-elle été rédigée?" *Romania* 82 (1961): 482–521.

Chapter Five. Thanatopathelin and the Art of Dying

1. For a discussion of forerunners, sources, and authorship, see Sr. Mary Catharine O'Connor, *The Art of Dying Well: The Development of the Ars moriendi* (New York: Columbia University Press, 1942), pp. 11–60. For its place in late medieval popular devotion, see Etienne Delaruelle, *La Piété populaire au Moyen Age* (Turin: Bottega d'Erasmo, 1975), pp. 422–23; 445–48; 457–59; 462.

2. Cited in translation from Emile Mâle, *L'Art religieux de la fin du Moyen Age en France: Etude sur l'iconographie du Moyen Age et ses sources d'inspiration* (Paris: Colin, 1922), p. 381.

3. O'Connor provides a lengthy account of both versions, *Art of Dying Well*, pp. 7–17.

4. The theme of death in late medieval culture has been extensively discussed. See Johan Huizinga, *The Waning of the Middle Ages* (New York: Doubleday, 1954), Ch. 11: "The Vision of Death," pp. 138–51. First published in 1924, this study was frequently cited in subsequent studies of death in the later Middle Ages. See also Mâle, *L'Art religieux* pp. 347–79; Alberto Tenenti, *Il Senso della morte e l'amore della vita nel rinascimento (Francia e Italia)* (Turin: Einaudi, 1957), pp. 21–184; Edelgard Dubruck, *The Theme of Death in French Poetry of the Middle Ages and the Renaissance* (The Hague: Mouton, 1964), pp. 9–99; Joël Saugnieux, *Les Danses macabres de France et d'Espagne et leurs prolongements littéraires* (Lyon: Vitte, 1972), pp. 13–137; T.S.R. Boase, *Death in the Middle Ages: Mortality, Judgment and Remembrance* (New York: McGraw-Hill, 1972), esp. Ch. 5, "The Art of Dying," pp. 118–29; Philippe Ariès, *Western Attitudes toward Death: From the Middle Ages to the Present*, trans. Patricia M. Ranum (Baltimore, Md.: The Johns Hopkins University Press, 1974), pp. 27–52; and Pierre Chaunu, *La Mort à Paris: XVIe, XVIIe et XVIIIe siècles* (Paris: Fayard, 1978), pp. 28–161.

5. Ariès, *Western Attitudes*, says that there was a gradual suppression of "the eschatological time between death and the end of the world . . ." so that the judgment was no longer situated "in space at the Second Coming, but in the bedchamber, around the deathbed" (p. 33). "Thus the great gathering which in the twelfth and thirteenth centuries had taken place on the last day, in the fifteenth century had moved to the sickroom" (p. 34). "God and his court are there to observe how the dying man conducts himself during this trial—a trial he must endure before he breathes his last and which will determine his fate in eternity. This test consists of a final temptation. The dying man will see his entire life as it is contained in the book, and he will be tempted either by despair over his sins, by the 'vainglory' of his good deeds, or by the passionate love for things and persons. His attitude during this fleeting moment will erase at once all the sins of his life if he wards off temptation or, on the contrary, will cancel out all his good deeds if he gives way. The final test has replaced the Last Judgment" (pp. 36–37).

6. See O'Connor, *Art of Dying Well*, for an inventory of extant MSS (pp. 61–112), xylographic editions (pp. 113–33), and editions from movable type (pp. 133–71).

7. Ibid., pp. 1–2 and 172–219. For a useful analysis of the circulation and survival of the *Ars moriendi* and its iconography, see Roger Chartier, "Les Arts de mourir, 1450–1600," *Annales: Economies, Sociétés, Civilisations* 31 (1976): 51–75. See also Chaunu, *La Mort à Paris*, pp. 275–87, for the later development of the treatise.

8. Lucien Febvre and Henri-Jean Martin, *L'Apparition du livre* (Paris: Albin Michel, 1971), p. 362.

9. The juxtaposition of *Pathelin* with the *Faintes du monde* is also noteworthy, for Guillaume Alexis has been proposed as the likely author of the play. See Richard T. Holbrook, *Guillaume*

Alecis et Pathelin (Berkeley: Univ. of California Press, 1928); Louis Cons, *L'Auteur de la farce de Pathelin,* Elliott Monographs in the Romance Languages and Literatures, No. 17 (Princeton, N. J.: Princeton University Press, 1926).

   10. J. L. de Altamira, "La Vision de la mort dans 'Maître Pathelin,' " *Dissonances* 1 (1977): 119–31.

   11. Mâle, *L'Art religieux* p. 388; Febvre and Martin, *L'Apparition* p. 66; Chartier, "Les Arts," p. 53.

   12. According to Henri Zerner in *"L'Art au morier," Revue de l'art* 11 (1971): 7.

   13. Richard T. Holbrook, *Etude sur Pathelin,* Elliott Monographs in the Romance Languages and Literatures, No. 5 (Baltimore, Md.: Johns Hopkins University Press, 1917), pp. 81–92. Cf. Cons, *L'Auteur,* pp. 18–21, who maintains that the play appeared between 1464 and 1469; see also E. Cazalas, "Où et quand se passe l'action de *Maistre Pierre Pathelin,*" *Romania* 57 (1931): 573–77, who, on the basis of monetary values in the play, dates it prior to 1474.

   14. Zerner, "*L'Art au morier,*" pp. 7–30, esp. pp. 11–14. This is known as Edition IB, after the classification of the xylographic editions by Wilhelm Schreiber, in *Manuel de l'amateur de la gravure sur bois et sur métal au XVe siècle* (Berlin, 1911), vol 4, p. 257. See O'Connor, *Art of Dying Well* pp. 124–33, for discussion of this classification.

   15. See Arthur M. Hind, *An Introduction to a History of Woodcut, with a Detailed Survey of Work Done in the Fifteenth Century* (Boston: Houghton Mifflin, 1935), vol. 1, p. 227, though Schreiber says 1465. Cf. Zerner, "*L'Art au morier,*" p. 14.

   16. Zerner, "*L'Art au morier,*" p. 18.

   17. The eleven illustrations conform to a relatively fixed tradition followed by woodcutters and engravers, though iconographic details vary considerably from one designer to another. See, for example, the edition of *L'Art au morier* by Zerner, "*L'Art au morier,*" pp. 18–30, which contains its woodcuts in photographic reproduction, as well as photos of the eleven illustrations of MS. Wellcome 49 and of selected illustrations in other editions.

   18. For an inventory of printed editions of *Pathelin* prior to 1515, including information on illustrations, see Marion de Malaunoy, *Maistre Pierre Pathelin hystorié, reproduction en fac-similé de l'edition imprimée vers 1500,* SATF (Paris: Didot, 1904), pp. 3–11.

   19. The function of Guillemette's comments on the degenerating condition of her spouse will be taken up in the discussion of manipulative strategies and their illocutionary value (Chapter 8).

   20. The same series of woodcuts adorns both the first Latin and first French block-books, editions IA and IB, respectively. The five temptation scenes and the final death scene reproduced here are all from a facsimile edition of IA, housed in the British Museum. See *The Ars moriendi (Editio Princeps, circa 1450). A Reproduction of the Copy in the British Museum.* Ed. W. Harry Rylands, F.S.A. With an Introduction by George Bullen, F.S.A., Keeper of the Printed Books in the British Museum (London: Wyman, 1881). Useful interpretive commentary on the illustrations is provided by Mâle, *L'Art religieux,* pp. 383–88; and O'Connor, *Art of Dying Well,* pp. 115–20.

   21. See the text of *L'Art au morier* in Zerner, "*L'Art au morier,*" p. 20.

   22. Richard T. Holbrook, "Exorcism with a Stole," *MLN* 19 (1904): 235–37; ibid., 20 (1905): 111–15.

   23. See *L'Art au morier,* p. 22, for the text.

   24. See Cons, *L'Auteur,* pp. 32–33; Rita Lejeune, "Pour quel public la farce de *Maistre Pierre Pathelin* a-t-elle été rédigée?" *Romania* 82 (1961): pp. 495–96.

   25. "Le mot *guiterne* est employé ici au figuré et désigne évidemment un personnage féminin de moeurs légères, une 'fille de joie' pour user d'un euphémisme, dont les *guiterneaux* sont les bâtards. . . ." Fabienne Gégou, "Argot et expressions argotiques dans *Maistre Pierre Pathelin,*" *Actes du XIIIe Congrès International de Linguistique et Philologie Romanes* (Quebec: Presses de l'Université Laval, 1976), pp. 691–96.

   26. *L'Art au morier,* p. 19.

   27. Ibid., p. 24, for the accompanying text.

   28. Mâle, *L'Art religieux,* p. 385; O'Connor, *Art of Dying Well,* p. 117.

   29. Jean Frappier and A.-M. Gossart, eds. *Le Théâtre comique au Moyen Age* (Paris: Larousse, 1935), p. 73n3.

   30. Cf. the commentary by Bullen in the introduction to the *Ars moriendi* (ed. IA) facsimile, *The Ars moriendi,* p. 12: "In front of the bedstead, and towards the left of the engraving, is a

full-length figure of a female, handsomely dressed, probably the dying man's daughter, holding in her right hand a plate containing the leg of a goose or a fowl. . . ."

31. *L'Art au morier,* p. 26, contains the accompanying text of IB.

32. Ibid., p. 28.

33. E.g., the caution against allowing the sufferer to recall the past, in *L'Art au morier,* p. 28.

34. Ibid., p. 30.

35. ". . . chacun se doit soingneusement pourveoir dun bon devot sochon feal et ydoine ami qui lui assiste en ceste necessite et conforte a constance de vraie foy pacience. devotion et perseverance lesmouvant et incitant a bon devot corage et adrechement de ceur a dieu la sus sa doulce mere et cetera" (p. 30).

36. "Mais laz on troeve pau de telz qui en la mort ensi feablement assistent et secourrent a leur proximos et amis les interroguans exhortans remonstrant et amonestant a leur darrain salut et perpetuelle saulvacion et pour ce pryent lors et apres ayent oire de pryer et fere pryer come besoingz est par especial quant se morisant ne si adonne et ne veut bonnement encore morir" (p. 30).

37. Emmanuel Philipot, "Remarques et conjectures sur le texte de *Maistre Pierre Pathelin,*" *Romania* 56 (1930): 576.

38. Jean Frappier, "La Farce de 'Maistre Pierre Pathelin' et son originalité," *Mélanges de littérature comparée et de philologie offerts à Miczyslaw Brahmer,* ed. R. Brandwajn et al. (Warsaw: PWN—Editions scientifiques de Pologne, 1967), p. 214.

39. Chartier, "Les Arts," p. 69.

40. The prayers of the *Commendatio animae* are "mostly of early medieval Frankish origin." Gerhard Podhradsky, *New Dictionary of the Liturgy* (London: Chapman, 1966), pp. 125–26. Its liturgical use antedates *Pathelin* by several centuries. See Josef Höfer and Karl Rahner, *Lexikon für Theologie und Kirche* (Freiburg: Herder, 1959), p. 19. The "commendacions" mentioned in *L'Art au morier,* p. 20, most likely refer to this rite.

41. This specialized conceptualization of the "intertext" as a set of properties shared by two texts differs from but in no way challenges the notion of intertext proposed by Michael Riffaterre: "L'intertexte est l'ensemble des textes que l'on peut rapprocher de celui que l'on a sous les yeux, l'ensemble des textes que l'on retrouve dans sa mémoire à la lecture d'un passage donné." "L'intertexte inconnu," *Littérature* 41 (1981): 4–7.

42. See Julia Kristeva, *Le Texte du roman: Approche sémiologique d'une structure discursive transformationnelle* (The Hague/Paris: Mouton, 1970); Paul Zumthor, *Le Masque et la lumière: La Poétique des Grands Rhétoriqueurs* (Paris: Seuil, 1978); Mikhail Bakhtine, *L'Oeuvre de François Rabelais et la culture populaire au Moyen Age et sous la Renaissance* (Paris: Gallimard, 1970).

43. For satirical elements in the *sottie,* see Jean-Claude Aubailly, *Le Monologue, le dialogue et la sottie: Essai sur quelques genres dramatiques de la fin du Moyen Age et du début du XVIe siècle* (Paris: Champion, 1976), pp. 413–42; and, esp., Heather Arden, *Fools' Plays: A Study of Satire in the Sottie* (Cambridge: Cambridge University Press, 1980).

44. J. L. de Altamira, p. 128.

45. This is demonstrated in the semiological analysis of the mercantile systems of coherence by Larry S. Crist, "Pathelinian Semiotics: Elements for an Analysis of *Maistre Pierre Pathelin,*" *ECr* 18 (1978): 69–81.

46. Mâle, *L'Art religieux,* pp. 35–84, surveys what he believes to be the extensive influence of staging in the *Mystères* on late medieval art. See also Grace Frank, "Popular Iconography of the Passion," *PMLA* 46 (1931): pp. 333–40, for 12 plates from Vatican MS Cod. Reg. 473 (late 14th or early 15th c.) that accompany a MS of the Passion and are based on the staging of religious drama. G. R. Kernodle, in *From Art to Theatre, Form and Convention in the Renaissance* (Chicago: Chicago University Press, 1944), inverts the hypothesis of Mâle; the plastic arts would have influenced the visual arts, including the staging of drama. See Elie Konigson, *L'Espace théâtral médiéval* (Paris: Centre National de la Recherche Scientifique, 1975), pp. 231 ff., for a discussion of the relative merits of the two positions.

Chapter Six. Antipathiquelin and the Rhetoric of Torts

1. See R. Howard Bloch, *Medieval French Literature and Law* (Berkeley and Los Angeles: University of California Press, 1977), for a study of epic and courtly works in relation to the

transformation of judicial institutions, with emphasis on trial procedure from the feudal court to the advent of inquisitory judicial systems. For an early literary reflection of feudal succession laws, see my "'E Baldewin mun filz': La Parenté dans la *Chanson de Roland*," *Société Rencesvals: Actes du VIIIe Congrès International* (Pamplona, 1981), pp. 299–304. In the late fifteenth-century *Arrests d'Amour*, Martial d'Auvergne depicts judgments of courtly conduct in terms of juridical procedure.

2. One thinks in particular of the Icelandic sagas, of certain courtly texts in Middle High German, and of numerous medieval English works from the twelfth century and later. For an incisive survey of the latter, see John A. Alford, "Literature and Law in Medieval England," *PMLA* 92 (1977): 941–51.

3. In the opening scene of the play, Figura expresses higher law in terms of specific positive interdictions and prescriptions regarding temporal power, obedience, use of natural resources, and marriage. The relation between God and man is depicted in terms of a contract based on fealty and homage.

4. In the *procès de paradis*, the soul of man is disputed by Lucifer and the Virgin. The figures of Justice, Vérité, Miséricorde, and Paix each enter pleas, and the verdict normally favors the latter two. See exemplary occurrences of this scene in *The Castle of Perseverance* and the *Mystère de la Passion* of Arnoul Gréban. On the Augustinian definition of divine or eternal law, see Alford, "Literature and Law," pp. 942–43.

5. See H. G. Harvey, *The Theatre of the Basoche: The Contribution of the Law Societies to French Mediaeval Comedy* (Cambridge, Mass.: Harvard University Press, 1941). Harvey comments only briefly on the role of judges, lawyers, and law officers in the miracle plays, pp. 5–6, but devotes extended analysis to the moralities, farces, and *sotties*, 1450–1550, that deal more frequently with the law and lawyers, pp. 39–201.

6. H. G. Harvey, "The Judge and the Lawyer in the *Pathelin*," *RR* 31 (1940): 313–33; P. Lemercier, "Les Eléments juridiques de *Pathelin* et la localisation de l'oeuvre," *Romania* 73 (1952): 200–226; Rita Lejeune, "Le Vocabulaire juridique de *Pathelin* et la personnalité de l'auteur," *Fin du Moyen Age et Renaissançe: Mélanges de Philologie Romane offerts à Robert Guiette* (Antwerp, 1961), pp. 185–94; idem, "Pour quel public la farce de *Maistre Pierre Pathelin* a-t-elle été rédigée?" *Romania* 82 (1961): 482–521.

7. Harvey, "The Judge," p. 316 and *passim*. See also *The Theatre of the Basoche*, pp. 145–71.

8. These matters have been extensively, though inconclusively, debated in the previously cited articles by Harvey, Lemercier, and Lejeune.

9. A. J. Greimas, en collaboration avec Eric Landowski, "Analyse sémiotique d'un discours juridique," in A. J. Greimas, *Sémiotique et sciences sociales* (Paris: Seuil, 1976), pp. 79–128. Although the juridical discourse analyzed pertains to modern aspects of commercial law, the article deals with general characteristics of juridical discourse. As we shall see, certain of these observations are pertinent even to late medieval statutory law and judicial procedures.

10. Ibid., p. 92.

11. On the development of inquisitory procedures in medieval law, see R. H. Bloch, *Medieval French Literature* pp. 108–61.

12. Greimas and Landowski, "Analyse sémiotique," pp. 90–91.

13. In "Literature and Law in Medieval England," p. 948, Alford says that negative portrayals of officers of the law in late medieval English literature reflect the anxiety generated by this productive aspect of legal verification: "At bottom, the problem was not the officers of the law—they were simply the most visible and convenient targets—but rather the stress and strain exerted upon the traditional view of justice and morality by the slow, shifting movement of a legal system bound to discover and implement, case by case, its own inherent logic."

14. Greimas and Landowski, "Analyse sémiotique," p. 94.

15. Lejeune, "Vocabulaire juridique," p. 189.

16. R. T. Holbrook, ed., *Pathelin*, p. 118.

17. Lemercier, "Eléments," p. 206.

18. Ibid., pp. 206–7.

19. R. T. Holbrook, ed., *Pathelin*, p. 112; Lejeune, "Vocabulaire," p. 190, reads this expression as a desire on the part of the shepherd to secure an out-of-court settlement. In context, however, the shepherd is offering to pay the lawyer to find a legal technicality *(clause)* that will ensure a decision in favor of the defendant.

20. Lejeune, "Vocabulaire," p. 191: "Suivons encore Littré: 'en termes de droit, *absoudre* et

acquitter ne sont pas synonymes. Le tribunal absout une personne qui est reconnue coupable du délit à elle imputée, mais dont le délit n'est pas qualifié punissable par la loi. Il acquitte un accusé reconnu innocent.'"

21. Lejeune, "Vocabulaire," p. 186: ALOUÉ: personne liée par un contrat de louage de services; cf. Holbrook, ed., *Pathelin*, p. 112; and Lemercier, "Eléments," p. 206.

22. Greimas and Landowski, "Analyse sémiotique," p. 88, single out this syntactic structure as fundamental to juridical grammar, which in their view gives priority to correct formation of utterances while neglecting the taxonomy of categories with which they are invested. This, of course, was a critique also leveled at the medieval ordeal predicated upon an oath.

23. H. G. Harvey, "The Judge," p. 321.

24. Lemercier, "Eléments," p. 206n1.

25. On the production of truth and veridictory criteria in discourse, see A. J. Greimas and Joseph Courtés, "The Cognitive Dimension of Narrative Discourse," *NLH* 7 (1976): pp. 443–47.

26. *La Chanson de Roland*, éd. G. Moignet (Paris: Bordas, 1969), vv. 3742–974.

27. On Augustinian views and medieval law, see Alford, "Literature and Law," pp. 942–44.

28. Thomas d'Angleterre, *Le Roman de Tristan*, éd. J. Bédier (Paris: SATF, 1903 and 1905), 2 vols.

29. Cf. R. H. Bloch, *Medieval French Literature*, pp. 108–61.

30. Alford, "Literature and Law," pp. 948–49.

31. The possible prototypes are set forth in the articles, cited above, by Harvey and Lemercier.

32. Alexander Fischler suggests that "a series of veiled Biblical allusions [anticipate] the conclusion in the triumph of the true Shepherd to follow that of the thieving Agnelet." The discrepancy between fallible human judgment and ultimate divine justice—on Judgment Day—is indeed a possible reading of the farce, though the alleged Biblical "allusions" are tenuous and not at all necessary to convey this view. See "The Theme of Justice and the Structure of *La Farce de Maistre Pierre Pathelin*," *Neophil* 53 (1969): 261–73.

Chapter Seven. Manipathulin, the Delusive Persuader

1. Latin *manipulus* ("handful"), from *manus* ("hand"), subtends French *manipule* (1380), meaning: I. A band of cloth worn on the left forearm by the celebrant of Mass (1380); II. A handful of plants or grains used in the composition of remedies (16th c.); III. Primitive insignia of a military company, or tactical unit of the Roman army (17th c.). From the second, pharmaceutical sense of *manipule* derives French manipulation (1716) and *manipuler* (1765), meaning: I. To work with the hands (substances) or to operate (devices); used in chemistry, physics, technology, or pharmaceutics. [Paul Robert, *Dictionnaire alphabétique et analogique de la langue française* (Paris: Société du Nouveau Littré, 1966), vol. 4, p. 260].

2. For a popular survey of "subliminal" manipulation in media, see Vance Packard, *The Hidden Persuaders* (New York: McKay, 1957). The same author explores eugenics and behavior modification in *The People Shapers* (Boston: Little, Brown, 1977).

3. The figurative and pejorative sense of "manipulation," meaning a maneuver aiming to deceive, is first documented in French in 1872: "La comédie des manipulations électorales" (Gautier). *Grand Larousse de la langue française en sept volumes* (Paris: Larousse, 1975), vol. 4, p. 3214. For an excellent study of early Romance usage of the term, see Germán Colón, "*Manipulation*, mot à la mode et hispanisme," *Mélanges de langues et de littératures romanes offerts à Carl Théodor Gossen*, ed. G. Colón and R. Kopp (Bern: Francke Verlag; Liège: Marche Romane, 1976), pp. 155–68.

4. A more systematic effort is reflected in the interdisciplinary Congress of European Moralists on the subject of manipulation held at the University of Strasbourg in 1973, with perspectives from philosophy and theology, as well as from the biological and social sciences. See the proceedings in Charles Robert, ed., *L'Homme manipulé: Pouvoir de l'homme sur l'homme, ses chances et ses limites, Recherches européennes, Strasbourg 24–29 septembre 1973*, Université des Sciences Humaines de Strasbourg, Hommes et Eglise, 6 (Strasbourg: CERDIC Publications, 1974). Included in the proceedings is a 240-item bibliographical inventory of related studies, 1970–73, with emphasis on bioethical problems as well as on human manipulation in general.

5. For a general account of the Greimas seminar of 1976–77, see Diana Luz Pessoa de

Barros, "Vers une sémiotique de la manipulation," in *Le Bulletin du Groupe Greimas*, I (1977), pp. 1–13; in the same issue: "Sémiotique de la manipulation et sémiotique des passions," a synthesis by A. J. Greimas on the occasion of a seminar presentation by Umberto Eco, pp. 11–13. For a literary application of the model, see J. Fontanille, D. Pessoa de Barros, J. Sacré, and F. Thurlemann, "La Fontaine et la manipulation: Analyse de la fable 'Le Dépositaire infidèle,'" in *Le Bulletin du Groupe Greimas*, II–III (1978), pp. 24–30. See also the useful article, "Manipulation," in A. J. Greimas and J. Courtés, *Sémiotique: Dictionnaire raisonné de la théorie du langage* (Paris: Hachette université, 1979), pp. 220–22.

6. Pessoa de Barros, "Vers une sémiotique," p. 4. See also Greimas and Courtés, *Dictionnaire*, p. 221.

7. On "operation," a "making to be," as opposed to "manipulation," a "making to do," see Greimas and Courtés, *Dictionnaire*, under "Opération" and p. 220.

8. Pessoa de Barros, "Vers une sémiotique," pp. 5–6; Greimas and Courtés, *Dictionnaire*, p. 221.

9. Cognitive persuasive tactics are characteristic of provocation and seduction, while pragmatic tactics, such as the offer of gifts or threats, typify temptation and intimidation, respectively. See Pessoa de Barros, "Vers une sémiotique," pp. 6–7; Greimas and Courtés, *Dictionnaire*, p. 221.

10. Pessoa de Barros, "Vers une sémiotique," pp. 4–5; Greimas and Courtés, *Dictionnaire*, pp. 220–21.

11. Pessoa de Barros, "Vers une sémiotique," pp. 5–6.

12. Ibid., pp. 7–8; Greimas and Courtés, *Dictionnaire*, p. 221.

Chapter Eight. Illocupathelin, Speech Actor

1. J. L. Austin, in *How to Do Things with Words* (Oxford: Oxford University Press, 1962), identified "illocutionary", or speech, acts as utterances that perform a specific function in addition to reference and predication, such as asserting, questioning, commanding, expressing a wish or a desire, etc. He maintained that the English language contains more than a thousand such utterances. As we shall see in this chapter, it is an "illocutionary force" which ensures that Pathelin may portray, plead and "perish" successfully, i.e., deceptively.

2. John R. Searle, *Speech Acts: An Essay in the Philosophy of Language* (Cambridge: Cambridge University Press, 1969), p. 78.

3. See Richard Ohmann, "Speech Acts and the Definition of Literature," *Philosophy and Rhetoric* 4 (1971): 1–19, who observes that "a literary work is discourse abstracted, or detached, from the circumstances and conditions which make illocutionary acts possible—hence it is a discourse without illocutionary force" (p. 13). "A literary work is a discourse whose sentences lack the illocutionary forces that would normally attach to them. Its illocutionary force is mimetic" (p. 14). In fiction, then, represented speech acts mime the conventional social context of communication.

4. "The illocutionary force indicator shows how the proposition is to be taken, or . . . what illocutionary act the speaker is performing in the utterance of the sentence." Searle, *Speech Acts*, p. 30.

5. Umberto Eco, *A Theory of Semiotics* (Bloomington and London: Indiana University Press, 1976), p. 156.

6. As in Edward T. Hall, *The Silent Language* (New York: Doubleday, 1959).

7. Anne Ubersfeld, *Lire le théâtre*, Classiques du peuple, "Critique" (Paris: Editions Sociales, 1978), p. 257.

8. John Searle, "A Classification of Illocutionary Acts," *Language in Society* 5 (1976): 1–23; idem, "A Taxonomy of Illocutionary Acts," *Language, Mind, and Knowledge*, Minnesota Studies in the Philosophy of Science, 7. Ed. K. Gunderson (Minneapolis: University of Minnesota Press, 1975), pp. 344–69.

9. Michael Hancher, "Beyond a Speech Act Theory of Literary Discourse," *MLN* 92 (1977): 1087.

10. Searle, *Speech Acts*, p. 67.

11. Ibid., pp. 50–53.

12. P. Lemercier, "Les Eléments juridiques de *Pathelin* et la localisation de l'oeuvre," *Romania* 73 (1952): 204.

13. Lemercier, "Elèments," p. 204, says that the *engagement par la foi* took two forms, the *serment* and the *paumée*. Pathelin would seem to be familiar with varieties of these gestures in use in mercantile fairs.

14. Searle, *Speech Acts*, pp. 54–61.

15. Searle excludes "parasitic forms of communication such as . . . acting in a play" (ibid., p. 57). However, we are considering the speech act *within* the play as an autonomous mimetic replica of communication. For a discussion of the limitations and problems presented by this approach, which is commonly taken by those who apply speech act theory in literary studies, see Martha Woodmansee, "The Dogma of Literary Autonomy," and Joseph Margolis, "Literature and Speech Acts," both unpublished papers delivered at the workshop on Speech Act Theory of the Modern Language Association Annual Convention, December 26–29, 1978.

16. Searle, *Speech Acts*, p. 62.

17. See Mary Louise Pratt, *Toward a Speech Act Theory of Literary Discourse* (Bloomington: Indiana University Press, 1977), p. 80.

18. Searle, *Speech Acts*, p. 62.

19. See vv. 642–47, and Omer Jodogne, "Notes sur *Pathelin*," *Festschrift Walter von Wartburg zum 80. Geburtstag. 18. mai 1968*, ed. K. Baldinger (Tübingen: Niemeyer, 1968), pp. 440–41.

20. The very name of Pathelin's spouse signifies deceit, *guille* being synonymous with "tromperie, superchérie." Godefroy and Greimas list numerous instances of *guiler* and *guile* from as early as the twelfth century. Likewise, Guillaume may connote an individual who is vulnerable to deceit, as it does in v. 772: "Et tient il les gens pour Guillaumes?" (cf. vv. 389; 996). On the literary analysis of proper names, see Michel Grimaud, "Hermeneutics, Onomastics, and Poetics in English and French Literature," *MLN* 92 (1977): 888–921.

21. Searle, *Speech Acts*, p. 66.

22. Cf. ibid., p. 45.

23. Ibid., pp. 44–45.

24. See Eco, *A Theory of Semiotics*, pp. 54–57.

25. H. P. Grice, "Logic and Conversation," in *Speech Acts, Syntax and Semantics*, 3, ed. Peter Cole and Jerry L. Morgan (New York: Academic Press, 1975), pp. 41–58. Grice establishes conversational maxims that make ordinary verbal communication timely, informative, correct, relevant, unambiguous, etc. Deliberate violation of any of these maxims may communicate by implication more than is literally being said, sometimes to produce effects of irony, metaphor, understatement, etc. For a discussion of Gricean implicatures and literary analysis, see "Grice through the Looking Glass" and "Grice's 'Implicature' and Literary Interpretation: A Synopsis," both unpublished papers by Michael Hancher delivered at the Workshop on Speech Act Theory of the Modern Language Association Annual Convention, December 26–29, 1978.

26. See Eco, p. 55.

27. See Emmanuel Philipot, "Remarques et conjectures sur le texte de *Maistre Pierre Pathelin*," *Romania* 56 (1930): 575–76.

28. Searle, *Speech Acts*, p. 25.

29. As Jean Frappier suggested, in "La Farce de *Maistre Pierre Pathelin* et son originalité," ed. R. Brandwajn et al. *Mélanges de littérature comparée et de philologie offerts à Miczyslaw Brahmer* (Warsaw: PWN—Editions Scientifiques de Pologne, 1967), p. 214.

30. On the notion of "surplus of signifier," see Fredric Jameson, *The Prison-House of Language: A Critical Account of Structuralism and Russian Formalism* (Princeton, N.J.: Princeton University Press, 1972), pp. 132–33.

31. Cf. Claude Lévi-Strauss, *Anthropologie structurale* (Paris: Plon, 1958), p. 211: "Le texte que nous avons analysé apporte une contribution exceptionnelle à la solution du problème. [The text being from the Cuna Indians of Panama.] Il constitue une médication purement psychologique, puisque le chaman ne touche pas au corps du malade et ne lui administre pas de remède; mais en même temps, il met directement et explicitement en cause l'état pathologique et son siège: nous dirions volontiers que le chant constitue une *manipulation psychologique* de l'organe malade, et que c'est de cette manipulation que la guérison est attendue." Contrast with this shamanistic cure the effects of psychiatric manipulation: "Nous retrouvons . . . la notion de manipulation, qui nous avait paru essentielle à l'intelligence de la cure chamanique,

mais dont nous voyons que la définition traditionnelle doit être très élargie; car c'est tantôt une manipulation d'idées, et tantôt une manipulation des organes, la condition commune restant qu'elle se fasse à l'aide de symboles, c'est-à-dire d'équivalents significatifs du signifié, relevant d'un autre ordre de réalité que ce dernier."

Chapter Nine. Protopathelin: The Medieval Dramatic Heritage of Deceit

1. Cf. Greimas and Courtés, "The Cognitive Dimension of Narrative Discourse," p. 441: "It goes without saying that the four categorial terms [True, False, Secret, Delusion] can be defined as such only within discourse: the problem of truth, as we treat it here, is totally independent of an *external designatum* [*référant*]. By that, we mean that from a semiotic point of view the narrative establishes its own 'intrinsic truth'. . . ."

2. Roland Barthes, "L'Effet de réel," *Communications* 11 (1968): 84–89. This effect fosters understanding of represented reality as a fiction. Cf. Roman Ingarden, "The Functions of Language in the Theatre," in *The Literary Work of Art*, trans. G. C. Gaborowicz (Evanston, Ill.: Northwestern University Press, 1973), pp. 377–96. See also Jiri Veltrusky: "In the theatre . . . the action is an end in itself and lacks an external practical purpose. . . . its purpose is a semiological matter and not a matter of practical life." "Man and Object in the Theatre," in *A Prague School Reader*, ed. P. L. Garvin (Washington, D.C.: Georgetown University Press, 1964), p. 84.

3. Patrice Pavis, *Problèmes de sémiologie théâtrale* (Quebec: Les Presses de l'Université du Québec, 1976), pp. 127–29; 137. Cf. Keir Elam: "What converts objects, people and action into signs on stage . . . is the removal of the performance from praxis. . . . upon this simple act of severance rests the whole power of theatrical semiosis, indeed its very existence." "Language in the Theater," *Sub-Stance* 18/19 (1977): 144.

4. Antonin Artaud, *The Theater and Its Double*, trans. M. C. Richards (New York: Grove, 1968), p. 51.

5. See esp. chapters 2, "Metaphysics and the Mise en Scène," pp. 33–47, and 3, "The Alchemical Theater," pp. 48–52.

6. On the staging of *Perseverance*, see Richard Southern, *The Medieval Theater in the Round* (London: Faber & Faber, 1957). For archaeological evidence of circular theaters in Europe, see Henri Rey-Flaud, *Le Cercle magique: Essai sur le théâtre en rond à la fin du Moyen Age* (Paris: Gallimard, 1973), and Elie Konigson, *L'Espace théâtral médiéval (Paris: Editions du CNRS, 1975)*, pp. 178–95.

7. Thus, the notion of "text" is not confined to the literary dimension alone, but rather comprehends "systems of signs" that may be oral, social, or unconscious, as well as literary. Intertextuality is thus a matter of the *transposition* of one or more systems of signs into another. See Julia Kristeva, *La Révolution du langage poétique* (Paris: Seuil, 1974), p. 60.

8. Secondary modeling systems are secondary languages constructed on the model of natural languages. Human consciousness being essentially linguistic, natural languages invariably provide the structural stereotypes of systems secondary to them, such as those of artistic expression. See Iouri Lotman, *La Structure du texte artistique*, trans. A. Fournier et al. (Paris: Gallimard, 1973), pp. 36–37. In the present context, the nondramatic source of the medieval veridictory play is by definition a modeling system, while the play is a transposition into yet another modeling system.

9. On this figure in modern literature, see Lucien Dällenbach, *Le Récit spéculaire: Essai sur la mise en abyme* (Paris: Seuil, 1977).

10. The relationship between early liturgical drama and the "sacred drama" of the Mass itself is discussed at length by O. B. Hardison, Jr., in *Christian Rite and Christian Drama in the Middle Ages* (Baltimore, Md.: Johns Hopkins University Press, 1965). See also Robert Guiette, "Réflexions sur le drame liturgique," in *Mélanges offerts à René Crozet* (Poitiers, 1966), vol. 1, pp. 197–202.

11. E.g.: "Or nous faites pais, si l'orrés," v. 114 of the prologue to the *Jeu de Saint Nicolas*. The lengthy prologue to *La Seinte Resureccion* details the manner in which the stations are disposed on the playing area. If spoken, these verses would have served to attract and orientate the attention of the spectators. The late medieval tradition of preceding a mystery or a morality by a comic debate or a *sottie* places the latter in the function of a crowd-gathering,

quasi-exordial device. See Alan E. Knight, "The Medieval Theater of the Absurd," *PMLA* 86 (1971): 183. Other techniques for quieting the public, including musical preludes, dances, sermons, even recitation of a Mass, are mentioned by Omer Jodogne, "Le Théâtre français du Moyen Age: Recherches sur l'aspect dramatique des textes," in *The Medieval Drama*, ed. Sandro Sticca (Albany, N.Y.: SUNY Press, 1972), pp. 2–5.

12. "Et pour ce que plus est meü / Le cuer de l'omme par vëoir / Que par lire, sanz plus savoir, / Et mieux s'i mettent les coraiges, / Sera ci fait par personnages. . . ." *L'Estoire de Griseldis*, ed. Barbara M. Craig (Lawrence: University of Kansas Press, 1954), vv. 26–30. See also my "Early Secular Courtly Drama in France: *L'Estoire de Griseldis*," in *The Expansion and Transformation of Courtly Literature*, ed. N. B. Smith and J. T. Snow (Athens: University of Georgia Press, 1980), pp. 156–70, esp. 160–61.

13. Sr. Mary Faith McKean, R.S.M., *The Interplay of Realistic and Flamboyant Art Elements in the French Mystères* (Washington, D.C.: The Catholic University of America Press, 1959).

14. The manner in which the play is amplified is indicative of a significant step toward secular drama. See Laurent Romero, "*Courtois d'Arras* et la liberté naissante," *RN* 13 (1971–72): 168–76.

15. Cf. Genesis 4, and *Le Mystère d'Adam*, ed. P. Aebischer (Geneva: Droz, 1964), vv. 603–6; 615–18; 639–61.

16. Ibid., vv. 61–62; 76–77; 227–30. On the Augustinian view of the Fall, see D. W. Robertson, Jr., "The Doctrine of Charity," p. 24ff.

17. Rainer Warning, "On the Alterity of Medieval Religious Drama," *NLH* 10 (1979): 265–92.

18. Georges Duby, "Les 'jeunes' dans la société aristocratique dans la France du Nord-Ouest au XIIe siècle," in *Hommes et structures du Moyen Age* (Paris and The Hague: Mouton, 1973), pp. 213–25.

19. *Le Mystère de la Passion d'Arnoul Gréban*, ed. Gaston Paris and Gaston Raynaud (Paris: Vieweg, 1878), p. 261: Tierce Journee de la Passion Nostre Saulveur Jhesu Christ Prologue . . .

> Ainsi va son veil moderant
> en ce miroir considerant
> ou tout cueur pour son dueil mirer
> se doit doulcement remirer;
> et affin que vous y mirez
> et humblement la remirez,
> ce devost miroir pour le mieulx
> vous ramenons devant les yeulx
> sensiblement par parsonnages:
> mirez vous, si serez bien sages;
> chacun sa forme y entrevoit;
> qui bien se mire, bien se voit.
> Dieu doint que si bien nous mirons
> que par mirer nous remirons
> après ceste vie mortelle
> l'essence divine immortelle,
> qui règne sans jamais tarir.
>   (vv. 19989–20005)

20. The relative importance of the written text in dramatic performance remains a matter of great theoretical interest among semioticians. See, notably, Régis Durand, "Problèmes de l'analyse structurale et sémiotique de la forme théâtrale," in *Sémiologie de la représentation: Théâtre, télévision, bande dessinée*, ed. André Helbo (Brussels: Complexe, 1975), pp. 112–20; André Helbo, "Theater as Representation," *Sub-Stance*, 18/19 (1977), pp. 172–81; Ann Ubersfeld, *Lire le théâtre* (Paris: Editions Sociales, 1978), pp. 13–40. There is a general tendency to maintain that a semiology of theater must consider not only textual signs but those of representation, as well as their complex interrelations. See Jean Alter, "Coding Dramatic Efficiency in Plays: From Text to Stage," *Semiotica*, 28 (1979), pp. 247–58.

21. It goes without saying that Artaud is a precursor of theatrical semiology and not himself a semiotician in the strictest sense, though the passage quoted here might well serve as a miniature manifesto for a truly semiological approach to theater. Cf. my "Antonin Artaud and

a Semiotics of Theater," a paper presented at the Twentieth-Century French Division of the Modern Language Association Annual Convention, Los Angeles, December 28, 1982, forthcoming.

22. This model is amply discussed by A. J. Greimas and François Rastier in A. J. Greimas, *Du Sens: Essais sémiotiques* (Paris: Seuil, 1970), "Les jeux des contraintes sémiotiques," pp. 135–55.

23. See the Introduction to this essay, note 1, and Edmund Reiss, "Nationalism and Cosmopolitanism as Subject and Theme in Medieval Narratives," *Actes du IVe Congrès de l'Association Internationale de Littérature Comparée* (The Hague: Mouton, 1966), pp. 619–27.

24. The extensive relationship between the *mise en scène* of vernacular French plays and the medieval world view has recently been discussed by Paul Verhuyck and Anneli Vermeer-Meyer, in "La Plus ancienne scène française," *Romania* 100 (1979): 402–12. The authors quite justifiably suggest that the "bipolar" opposition of good and evil in these plays is signified by their staging, which is "d'ordre sémiotique: elle a valeur de signe" (p. 412).

25. The "figure of veridiction" is akin to the "absolute point of view of the narrator whose views are those of a god or of a community" in what Kristeva has termed "epic monologism," after Bakhtine. Like the veridictory configuration, this narrator imposes a clear disjunction between good and evil, whence a "monological" discourse which excludes perspectives that deviate from the absolute standard. See Julia Kristeva, *Sèméiotiké: Recherches pour une sémanalyse* (Paris: Seuil, 1969), Chapter 4, "Le Mot, le dialogue et le roman," pp. 82–112. We shall return to this matter in the concluding chapter.

26. *Assimilatio* "asserts two things—first, that the relations internal to language are the same as the one which relates it to the real world, and second, that this relation is analogical—it is a relation of likening. Accepting these two assertion, we must see language as an analogising system which includes, rather than excludes, the world. The inclusion works because in the Middle Ages the worlds of nature and of human action were understood as things whose very being was linguistic." Judson B. Allen, "The *Grand Chant Courtois* and the Wholeness of the Poem: The Medieval Assimilatio of Text, Audience, and Commentary," in *Medieval Poetics and Semiotic Theory,* ed. D. Maddox and S. Sturm-Maddox, *ECr* 18 (1978): 6. Cf. Pierre Guiraud, *Semiology,* trans. G. Gross (London: Routledge & Kegan Paul, 1975), pp. 59–68, who cites astrology, cartomancy, palmistry, oneiromancy, etc., as coded sign systems that assimilate unknown structures to known ones in primitive thought. In medieval veridictory drama, the principle of *assimilatio* relates specific systems of language, representation, social organization, religious belief, and history.

27. *Sèméiotikè*, p. 56.

28. In 1548, the Parliament of Paris forbade *mystères sacrés*, though they continued to be played and their influence was felt for a century thereafter. See Grace Frank, *The Medieval French Drama,* p. 270, and Raymond Lebègue, "Quelques survivances de la mise en scène médiévale," *Mélanges offerts à M. Gustave Cohen à l'occasion de son 70e anniversaire* (Paris, 1950), pp. 219–26. On cruelty and violence in the Passion scenes in fifteenth-century French mysteries, see Warning, "Alterity," pp. 278–85.

29. Warning, "Alterity," pp. 271–78. The author develops the background of this perspective in his *Funktion und Struktur: Die Ambivalenzen des geistlichen Spiels* (Munich: Fink, 1974).

30. The cognitive model appears in Greimas and Courtés, "The Cognitive Dimension of Narrative Discourse," p. 440. Its pertinence to this essay is established above, at the end of Chapter 1. In the present adaptation, the Deixis of Delusion or Lie (A + $\bar{B}$) becomes the Deixis of *Illusion* in keeping with the representational illusion of dramatic performance. Unlike a delusion or lie, the dramatic illusion is a conventional mode entailing a "willing suspension of disbelief" on the part of the spectator.

31. See Eco, *Theory,* p. 55. The model is also applied above in Chapter 8.

32. In information theory, *entropy* is occasioned by disorder and "noise" which interferes with or impedes the transmission of information. See Lotman, *Structure,* pp. 58–65; 124–27. The zone of entropy designates "what does not fit into the model [and] does not exist at the level of signs, the only level which in . . . cultural terms is endowed with meaning. . . ." Maria Corti, "Models and Antimodels in Medieval Culture," *NLH* 10 (1979): 341. In terms of the model of representation proposed here, entropy is the zone of exclusion of that which is not

pertinent to the coherence of dramatic discourse. In negative terms, it consists of potential detractors from the communicative relation between producers and receptors. In positive terms, its existence as a realm of nonpertinence and exclusion assures the discursive coherence of representation. In some modern types of drama—such as Theater of the Absurd or the Living Theater—elements from the zone of entropy may be recuperated for esthetic or ideational effects. Cf. Lotman, p. 124, who says that art is capable of transfiguring noise into artistic information.

33. Drawing a distinction between two types of intertextuality, one conservative and integrative, the other characterized by transgression and exclusion, Paul Zumthor identifies the latter type as nascent in fifteenth-century Europe. "Le Carrefour des rhétoriqueurs: Intertextualité et rhétorique," *Poétique* 27 (1976): 317–37.

34. Guiette, "Réflexions," p. 197: Liturgical drama "doit signifier, plus qu'il ne représente."

Chapter Ten. Ideopathelin: The Signs of the Times

1. On the "impossibility" of formalism—"a 'text by itself' is no text at all"—see Walter Benn Michaels, "Against Formalism: The Autonomous Text in Legal and Literary Interpretation," *Poetics Today* 1 (1979): 23–34. The interrelationship of sign systems and the nonautonomy of the work of art were key points made by the Prague Linguistic Circle. See Roman Jakobson and Jurij Tynjanov, "Problemy izučenija literatury i jazyka," *Novyi Lef* 12 (1928): 35–37, and Thomas G. Winner, "Some Fundamental Concepts Leading to a Semiotics of Culture: An Historic Overview," in *Semiotics of Culture*, a special issue of *Semiotica*, ed. Irene Portis Winner and Jean Umiker-Sebeok, 27, nos. 1–3 (1979), pp. 75–82.

2. On codes, see Eco, *Theory*, pp. 48–150. See also Irene Portis Winner, "Ethnicity, Modernity, and Theory of Cultural Texts," in Winner and Umiker-Sebeok, p. 106: "Culture is understood as a process and a mechanism characterized by the struggle for information which is received, accumulated, preserved, and coded, decoded and translated from one system into another, as well as exchanged."

3. For a thorough study of literature as information and communication linking "senders" and "receivers", see Maria Corti, *An Introduction to Literary Semiotics*, trans. M. Bogat and A. Mandelbaum (Bloomington and London: Indiana University Press, 1978), esp. p. 19.

4. Cf. ibid. pp. 144–45; Cesare Segre, " Culture and Modeling Systems," *Critical Inquiry* 4 (1978): 525–37.

5. Cultural elements are recombined in the discursive registers of the play. Study of the cultural dimension necessitates analysis of the types of discourse involved and of the unique coherence achieved through this recombination. Cultural history is less a matter of objective fact than of the types of discourse in which it is presented. See Hayden White, *Tropics of Discourse: Essays in Cultural Criticism* (Baltimore, Md.: Johns Hopkins University Press, 1978). On the importance of a typology of discourse to literary study, see Tzvetan Todorov, *Les Genres du discours* (Paris: Seuil, 1978), pp. 13–26.

6. Cited from the "Theses on the Semiotic Study of Culture" of the Tartu-Moscow group [Lotman, Uspenskij, Toporov, Ivanov, Pjatigorskij], (1.0.0), in *The Tell-Tale Sign: A Survey of Semiotics*, ed. Thomas A. Sebeok (Lisse: Peter de Ridder, 1975), pp. 57–83. Another English translation is available in *The Structure of Texts and the Semiotics of Culture*, ed. Jan van der Eng and Mojmir Grygar (The Hague: Mouton, 1973). For extended analysis of the "Theses", see Irene Portis Winner and Thomas G. Winner, "The Semiotics of Cultural Texts," *Semiotica* 18 (1976): 101–56.

7. Julia Kristeva, "Le Texte clos," *Langages* 12 (1968): 103.

8. See Winner and Winner, "Semiotics of Cultural Texts," pp. 108–9.

9. Clifford Geertz, "Deep Play: Notes on the Balinese Cockfight," *Daedalus*, Winter (1973), p. 26.

10. Segre, "Cultural Modeling Systems," p. 534.

11. Ibid., p. 535.

12. Konigson, *Espace théâtral médiéval*, p. 104, contrasts the "mythic time" of the medieval religious plays with the "urban time" of the fourteenth-century public striking clocks towering

above the spectacle. See also Jean Leclercq "Experience and Interpretation of Time in the Early Middle Ages," *SMC* 5 (1975): 9–19.
13.

Intérieur bourgeois anglais, avec des fauteuils anglais. Soirée anglaise. M. Smith, Anglais, dans son fauteuil et ses pantoufles anglais, fume sa pipe anglaise et lit un journal anglais, prés d'un feu anglais. Il a des lunettes anglaises, une petite moustache grise, anglaise. A côté de lui, dans un autre fauteuil, Mme Smith, Anglaise, raccommode des chaussettes anglaises. Un long moment de silence anglais. La pendule anglaise frappe dix-sept coups anglais. Mme Smith.—Tiens, il est neuf heures.

Eugène Ionesco, *Théâtre*, I (Paris: Gallimard, 1954), p. 17.

14. Pavis, *Problèmes de sémiologie théâtrale*, p. 82: "Contrairement à l'opinion habituelle, les icônes visuelles ne sont pas monosémiques et dénotantes, mais polysémiques, car si on reconnaît clairement un objet du décor, on ne sait pas pour autant quelle sera sa fonction dans l'ensemble de la pièce."

15. Cf. Jameson, *Prison-House of Language*, p. 133.

16. Zumthor, *Le Masque et la lumière*, p. 213.

17. Kristeva, *Le Texte du roman* (The Hague and Paris: Mouton, 1970). See also "Le texte clos," pp. 105–9: "Du Symbole au signe".

18. Zumthor, p. 55.

19. Kristeva, *Sèméiotikè, recherches pour une sémanalyse*, p. 67. For an illuminating study of the traitor along related lines, see Louis Marin, *Sémiotique de la Passion, topiques et figures* (Paris: Bibliothèque des Sciences Religieuses, 1971).

20. Kristeva, *Sèméiotikè*, p. 67.

21. Pierre Van Nuffel, "Problèmes de sémiotique interprétative: l'Epopée," *LR* 27 (1973): 150–62; Larry S. Crist, "Deep Structures in the *chansons de geste:* Hypotheses for a Taxonomy," *Olifant* 3 (1975): 3–35. See my "Greimas in the Realm of Arthur: Toward an Analytical Model for Medieval Romance," *ECr* 17 (1977): 179–94, and *Structure and Sacring*, pp. 41–176.

22. For a penetrating study of the deceptive function in the *fabliaux*, see Mary Jane Schenck, "Functions and Roles in the Fabliau," *CL* 30 (1978): 22–34; by the same author, "Toward a Typology of Narrative: Actantial Analysis and the Fabliau," a paper presented at the annual meeting of the Modern Language Association of America, December, 1975 (unpublished).

23. Kristeva, "Le Texte clos," p. 107.

24. On the *Testament de Pathelin* and the *Nouveau Pathelin à troys personnages, Pathelin, le pelletier, le prebstre*, see Aubailly, *Théâtre médiéval*, pp. 156–58.

25. Kristeva, *Sèméiotikè*, p. 98. On "presence", see Jacques Derrida, *L'Ecriture et la différence* (Paris: Seuil, 1967), and Jameson, *Prison-House of Language*, pp. 173–86.

26. Kristeva, *Sèméiotikè*, p. 101. Mikhail Bakhtine, *L'Oeuvre de François Rabelais et la culture populaire au Moyen Age et sous la Renaissance* (Paris: Gallimard, 1970).

27. *Sèméiotikè*, p. 101.

28. Cf. Eco, *Theory*, pp. 71–72.

29. Emile Mâle, *L'Art religieux de la fin du Moyen Age*, pp. 380–88.

30. Kristeva, *Sèméiotikè*, p. 55; "Le Texte clos," p. 105.

31. See Fabienne Gégou, "Argot et expressions argotiques dans *Maistre Pierre Pathelin*," *Actes du XIIIe Congrès International de Linguistique et Philologie Romanes* (Quebec: Presses de l'Université de Laval, 1976), pp. 691–96, esp. 693–94.

32. On lamb and shepherd as symbols, see George Ferguson, *Signs and Symbols in Christian Art* (New York: Oxford University Press, 1961), pp. 20–21.

33. On the structures of exchange in *Pathelin*, see Crist, "Pathelinian Semiotics: Elements for an Analysis of *Maistre Pierre Pathelin*," *ECr* 18 (1978): 69–81. On the valuation of currency in the play, see R. T. Holbrook, *Etude sur Pathelin: Essai de bibliographie et d'interprétation*,Elliott Monographs in the Romance Languages and Literatures, 5 (Baltimore, Md.: Johns Hopkins University Press, 1917), p. 83; L. Cons, *L'Auteur de la farce de Pathelin*, Elliott Monographs in the Romance Languages and Literatures, 17 (Princeton, N.J.: Princeton University Press; Paris: PUF, 1926), pp. 26–30; E. Cazalas, "Où et quand se passe l'action de *Maistre Pierre Pathelin?*" *Romania* 57 (1931): 573–77; cf. L. Foulet, *Romania* 45 (1919): 454; Halina Lewicka,

"Le Lieu d'origine de *Pathelin*," in *Etudes sur l'ancienne farce française*, Bibliothèque française et romane (Paris: Klincksieck; Warsaw: Editions Scientifiques de Pologne, 1974), pp. 96–98.

34. Kristeva, *Sèméiotikè*, p. 62.

35. Ibid., p. 73.

36. Especially the printed book, a development of the fifteenth century. It was at once a tangible, marketable commodity and the purveyor of virtually every sort of discourse, from the most pious or abstract to the most trivial. See Febvre and Martin, *L'Apparition du livre*, for a full treatment of the scope of early printed books.

37. The place of drama in late medieval secular, mercantile, urban contexts is detailed by Konigson, *L'Espace théâtral médiéval*, pp. 55–305. See also Alfred Simon, *Les Signes et les songes: Essai sur le théâtre et la fête* (Paris: Seuil, 1976), pp. 120–89.

38. Kristeva, *Sèméiotikè*, p. 57

39. The significance of analogy to the aesthetics of the high Middle Ages is discussed by Eugene Vinaver, *The Rise of Romance* (New York & Oxford: Oxford University Press, 1971), ch. 6: "Analogy as the Dominant Form," pp. 99–122.

40. Michel Foucault, *Les Mots et les choses: Une Archéologie des sciences humaines* (Paris: Gallimard, 1966). From the time of the Stoics, Western sign theory was ternary, consisting of signifier, signified, and their "conjuncture." Following the seventeenth-century emphases of Port Royal theoreticians, the binary relation of signifier to signified marks a significant turning point in the history of sign theory (p. 57). At the end of the Renaissance, ". . . le langage, au lieu d'exister comme l'écriture matérielle des choses, ne trouve plus son espace que dans le régime général des signes représentatifs. . . . On s'était demandé comment reconnaître qu'un signe désignait bien ce qu'il signifiait; à partir du XVIIe siècle on se demandera comment un signe peut être lié à ce qu'il signifie. Question à laquelle l'âge classique répondra par l'analyse de la représentation; et à laquelle la pensée modern répondra par l'analyse du sens et de la signification. . . . Le langage ne sera rien de plus qu'un cas particulier de la représentation (pour les classiques) ou de la signification (pour nous). La profonde appartenance du langage et du monde se trouve défaite. . . . Le discours aura bien pour tâche de dire ce qui est, mais il ne sera rien de plus ce que ce qu'il dit" (p. 58).

41. Zumthor, "Le Carrefour des rhétoriqueurs: Intertextualité et rhétorique," p. 336, and *Masque*, p. 196. The fifteenth century marks a shift from "integrative" to "*exilique*" intertextuality. On the role of "transgression" in the development of "new signifying chains," see Kristeva, "The System and the Speaking Subject," in Sebeok, *Tell-Tale Signs*, p. 51.

42. Cf. Bakhtine, *Rabelais*, pp. 151–53.

Index

Actant, 23, 204
Actantial model, 204
Adam de la Halle: *Jeu de la feuillée*, 18, 69, 145; *Jeu de Robin et Marion*, 18
Agent, 204
Alford, J., 108, 214n, 215n
Allen, J. B., 150, 220n
Altamire, J. L., de, 93, 212n, 213n
Alter, J., 219n
Antoine de la Sale, 92; *Jehan de Saintré*, 161, 166
Arden, H., 213n
Ariès, P., 211n
Arnoul Gréban: *Mystère de la Passion*, 141, 157, 214n, 219n
Ars moriendi, 9, 62, 72–93, 126, 152, 157, 164
Artaud, A., 137–39, 140, 141–43, 218n, 219–20n
Art au morier, 74, 81, 212n, 213n
Assimilatio, 150, 170, 220n
Aubailly, J.-C., 207n, 213n, 222n
Aucassin et Nicolette, 69, 146
Augustine, Saint, 17, 138, 206n
Austin, J. L., 130, 216n
Axiology, 143f, 148, 152, 162
Axis: of contraries, 202–3; of subcontraries, 202–3

Bakhtine, M., 163, 213n, 220n, 222n, 223n
Barthes, R., 171, 208n, 218n
Basoche, 96, 157
Beckett, Samuel, 11, 172
Blasonner, 63, 68
Bloch, R. H., 213n, 214n, 215n
Bloomfield, M. W., 207n
Boase, T. S. R., 211n
Bonno, G., 206n
Bosch, Hieronymus, 138
Bremond, C., 29, 34, 162, 205, 208n

Bullen, G., 212n
Buridant, C., 209n

Carnival, 92, 163, 170
Castle of Perseverance, 138, 214n
Cazalas, E., 212n, 222n
Cerquiglini, B. and J., 209n, 210n
Chanson de Roland, 107, 145, 162–63, 166, 215n
Chansons de geste, 44, 145, 166
Chartier, R., 91, 211n, 213n
Chatman, S., 29, 205, 209n
Chaunu, P., 211n
Chevaldin, L.-E., 206n
Chrétien de Troyes, 22; *Cligés*, 163; *Conte del graal*, 69; *Yvain*, 69
Cicero, 70
Classeme, 20f, 31, 49–58, 171, 201
Cognition, in narrative, 24–25
Cognitive dimension, 32f, 115–16, 204
Colby, A., 69, 210n, 211n
Colón, G., 215n
Comportment, 34, 201
Concatenation, 34, 203
Conjointe, 22–23, 41
Conjunction, 204
Cons, L., 206n, 213n, 222n
Contract, fiduciary, 24, 30–32, 113
Corpus Christi Cycle, 150
Corti, M., 220n, 221n
Courtés, J., 24–25, 29–31, 205, 207n, 208n, 215n, 216n, 218n, 220n
Courtois d'Arras, 18, 139, 141, 145, 147
Crist, L. S., 54, 162, 211n, 213n, 222n
Curtius, E. R., 207n, 208n

Dällenbach, L., 209n, 218n
/Deceit/, 20–26, 29–33, 49, 135–36, 170, 201f
Deception, cognitive and pragmatic, 32–39

224

Deixis, 25, 144–47, 202–3, 220n
Delaruelle, E., 211n
Deroy, J., 206n
Derrida, J., 163, 222n
Discourse, of deceit, 41; dialogical, 163–64; epideictic, 41, 63–71; illocutionary, 41, 118–31; juridical, 41, 95–107; manipulative, 41, 109–17; monological, 163–64; narrative, 29–30; paremiological, 41; 43–58; thanatological, 41, 72–93, 126
Disjunction, 204
Disposition, 22–23, 29, 39, 41, 46, 53, 56
Doubles, model of, 139–42
Dubruck, E., 211n
Duby, G., 141, 219n
Dundes, A., 207n
Durand, R., 219n

Eco, U., 19–20, 119, 127, 151, 207n, 216n, 217n, 220n, 221n, 222n
Elam, K., 218n
El Greco, 138
Entropy, 158, 220–21n
Epiphonema, 57–58
Estienne, H., 22, 29, 37, 44, 56, 209n
Exchange, 204

Fable, 52–58, 62–63
Faral, E., 66, 210n
Farce, 22, 61, 96, 136, 150
Farce des femmes qui font acroire à leurs marys de vecies que ce sont lanternes, 57
Febvre, L., 211n, 212n, 223n
Ferguson, G., 222n
Figure, 201, 207n
Fischler, A., 215n
Fontanille, J., 216n
Form of content, 201
Foucault, M., 170, 223n
Foulet, L., 222n
Frank, G., 44, 209n, 210n, 213n, 220n
Frappier, J., 21, 91, 210n, 212n, 213n, 217n
Functions, 23, 30–39, 53–56, 203–4

Garçon et l'aveugle, Le, 61
Geertz, C., 158, 221n
Gégou, F., 212n, 222n
Genette, G., 208n
Godefroy, F., 210n, 217n
Grands Mystères, 92, 95

Grands Rhétoriqueurs, 58, 92, 161, 170
Greimas, A. J., 23–25, 29–31, 38–39, 97–98, 110–15, 129–32, 151, 162–63, 171, 201–5, 207n, 208n, 209n, 214n, 215n, 216n, 217n, 218n, 220n
Grice, H. P., 127, 217n
Grimaud, M., 217n
Gringore, P., 210n
Guiette, R., 153, 218n, 221n
Guillaume Alexis, *Faintes du Monde*, 73
Guillaume de Machaut, *Remede de Fortune*, 57
Guiraud, P., 220n

Hall, E. T., 216n
Hamon, P., 208n
Hancher, M., 216n, 217n
Hardison, O. B., Jr., 218n
Harvey, H. G., 96, 104, 214n, 215n
Heft, D., 209n
Helbo, A., 219n
Hind, A. M., 212n
Höfer, J., 213n
Holbrook, R. T., 9, 74, 78, 100, 101, 206n, 207n, 210n, 211n, 212n, 214n, 222n
Huizinga, J., 211n

Illocution, 118–31
Ingarden, R., 218n
Intention, 22–23, 41, 46, 53, 56
Intertextuality, 92–93, 158–59
Invention, 22
Ionesco, Eugène, *La Cantatrice chauve*, 159–61, 169, 172, 222n
Isotopy, 201

Jakobson, R., 221n
Jameson, F., 217n, 222n
Jauss, H. R., 57, 209n, 210n
Jean Bodel, *Jeu de Saint Nicolas*, 18, 139, 141, 145, 148, 218n
Jeux-partis, 57
Jodogne, O., 210n, 217n, 219n
Joyce, J., 11, 87

Kaisergruber, D., 208n
Kelly, D., 207n
Kernodle, G. R., 213n
Knight, A. E., 13; *Master Pierre Pathelin* (translation), 173–99, 219n
Köhler, E., 210n

Konigson, E., 213n, 218n, 221n, 223n
Kristeva, J., 92–93, 139, 150, 158, 161–62, 213n, 218n, 220n, 221n, 222n, 223n

Landowski, E., 97–98, 214n, 215n
Laus, 69–70
Leach, E., 69, 211n
Lebègue, R., 220n
Leclercq, J., 222n
Lejeune R., 100, 102, 211n, 212n, 214n, 215n
Lemercier, P., 100, 104, 120–21, 214n, 217n
LeRoux de Lincy, M., 44–46, 48–49, 209n
Lévi-Strauss, C., 217n
Lewicka, H., 206n, 222n
Li Rois de Cambrai, *Descrission des religions*, 57
Locke, J., 20
Lotman, I., 218n, 220n
Lucas van Leyden, 138

McKean, Sr. M. F., 140, 219n
Maddox, D., 208n, 210n, 214n, 219–20n, 222n
Malaunoy, M. de, 212n
Mâle, E., 83, 164, 211n, 212n, 213n, 222n
Manger l'oie, 43, 46f, 111
Manipulation, 12–13, 33, 41, 60, 106–7, 109–17, 129–32, 205, 215n
Margolis, J., 217n
Marin, L., 222n
Martial d'Auvergne, *Arrests d'amour*, 214n
Martin, H.-J., 211n, 212n, 223n
Mésangère, M. de la: 46, 209n
Meschonnic, H., 209n
Michaels, W. B., 221n
Miner, D., 209n
Miracles de Nostre Dame, 18, 139
Mise en abyme, 46, 139
Modalities, 112, 204–5
Molière, 11
Morphology, 23
Mystère d'Adam, 17, 95, 139, 141, 144, 146, 147, 219n

Narrative program, 204
Narrative syntax, 29–39, 204

Nature topos, 65–67
Nouveau Pathelin à troys personnages, Pathelin, le pelletier, le prebstre, 222n

O'Connor, Sr. M. C., 83, 211n, 212n
Ohmann, R., 216n
Ollier, M.-L., 207n, 209n
Oudin, A., 46, 49

Packard, V., 215n
Paistre, 48f, 111
Paremiology, 41–58
Parody, 93
Passion d'Autun, 139
Passion des Jongleurs, 140
Passion du Palatinus, 139
Pateliner, 45
Pathegyric, 13
Pathelin, 12
Paulhan, J., 209n
Pavel, T., 34–35, 208n
Pavis, P., 30, 208n, 218n, 222n
Pèlerinage de Charlemagne, 163
Perlocutionary effect, 130
Permjakov, G. L., 209n
Pessoa de Barros, D. L., 215–16n
Philipot, E., 91, 210n, 213n, 217n
Philippe de Mézières: *L'Estoire de Griseldis*, 140, 147, 219n
Podhradsky, G., 213n
Poirion, D., 12, 206n
Pragmatic dimension, 32f, 115–16, 204
Pratt, M. L., 217n
Prince, G., 208n
Priscian, 70
Procès de paradis, 214n
Propp, V., 22–23, 29, 162, 207n, 208n
Proverbe au conte de Bretaigne, 57
Proverbe au vilain, 57
Proverbes en rimes, 57
Proverbs, 41, 43–58, 157, 167
Proxemics, 143
Psychomachia, 138, 164

Quintilian, 70

Rabelais, François, 11, 44
Rahner, K., 213n
Rastier, F., 220n
Récit, 23; *mythique*, 38–39
Reiss, E., 220n

Rey-Flaud, H., 218n
Rhetorica ad Herennium, 70
Riffaterre, M., 213n
Robertson, D. W., Jr., 207n, 219n
Roman de Renart, 163
Romero, L., 219n
Roques, M., 48–49, 206n, 209n
Rousse, M., 33, 206n, 207n, 208n
Rutebeuf, *Miracle de Théophile,* 139
Rylands, W. H., 212n

Sacré, J., 216n
Satire, 93
Saugnieux, J., 211n
Schema, 202
Schenck, M. J., 222n
Schreiber, W., 212n
Searle, J., 118–19, 122f, 130, 216n, 217n
Segment, 33–39
Segre, C., 158–59, 221n
Seinte Resureccion, 139, 144, 218n
Seme, 201
Semiopath, 12–13, 172
Semiotics, 12, 20, 22–26; narrative and discoursive, 22–23, 200–5; of culture, 12, 157f, 171–72; of manipulation, 110f; of theater, 137f
Semiotic square *(carré sémiotique),* 24–25, 143–46, 202
Sémiotique et Bible, 205
Sententiae, 47–48, 57
Simon, A., 223n
Sottie, 93, 96, 150
Southern, R., 218n
Stevenson, R. L., 59, 210n
Sturm, H., 210n
Sturm-Maddox, S., 208n
Subject, 204

Syntax, narrative, 34–39

Tacitus, 70
Tartu-Moscow Group, 172, 221
Taylor, A., 210n
Tenenti, A., 211n
Testament de Pathelin, 222n
Thomas d'Angleterre: *Roman de Tristan,* 107, 215n
Thompson, S., 37, 208n
Thurlemann, F., 216n
Todorov, T., 208n, 211n, 221n
Tynjanov, J., 221n

Ubersfeld, A., 119, 216n, 219n
Utley, F. L., 207n

Van Nuffel, P., 162, 222n
Veltrusky, J., 218n
Verhuyck, P., 220n
Veridiction, 136–54, 168, 201; model of, 24–26, 201–2
Vermeer-Meyer, A., 220n
Villon, François, 11, 81, 92
Vinaver, E., 223n
Vituperatio, 69–70

Warning, R., 141, 150, 219n, 220n
White, H., 221n
Winner, I. P., 221n
Winner, T. G., 221n
Woodmansee, M., 217n

Zerner, H., 212n
Zolkovskij, A. K., 209n
Zumthor, P., 57, 161, 170, 207n, 208n, 209n, 210n, 213n, 221n, 222n, 223n 223n